369 0121533

D1447605

616

3)

Phobic and Anxiety Disorders in Children and Adolescents

DATE DUE

14/8/15			
			PRINTED IN U.S.A.

About the Authors

Amie Grills-Taquechel, Associate Research Professor of Psychology at the University of Houston, has published in the area of childhood anxiety for the past 10 years. She has also given numerous conference presentations, secured grants, and received prestigious awards, including selection as a 2011 American Psychological Society Rising Star.

Thomas H. Ollendick, University Distinguished Professor at Virginia Tech, has published widely in the childhood anxiety disorders arena. In September 2011, he received an honorary doctorate from the University of Stockholm for his work in the field of childhood anxiety. Prof. Ollendick has been actively involved in grantsmanship and has conducted several randomized controlled trials on the efficacy and effectiveness of cognitive behavior treatments with young people and children.

Advances in Psychotherapy – Evidence-Based Practice

Series Editor
Danny Wedding, PhD, MPH, Professor of Psychology, California School of Professional
  Psychology / Alliant International University, San Francisco, CA

Associate Editors
Larry Beutler, PhD, Professor, Palo Alto University / Pacific Graduate School of Psychology,
  Palo Alto, CA
Kenneth E. Freedland, PhD, Professor of Psychiatry and Psychology, Washington University
  School of Medicine, St. Louis, MO
Linda C. Sobell, PhD, ABPP, Professor, Center for Psychological Studies, Nova Southeastern
  University, Ft. Lauderdale, FL
David A. Wolfe, PhD, RBC Chair in Children's Mental Health, Centre for Addiction and Mental
  Health, University of Toronto, ON

The basic objective of this series is to provide therapists with practical, evidence-based treatment guidance for the most common disorders seen in clinical practice – and to do so in a "reader-friendly" manner. Each book in the series is both a compact "how-to" reference on a particular disorder for use by professional clinicians in their daily work, as well as an ideal educational resource for students and for practice-oriented continuing education.

The most important feature of the books is that they are practical and "reader-friendly:" All are structured similarly and all provide a compact and easy-to-follow guide to all aspects that are relevant in real-life practice. Tables, boxed clinical "pearls," marginal notes, and summary boxes assist orientation, while checklists provide tools for use in daily practice.

Phobic and Anxiety Disorders in Children and Adolescents

Amie E. Grills-Taquechel
Department of Psychology, University of Houston, Texas

Thomas H. Ollendick
Virginia Polytechnic Institute and State University, Blacksburg, Virginia

Library of Congress Cataloging in Publication

is available via the Library of Congress Marc Database under the
Library of Congress Control Number 2012941492

Library and Archives Canada Cataloguing in Publication

Grills-Taquechel, Amie E., 1975-
      Phobic and anxiety disorders in children and
adolescents / Amie E. Grills-Taquechel, Thomas H. Ollendick.

(Advances in psychotherapy - evidence-based practice ; 27)
Includes bibliographical references.
ISBN 978-0-88937-339-6

      1. Anxiety in children. 2. Anxiety in adolescence.
3. Phobias in children. I. Ollendick, Thomas H. II. Title.
III. Series: Advances in psychotherapy--evidence-based
practice ; 27

RJ506.A58G75 2012   618.92'8522   C2012-904199-8

PUBLISHING OFFICES
USA: Hogrefe Publishing, 875 Massachusetts Avenue, 7th Floor, Cambridge, MA 02139
                  Phone (866) 823-4726, Fax (617) 354-6875; E-mail customerservice@hogrefe-publishing.com
EUROPE: Hogrefe Publishing, Merkelstr. 3, 37085 Göttingen, Germany
                  Phone +49 551 99950-0, Fax +49 551 99950-425, E-mail publishing@hogrefe.com

SALES & DISTRIBUTION
USA: Hogrefe Publishing, Customer Services Department,
                  30 Amberwood Parkway, Ashland, OH 44805
                  Phone (800) 228-3749, Fax (419) 281-6883, E-mail customerservice@hogrefe.com
EUROPE: Hogrefe Publishing, Merkelstr. 3, 37085 Göttingen, Germany
                  Phone +49 551 99950-0, Fax +49 551 99950-425, E-mail publishing@hogrefe.com

OTHER OFFICES
CANADA: Hogrefe Publishing, 660 Eglinton Ave. East, Suite 119-514, Toronto, Ontario, M4G 2K2
SWITZERLAND: Hogrefe Publishing, Länggass-Strasse 76, CH-3000 Bern 9

Hogrefe Publishing
Incorporated and registered in the Commonwealth of Massachusetts, USA, and in Göttingen, Lower Saxony,
Germany

Printed and bound in the USA
ISBN: 978-0-88937-339-6

Endorsements

"This informative book describes the various ways that anxiety can be detrimental and interfering for children and adolescents, and explores the course of anxiety development, methods for its assessment, and considerations in its treatment. The writing is concise and up-to-date, and guided by evidence-based clinical practice. No hocus pocus, just well-informed guidance."

Philip C. Kendall, Ph.D., ABPP, Distinguished University Professor, Laura H. Carnell Professor, and Director of the Child and Adolescent Anxiety Disorders Clinic, Department of Psychology, Temple University, Philadelphia, PA, USA

"Anxiety disorders of childhood in a perfect nutshell. If you are looking for a concise, thorough, and bang up-to-date book, then this is the one!"

Dr. Sam Cartwright-Hatton, NIHR Career Development Fellow, University of Sussex, UK

"This book contains a wealth of information about the nature of phobic and anxiety disorders in young people and their assessment and treatment. It will be of enormous value to mental health practitioners, providing them with clear and detailed information about state-of-the-art practice."

Sue Spence, PhD, Griffith University, Brisbane, Australia

"Research on anxiety disorders in children and adolescents has sky-rocketed during the last two decades and we now know much more about the etiology, prevalence, consequences, and treatment of these disorders. In just 90 pages this volume provides the reader with basic knowledge about background, diagnoses, assessment, psychological and pharmacological treatments, and their evidence-base. This book should be required reading for students interested in and professionals working with children and adolescents."

Lars-Göran Öst, Professor of Clinical Psychology, Stockholm University

"In recent years the number of scientific studies on anxiety disorders has grown exponentially. This book provides a comprehensive and thorough review of theoretical explanations, evaluation, and evidence-based treatments of anxiety disorders in children and adolescents. As expert researchers and practitioners, Grills-Taquechel and Ollendick provide an important resource and up-to-date reference work for professional psychologists and students alike."

Laura Hernández-Guzmán, Professor of Psychology and Chair of Continuing Education, Universidad Nacional Autónoma de México, Mexico City, Mexico

Dedication

For all the families who have been brave enough to seek treatment for their child's anxiety and trusted their children to our care. To my husband, parents, and friends for the support they provided while I tackled this project. And, most of all, to my daughter Francesca for the endless amounts of joy she brings to my life.

"I'm afraid that..."
"But what if..."
"I could never..."
"That's too scary for me..."

Preface

Fearful statements such as these and many others are commonly heard by clinicians working with anxious youths. As is discussed in this book, for a variety of reasons, children can come to view aspects of their world as overly frightening. In actuality, anxiety is a normal emotional response to a perceived threat to one's physical or emotional well-being. Feeling fearful and fleeing from a genuinely dangerous situation is adaptive. However, when a child experiences an anxiety response because of situations or objects that are not truly dangerous, then the anxiety and the avoidance associated with it are no longer adaptive. Just like adults, children and adolescents are usually quite distressed by excessive anxiety, and the avoidance behaviors they engage in frequently interfere with their ability to carry out developmentally appropriate tasks and activities. For many youths experiencing these difficulties, "normal" development has gone awry. In such instances, an anxiety disorder diagnosis is warranted when the anxiety response is excessive in frequency, intensity and/ or duration, and results in significant impairment in functioning. Alarmingly, anxiety disorders are among the most common psychological difficulties experienced by children and adolescents. The purpose of our book is to examine these disorders in more detail and to explore not only their developmental course and expression but also effective assessment and treatment approaches for them. In doing so, we hope to provide the reader with a summary of extant research and to illustrate how this research can be used in evidence-based clinical practice.

Before proceeding, however, we would like to provide the reader with a list of acronyms that will frequently be used throughout the book. These acronyms are listed alphabetically below:

Anxiety can range from normative to clinical levels in children and adolescents

Clinical anxiety is marked by excessively frequent, intense, and impairing anxious responses

Acronyms Commonly Used Throughout This Book	
ADHD	attention-deficit/hyperactivity disorder
ADJ	adjustment disorder
ADNOS	anxiety disorder not otherwise specified
AG	agoraphobia
ASD	acute stress disorder
BT	behavior therapy
CBT	cognitive behavior therapy

CBT+F	cognitive behavior therapy with family components
CD	conduct disorder
GAD	generalized anxiety disorder
GCBT	group cognitive behavior therapy
ICBT	individual cognitive behavior therapy
OCD	obsessive-compulsive disorder
ODD	oppositional defiant disorder
PD	panic disorder
PTSD	posttraumatic stress disorder
SAD	separation anxiety disorder
SM	selective mutism
SOCP	social phobia
SPP	specific phobia

Table of Contents

1

Description

In this section, we will first discuss the basic terminology and categorization of childhood diagnoses involving anxiety, as denoted in two of the major psychological/psychiatric classification systems used today. Table 1 lists all of these diagnoses to provide the reader with a comprehensive illustration of the diverse manifestations anxiety may take in children and adolescents. Descriptions, epidemiological information, and noted variations for each individual diagnosis are presented separately and summarized in Table 2. Following this, childhood anxiety disorders are discussed as a group regarding course and prognosis, differential diagnosis, comorbidities, and diagnostic procedures; however, specific disorder variations are also noted within each of these sections as appropriate.

Table 1
DSM-IV-TR and ICD-10 Diagnostic Codes for Childhood and Adolescence Anxiety and Related Conditions

DSM-IV-TR	ICD-10

Disorders Usually First Diagnosed in Infancy, Childhood, or Adolescence
  Separation anxiety disorder (309.21)
  Selective mutism (313.23)
	Disorders of Social Functioning With Onset Specific to Childhood and Adolescence
	  Elective mutism (F94.0)

Anxiety Disorders
  Specific phobia (300.29)
  Social phobia (300.23)
  Obsessive-compulsive disorder (300.3)
  Generalized anxiety disorder (300.02)
  Posttraumatic stress disorder (309.81)
  Acute stress disorder (308.3)
  Panic disorder without agoraphobia (300.01)
  Agoraphobia without history of panic disorder (300.22)
  Panic disorder with agoraphobia (300.21)
  Anxiety disorder due to a general medical condition (293.84)
	Emotional Disorders With Onset Specific to Childhood
	  Separation anxiety disorder of childhood (F93.0)
	  Phobic anxiety disorder of childhood (F93.1)
	  Social anxiety disorder of childhood (F93.2)
	  Other childhood emotional disorder (F93.8)
	
	Phobia Anxiety Disorders
	  Agoraphobia (F40.0)
	  Social phobias (F40.1)
	  Specific phobias (F40.2)
	  Other phobic anxiety disorders (F40.8)
	  Phobic anxiety disorder, unspecified (F40.9)

Table 1 continued

DSM-IV-TR	ICD-10
Substance-induced anxiety disorder (292.89) Anxiety disorder not otherwise specified (300.00) **Adjustment Disorders** with anxiety (309.24) with mixed anxiety and depressed mood (309.28) with disturbance of emotions and conduct (309.4)	**Other Anxiety Disorders** Panic disorder (F41.0) Generalized anxiety disorder (F41.1) Mixed anxiety and depressive disorder (F41.2) Other mixed anxiety disorders (F41.3) Other specified anxiety disorders (F41.8) Anxiety disorder, unspecified (F41.9) **Obsessive-Compulsive Disorder** Predominantly obsessional thoughts/ruminations (F42.0) Predominantly compulsive acts (F42.1) Mixed obsessional thoughts and acts (F42.2) Other obsessive-compulsive disorders (F42.8) Obsessive-compulsive disorder, unspecified (F42.9) **Reaction to Severe Stress and Adjustment Disorders** Acute stress reaction (F43.0) Posttraumatic stress disorder (F43.1) Adjustment disorders (F43.2) Other reactions to severe stress (F43.8) Reaction to severe stress, unspecified (F43.9) **Mixed Disorders of Conduct and Emotions** Other mixed disorders of conduct and emotions (F92.8) **Other Mental Disorders due to Brain Damage and Dysfunction and to Physical Disease** Organic anxiety disorder (F06.4) **Mental and Behavioural Disorders due to Psychoactive Substance Use (F10-F19)**

Note. DSM-IV-TR = *Diagnostic and Statistical Manual of Mental Disorders*, 4th edition, text revision; ICD-10 = *International Statistical Classification of Diseases and Related Health Problems*, 10th Edition.

Table 2
Brief Description, Noted Variations (Including Specifiers), and Childhood/ Adolescent Prevalence/Onset Information for DSM-IV-TR/ICD-10

Disorder name	DSM-IV-TR (ICD-10) codes

Section: Disorders Usually First Diagnosed in Infancy, Childhood, or Adolescence

Separation Anxiety Disorder   **309.21 (F93.0)**
Brief description: excessive and recurrent anxiety and distress regarding separation from the home or individuals to whom the child is attached
Noted variations: inconsistent findings regarding sex differences; *Specifier:* early onset
Prevalence/onset: ~2–4%, with decreasing prevalence into adolescence[a,b]

Selective Mutism 313.23 (F94.0)
Brief description: refusal to speak in specific social situations despite the ability to do so
Noted variations: slightly greater prevalence among females
Prevalence/onset: <1%, more common in early childhood[a,c,d]

Section: Anxiety Disorders

Specific Phobia   **300.29 (F93.1/F40.2)**
Brief description: excessive and persistent fear of a specific object or situation
Noted variations: similar rates but different content for boys and girls; *Specifier:* subtypes
Prevalence/onset: ~2-6%, often begins in childhood/early adolescence; [a,e]

Social Phobia   **300.23 (F93.2/F40.1)**
Brief description: excessive and persistent fear and avoidance of social situations or situations where the child may be scrutinized in a manner that could lead to embarrassment
Noted variations: inconsistent findings regarding sex differences; *Specifier:* generalized
Prevalence/onset: ~1–2%, typically begins in midadolescence[a,f]

Obsessive-Compulsive Disorder   **300.3 (F42.8)**
Brief description: obsessions and/or compulsions that cause distress, are time consuming, and interfere with the child's daily life
Noted variations: more prevalent and earlier onset in male children, equivalent in males/females by adolescence
Prevalence/onset: ~1–3%; onset typically gradual[g]

Generalized Anxiety Disorder   **300.02 (F41.1)**
Brief description: excessive and difficult to control anxiety/worry across a variety of domains along with at least one associated physical/somatic symptom
Noted variations: equivalent in males/females in childhood, greater in females by adolescence
Prevalence/onset: ~<1–7%; onset commonly reported to be in late childhood/ adolescence[a,h,i]

Posttraumatic Stress Disorder (PTSD)   **309.81 (F43.1)**
Brief description: following a traumatic event perceived as threatening to the self or others, the child or youth reacts with fear, helplessness, horror, agitation, or disorganization. Re-experiencing the event, avoidance of things associated with the event, numbing, and hyperarousal follow the event and remain present for at least one month.

Table 2 continued

Disorder name	DSM-IV-TR (ICD-10) codes

Posttraumatic Stress Disorder continued
Noted variations: inconsistent findings regarding child sex differences; *Specifiers:* acute, chronic, or with delayed onset
Prevalence/onset:~1–6% in community samples but significantly greater depending on the precipitating event[a,j,k,l,m]

Acute Stress Disorder   **308.3 (F43.0)**
Brief description: similar to PTSD, symptoms of disassociation, re-experiencing, avoidance, and hyperarousal that follow a traumatic event that is perceived as threatening to the self. Symptoms last between 2 days and 4 weeks and begin within 4 weeks of the traumatic event.
Noted variations: limited research, but appears to be equal in both sexes
Prevalence/onset: ~7–36% posttrauma (injury/burn, assault or motor vehicle accident) [j,k,l,n]

Agoraphobia (AG) Without History of Panic Disorder 300.22 (F40.00)
Brief description: anxiety resulting from situations in which escape or avoidance may be inhibited or in which help may not be available if panic symptoms were to occur.
Noted variations: limited research but appears more common in females
Prevalence/onset: ~<1–8% (higher in clinic samples)[r]

Panic Disorder
    Without Agoraphobia   **300.01 (F41.0)**
    With Agoraphobia   **300.21 (F40.01)**
Brief description: recurrent panic attacks occurring unexpectedly and followed by 1+ months of persistent concern about having another attack, worry about the consequences of the attack, or a change in behavior related to the attack. Occurs with/without the above-described agoraphobia.
Noted variations: more common in females; equally divided for with/without AG
Prevalence/onset: ~1–5% (higher in clinic samples); rare in childhood, increasing prevalence with age[p,q,r]

Anxiety Disorder due to a General Medical Condition   **293.84 (F06.4)**
Brief description: anxiety symptoms that occur but are determined upon examination to be the direct physiological result of a medical condition
Noted variations: varies by condition; *Specifiers:* with generalized anxiety, with panic attacks, or with obsessive-compulsive symptoms
Prevalence/onset: n/a (prevalence/onset based on etiology of the medical condition)

Substance Induced Anxiety Disorder   **Uses specific substance code**
Brief description: anxiety symptoms that occur but are determined upon examination to occur during or shortly after substance intoxication or withdrawal
Noted variations: varies by substance; *Specifiers:* with generalized anxiety, with panic attacks, with obsessive-compulsive symptoms, with phobic symptoms, with onset during intoxication, or with onset during withdrawal specifiers
Prevalence/onset: n/a (prevalence/onset based on etiology of the substance)

Anxiety Disorder Not Otherwise Specified   **300.00 (F41.9, F40.8, F40.9, F41.3, F41.8)**
Brief description: a catch-all category provided for instances where significant anxiety is present but criteria are not met for the other diagnostic categories
Prevalence/onset: ~2%[s,t]

Table 2 continued

Disorder name	DSM-IV-TR (ICD-10) codes

Section: Adjustment Disorders

Adjustment Disorder
 with Anxiety 309.24 (F43.28)
 with Mixed Anxiety and Depressed Mood 309.28 (F43.22)
 with Disturbance of Emotions and Conduct 309.4 (F43.25)
Brief description: significant anxiety (and/or other emotional/behavioral) symptoms that develop within 3 months of a major stressor and dissipate within 6 months of that stressor ending
Noted variations: occurs equally in male and female children and adolescents; acute and chronic specifiers
Prevalence/onset: ~2–8% for adjustment disorders as a group

Notes: Prevalence rates represent childhood/adolescent rates only and include the data from Table 3, as well as the references noted with superscripts and listed below. DSM-IV-TR = *Diagnostic and Statistical Manual of Mental Disorders,* 4th edition, text revision; ICD-10 = *International Statistical Classification of Diseases and Related Health Problems,* 10th Edition; n/a = not applicable.
[a]Egger & Angold, 2006; [b]Brückl et al., 2007; [c]Referred to as elective mutism in the ICD-10; [d]Egger et al., 2006; [e]Previously referred to as simple phobia; [f]Previously referred to as avoidant disorder; [g]Heyman et al., 2003; [h]Previously referred to as overanxious disorder; [i]Lavigne et al., 2009; [j]Kassam-Adams & Winston, 2004; [k]Daviss et al., 2000; [l]Meiser-Stedman, Smith, Glucksman, Yule, & Dalgleish, 2007; [m]Saxe et al., 2005; [n]Miller, Enlow, Reich, & Saxe, 2009; [p]Doerfler et al., 2007; [q]Ollendick, Birmaher, & Mattis, 2004; [r]Wittchen, Reed, & Kessler, 1998; [s]ICD-10 includes nine additional "other" and "unspecified" anxiety categories; [t]Esbjorn et al., 2010.

1.1 Terminology

The two primary diagnostic classification systems used today are the fourth, text-revision, edition of the *Diagnostic and Statistical Manual of Mental Disorders* (DSM-IV-TR; American Psychiatric Association [APA], 2000) and the chapter "Mental and Behavioural Disorders" in the 10th edition of the *International Statistical Classification of Diseases and Related Health Problems* (ICD-10; World Health Organization, 2007).

Two primary classification systems are currently used: DSM-IV-TR and ICD-10

Within each of these classification systems (the DSM-IV-TR and ICD-10), disorders involving anxiety that can be diagnosed in children can be found in several locations. First, in the DSM-IV-TR, two disorders (separation anxiety disorder and selective mutism) are listed in the "Disorders Usually First Diagnosed in Infancy, Childhood, or Adolescence" section. These disorders, as well as phobic anxiety disorder of childhood and social anxiety disorder of childhood are included in the ICD-10 in the "Behavioral and Emotional Disorders With Onset Usually Occurring in Childhood and Adolescence" section. Second, DSM-IV-TR includes two additional sections with diagnoses involving anxiety that can be made in children, adolescents, or adults: "Anxiety Disorders" and "Adjustment Disorders." In ICD-10, the remaining anxiety diagnoses are found in the "Neurotic, Stress-Related, and Somatoform Disorders" section.

Overall, the ICD-10 and DSM-IV-TR have roughly corresponding diagnostic categories; however, slightly different groupings are used (see Table 1). For example, while DSM-IV-TR includes specifiers for children within broader categories (e.g., specific phobia [SPP], social phobia [SOCP]), ICD-10 separates some disorders by age (e.g., F93.1 – phobia anxiety disorder of childhood, and F40.2 – specific phobias). In addition, ICD-10 separately groups agoraphobia, social phobias, and specific phobias (along with other phobic anxiety disorders and phobic anxiety disorder–unspecified) in a section titled "Phobic Disorders," while acute stress disorder, posttraumatic stress disorder (PTSD), and adjustment disorders are included in the "Reaction to Severe Stress and Adjustment Disorders" section. ICD-10 also lists several "other" categories (e.g., other phobic anxiety, phobic anxiety–unspecified, other mixed anxiety disorders, other obsessive-compulsive disorder, etc.) which are subsumed under the diagnosis of anxiety disorders not otherwise specified, in the DSM-IV-TR. Although these different "other" diagnoses will not be described in our book, additional information on them can be found by visiting the ICD-10 website (http://www.who.int/classifications/icd). Another difference is that mixed anxiety–depressive disorder is provided as an ICD-10 diagnosis for when symptoms of anxiety and depression are present to equivalent extents and neither significantly to the degree that an individual anxiety or depressive disorder diagnosis should be given. Although a similar disorder is provisionally listed under "Criteria Sets and Axes Provided for Further Study," the DSM-IV-TR indicates that children with these symptoms should currently be given a diagnosis of anxiety disorder not otherwise specified. Finally, both classification systems include separate diagnostic categories for anxiety disorders that are the result of medical conditions or substance use.

Overall, the various manifestations of anxiety included in the DSM-IV-TR and ICD-10 overlap considerably. Given this fact, unless otherwise noted for consistency and ease of reading, the remainder of this book will focus on DSM-IV-TR diagnostic categorizations and criteria.

1.2   Descriptions

All of the anxiety disorders share some common features and about half have specific diagnostic information regarding children

In line with the organization of the DSM-IV-TR, the different anxiety disorders that can be diagnosed in children are presented by subcategories below and in Table 2 (see Appendix 1). Except where noted, the information summarized was derived from the descriptions provided in the DSM-IV-TR (APA, 2000). Prevalence rates are listed in Table 2 and represent those for childhood/adolescence only, including data from Table 3, as well as from the references noted.

In general, all of the childhood disorders involving anxiety share several features. Most notably, they all have in common some element of persistent and excessive anxious arousal or fear. In addition, for each disorder it is noted that the symptoms "cause clinically significant distress or impairment in social, academic (occupational), or other important areas of functioning" (APA, 2000), and exclusionary criteria are provided for when symptoms do and do

Table 3
Lifetime, 12-Month, and 3-Month Prevalence Estimates From Worldwide Studies of Anxiety Disorders

	N	Age	PD	AG	SPP	SOCP	OCD	PTSD	GAD	SAD	AD-NOS	Any anx	Country
Lifetime													
Essau et al. (2000)	1,035	12–17	0.5%	4.1%	3.5%	1.6%	1.3%	1.6%	0.4%	–	11.9%	18.6%	Germany
Merikangas, He, Burstein, et al. (2010)	10,123	13–18	0.0%	0.0%	0.6%	1.3%	–	1.5%	0.9%	0.6%	–	8.3%	USA
Wittchen et al. (1998)	3,021	14–24	1.6%	2.6%	2.3%	3.5%	0.7%	1.3%	0.8%	–	5.2%	14.4%	Germany
Ranges			0–1.6%	0–2.6%	0.6–3.5%	1.3–3.5%	0.7–1.3%	1.3–1.6%	0.4–0.9%	0.6%	5.2–11.9%	8.3–18.6%	
12-month													
Canino et al. (2004)	1,897	4–17	0.5%	–	–	2.5%	–	0.8%	2.2%	3.1%	–	6.9%	Puerto Rico
Merikangas, He, Brody, et al. (2010)	3,042	8–15	0.3%	–	–	–	–	–	0.2%	–	–	–	USA
Roberts et al. (2007)	4,175	11–17	0.4%	1.6%	–	1.0%	–	0.5%	0.4%	–	–	3.4%	USA
Wittchen et al. (1998)	3,021	14–24	1.2%	1.6%	1.8%	2.6%	0.6%	0.7%	0.5%	–	2.7%	9.3%	Germany

Table 3 continued

	N	Age	PD	AG	SPP	SOCP	OCD	PTSD	GAD	SAD	AD-NOS	Any anx	Country
Wells et al. (2006)	1,535	16–24	2.4%	0.7%	9.3%	7.0%	1.5%	2.4%	1.6%	–	–	17.7%	New Zealand
Ranges			0.3–2.4%	0.7–1.6%	1.8–9.3%	1.0–7.0%	0.6–1.5%	0.5–2.4%	0.2–2.2%	No range	No range	3.4–17.7%	
3-month													
Egger et al. (2006)	1,073	2–5	–	–	2.3%	2.1%	–	0.6%	3.8%	2.4%	–	9.4%	USA
Lavigne et al. (2009)	796	4	–	–	–	–	–	–	0.6%	0.0%	–	–	USA
Costello et al. (2003)	6,674	9–16	0.2%	0.2%	1.0%	0.5%	0.1%	<0.1%	0.8%	1.0%	–	2.4%	USA
Angold et al. (2002)	920	9–17	1.2%	0.5%	0.4%	1.4%	0.2%	–	1.3%	3.0%	–	5.7%	USA
Gau et al. (2005)	3,156	13–17	0.1%	0.1%	3.8%	2.4%	0.2%	–	0.5%	0.1%	–	6.6%	Taiwan
Ranges			0.1–1.2%	0.1–0.5%	0.4–3.8%	0.5–2.4%	0.1–0.2%	<0.1–0.6%	0.5–3.8%	0–3.0%	–	2.4–9.4%	

Note. Dashes indicate data not reported. AD-NOS = anxiety disorder not otherwise specified; AG = agoraphobia; Anx = anxiety; GAD = generalized anxiety disorder; N = number; OCD = obsessive-compulsive disorder; PD = panic disorder; PTSD = posttraumatic stress disorder; SAD = separation anxiety disorder; SOCP = social phobia; SPP = specific phobia.

not occur (e.g., not during the course of schizophrenia). As previously noted, separation anxiety disorder and selective mutism are listed in the "Disorders Usually First Diagnosed in Infancy, Childhood, or Adolescence" section. In addition to these, five of the 12 diagnoses in the anxiety disorders section include symptom variation specifications for children. These specifications are made for SPP, SOCP, obsessive-compulsive disorder, generalized anxiety disorder, and PTSD. Each symptom variation is detailed within the descriptions below, but in general, these pertain to the expression of anxiety (e.g., anxiety may be expressed as clinging or crying in children), symptom duration, and/or the removal of criteria that the fear be recognized as excessive or unreasonable.

1.2.1   Disorders Usually First Diagnosed in Infancy, Childhood, or Adolescence

Separation anxiety disorder (SAD) refers to excessive and recurrent anxiety regarding separation from the home or individuals to whom the child is attached. Eight primary symptoms are noted, and children must exhibit at least three to receive a diagnosis of SAD. In addition, the child must be 18 years of age or younger, and the symptoms must persist for at least 4 weeks. Early onset is specified if the child meets SAD diagnostic criteria before age 6. Associated features include persistent reluctance to attend school, remain alone, or go to sleep without a major attachment figure present, as well as nightmares involving the theme of separation and the expression of a number of physical complaints when separation occurs or is anticipated.

Selective/elective mutism (SM) occurs in a small percentage of children who refuse to speak in specific social situations (e.g., school) despite the ability to do so. Refusal to speak must occur for at least 1 month, and interference occurs in educational/occupational achievement *or* social communication domains. However, SM is not diagnosed if the refusal to speak occurs in the first month of school or because of a lack of knowledge/comfort with the language. Children with SM often also experience significant social concerns, shyness, or other anxiety symptoms.

1.2.2   Anxiety Disorders

Specific phobias (SPP) are excessive and persistent fears of explicit objects or situations, which are typically avoided or endured with intense anxiety or distress. Exposure or anticipation of exposure to that feared generally results in extreme anxiety and potentially a panic attack. DSM-IV-TR specifically notes that children may not be cognizant of the unreasonable or excessive nature of their fears; that fears may be expressed through crying, tantrum, freezing, or clinging behaviors; and that the phobia must be present for 6 months or longer. At a clinical level, phobias tend to be involuntary, inappropriate, and limiting to a child's life (Essau, Conradt, & Petermann, 2000). SPPs can be specified as falling into one of the following subtypes: animal, natural environment, blood-injection-injury, situational, or other.

Social phobia (SOCP) refers to excessive and persistent fear and avoidance of social situations or situations where scrutiny could lead to embarrassment. Feared situations are typically avoided or endured with intense distress that may take the form of a panic attack. Additional criteria for children in DSM-IV-TR include that the child has age-appropriate social relationships with familiar people and that the child's anxiety occurs for interactions involving peers as well as adults. As it does for SPP, DSM-IV-TR specifically notes that children may not be cognizant of the unreasonable or excessive nature of their social fears; that they may express their distress by crying, tantrums, freezing, clinging, or shrinking from social situations with unfamiliar people; and that their symptoms must be present for at least 6 months. The descriptor *generalized* is used as a specifier when most social situations and interactions are feared.

Obsessive-compulsive disorder (OCD) is diagnosed when a child experiences obsessions and/or compulsions that cause distress, are time consuming (i.e., an hour or more each day), and interfere with the child's daily life. Obsessions are recurrent and intrusive thoughts, impulses, or images that the child attempts to neutralize or suppress with other thoughts or actions. Compulsions are repetitive behaviors or mental acts that are performed in response to an obsession or used to reduce or prevent distress of a dreaded event. Often the child feels driven to perform the compulsive acts and if interrupted or prevented from doing so may feel intense anxiety or panic. Children need not recognize the unreasonable or excessive nature of their obsessions and/ or compulsions. Washing, checking, and ordering rituals are most common, and children will more often perform rituals at home than in front of others. Common obsessions involve contamination, aggressive or harmful acts to self or others, urges for exactness, and religiosity (March & Mulle, 1998; Piacentini & Langley, 2004). In rare cases, OCD symptoms may be associated with pediatric autoimmune neuropsychiatric disorders associated with streptococcal infections (Swedo et al., 1998).

Generalized anxiety disorder (GAD) is characterized by excessive and difficult-to-control anxiety and worry about several different domains that occurs more days than not for at least 6 months. Children must also exhibit at least one of six physical/somatic symptoms. Some of the more common worries among children with GAD concern performances, evaluation by others, perfectionism, health of significant others, and catastrophic events.

Posttraumatic stress disorder (PTSD) and acute stress disorder (ASD) are diagnosed in children who have experienced or witnessed an event that is perceived as threatening or dangerous to the child or others and that involves a response of intense fear, helplessness, or disorganized or agitated behavior. Following the event, the child continues to re-experience it through distressing memories or physiological arousal resulting from internal or external cues that are associated with the event in some way. Additional symptoms include persistent avoidance of stimuli associated with the event, numbing of general responsiveness, and persistent symptoms of arousal that were not present prior to the event. For PTSD (but not ASD), several specifications or qualifications are made for potential symptom variations in children and include that children may respond to traumatic events with disorganized or agitated behaviors and may display different re-experiencing (e.g., nightmares in general, rather than trauma-specific) and/or physical (e.g., stomach aches) symptoms from adults. Specifiers are also provided for PTSD, with *acute* used if symptoms have been present for less than 3 months, *chronic* if the symptoms have been present for 3 or more months, and with *delayed onset* if symptoms developed 6 months or longer after the traumatic event occurred. ASD is diagnosed when symptoms begin within 4 weeks of a traumatic event and last between 2 days and 4 weeks.

Panic disorder (PD) can be diagnosed with **agoraphobia (AG),** or either disorder can be diagnosed without the other. PD is marked by recurrent panic attacks which are acute and extreme feelings of anxiety that occur unexpectedly and are followed by at least 1 month of persistent concern about having another attack, worry about the consequences of the attack, or a change in behavior related to the attack. AG is characterized by excessive anxiety resulting from situations in which escape or avoidance may be inhibited or in which help might not be available if panic symptoms were to occur.

Two additional diagnoses are provided for when anxiety, panic, or obsessive-compulsive symptoms occur but are determined upon examination to be the direct result of either a medical condition (**anxiety due to a general medical condition**) or substance use (**substance-induced anxiety disorder**). In these instances, the specific medical condition (e.g., anxiety due to hypoglycemia) or substance (e.g., cannabis-induced anxiety disorder) is indicated, and for both diagnoses, specifiers are used to denote the type of anxiety symptoms present (e.g., with panic attacks). An additional specifier is used with substance-induced anxiety disorder to indicate whether symptoms occur during intoxication or withdrawal.

Anxiety disorder not otherwise specified (ADNOS) is diagnosed when anxiety symptoms are significant, but criteria are not met for any of the other formal diagnostic categories. ICD-10 provides several categories that are subsumed under ADNOS in DSM-IV-TR, including other phobic anxiety, phobic anxiety disorder–unspecified, other mixed anxiety disorders, other specified anxiety disorders, anxiety disorder–unspecified, other obsessive-compulsive disorders, obsessive-compulsive disorder–unspecified, other reactions to severe stress, and reaction to severe stress–unspecified.

1.2.3   Adjustment Disorders

An **adjustment disorder (ADJ)** is diagnosed within 3 months of a major life stressor that a child responds to with significant emotional and/or behavioral symptoms which are beyond that expected given the stressor, or that cause impairment in the child's life. Symptoms cannot be better accounted for by, or serve as an exacerbation of, an Axis I diagnosis like the above-described anxiety disorders; cannot be due to bereavement; and cannot last more than 6 months after the stressor has ended. For children, stressors might include family (e.g., new sibling, parental divorce) or environmental (e.g., new school, family move) issues. Three of the ADJ subtypes concern anxiety and include with anxiety, with mixed anxiety and depressed mood, or with mixed disturbance of emotions and conduct. Finally, specifiers are used to indicate whether symptoms have been present for less than (acute) or greater than (chronic) 6 months.

1.3   Epidemiology

Anxiety disorders are among the most commonly diagnosed childhood concerns; prevalence estimates typically range from 6% to 19%

As is likely apparent from Tables 2 and 3, anxiety disorders are among the most prevalent mental health concerns reported by children. Examined as a group, recent prevalence rate estimates for anxiety disorders during childhood typically range from 6% to 19% (e.g., Costello, Mustillo, Erkanli, Keeler, & Angold, 2003; Egger & Angold, 2006; Kessler et al., 2005; Merikangas, He, Brody, et al., 2010; Merikangas, He, Burstein, et al., 2010; Wittchen, Nelson, & Lachner, 1998). Further, when impairment criteria are not considered, prevalence rates climb substantially higher (e.g., 32% in Merikangas, He, Burstein, et al., 2010; 27% in Wittchen et al., 1998). Thus, a large prevalence range has been noted to occur, in part, because of inconsistent use of impairment and distress severity criteria across studies, as well as from sampling or ascertainment issues (e.g., community versus clinic-referred versus anxiety-clinic referred).

Of course prevalence rates also vary considerably for individual anxiety disorders assessed with differing time references (e.g., 3-month, 12-month, lifetime prevalence) or youth demographics (e.g., age, gender, race). Table 3 illustrates the former with studies of DSM-IV-TR criteria that have examined 3-month, 12-month, or lifetime prevalence estimates. Overall, increasing estimates are noted for any anxiety disorder diagnosis from 3 months (2.4–9.4%) to 12 months (3.4–17.7%) to lifetime (8.3–18.6%).

Bimodal distribution for age with peaks noted in early/ middle childhood and adolescence

Table 4 shows prevalence rates by age. Interestingly, while it has been reported by those with restricted samples that anxiety disorders increase in prevalence with age, there may actually be a bimodal distribution. For example, Costello et al. (2003) reported on the 3-month prevalence of anxiety disorders in 6,674 youths aged 9–16 and showed decreasing overall anxiety (any anxiety disorder) from ages 9–12 (4.6% to 0.9%), then an increase at age 13 (2.0%) that remained stable through the adolescent years (1.6–2.8%). A similar finding can also be observed for lifetime prevalence (Essau et al., 2000) by comparing the rates of 12–13 versus 14–15 and 16–17 year olds in Table 4. Although other DSM-IV-TR studies have not been completed across childhood and adolescence to be compared with these findings, clinicians should be cognizant that early childhood and early adolescence may represent particular peaks in anxiety disorder onset. In addition, certain diagnoses, such as SAD, show decreasing prevalence rates with age (Costello et al., 2003; Esbjørn, Hoeyer, Dyrborg, Leth, & Kendall, 2010; Gau, Chong, Chen, & Cheng, 2005; Kaplow, Curran, Angold, & Costello, 2001), while others, such as SOCP, GAD, PD, and PTSD increase with age (Canino et al., 2004; Costello et al., 2003; Esbjorn et al., 2010; Essau et al., 2000; Merikangas, He, Burstein, et al., 2010).

Studies comparing boys and girls have typically found small or nonexistent differences for anxiety disorders during childhood (Bittner et al., 2007; Canino et al., 2004; Egger & Angold, 2006); however, such differences become increasingly apparent in adolescence and into adulthood, with girls more often diagnosed with anxiety (Costello et al., 2003; Esbjorn et al., 2010; Essau et al., 2000; Gau et al., 2005; Merikangas, He, Burstein, et al., 2010; Roberts, Roberts, & Xing, 2007; Wittchen et al., 1998). This is most apparent when anxiety disorders are considered together, as depicted in the "Any Anxiety Disorder" category of Table 5. Also notable in Table 5 are the varying gender differences observed for the individual diagnostic categories.

Table 4
Lifetime, 12-Month, and 3-Month Prevalence Estimates Grouped By Age From Worldwide Studies of Anxiety Disorder

	N	Age	PD	AG	SPP	SOCP	OCD	PTSD	GAD	SAD	AD-NOS	Any anx	Country
Lifetime													
Essau et al. (2000)	380	12–13	0.0%	2.4%	2.6%	0.5%	0.3%	0.3%	0.0%	–	11.6%	14.7%	Germany
	350	14–15	0.9%	4.9%	3.1%	2.0%	2.0%	2.3%	0.9%	–	11.4%	19.7%	
	305	16–17	0.7%	5.2%	4.9%	2.6%	1.6%	2.6%	0.3%	–	12.8%	22.0%	
	3,897	15–16	2.3%	2.5%	18.3%	9.7%	–	5.1%	2.8%	8.0%	–	32.1%	
	2,356	17–18	3.3%	2.0%	17.7%	10.1%	–	7.0%	3.0%	6.7%	–	32.3%	
12-month													
Merikangas, He, Brody, et al. (2010)[a]	1,148	8–11	0.3%	–	–	–	–	–	0.0%	–	–	–	USA
	1,894	12–15	0.2%	–	–	–	–	–	0.4%	–	–	–	
3-month													
Gau et al. (2005)	1,070	13–15	0.2%	0.2%	5.0%	3.4%	0.2%	–	0.7%	0.3%	–	9.2%	Taiwan
	1,051	14–16	0.1%	0.0%	5.6%	1.8%	0.2%	–	0.3%	0.1%	–	7.4%	
	1,035	15–17	0.0%	0.0%	0.7%	2.0%	0.2%	–	0.4%	0.0%	–	3.1%	

Table 4 continued

	N	Age	PD	AG	SPP	SOCP	OCD	PTSD	GAD	SAD	AD-NOS	Any anx	Country
Costello et al. (2003)	936	9–10	<0.1%	0.0%	0.2%	0.3%	0.1%	0.0%	0.7%	4.1%	–	4.6%	USA
	901	11	0.0%	0.5%	<0.1%	0.3%	<0.1%	<0.1%	0.9%	1.2%	–	2.6%	
	854	12	0.1%	<0.1%	0.1%	0.1%	<0.1%	0.1%	0.3%	0.6%	–	0.9%	
	833	13	0.0%	0.1%	0.2%	1.2%	0.2%	0.0%	0.3%	0.5%	–	2.0%	
	913	14	0.1%	0.1%	0.1%	0.2%	0.4%	0.0%	1.3%	0.2%	–	1.8%	
	1,136	15	0.5%	0.4%	0.7%	1.1%	0.1%	<0.1%	0.8%	0.3%	–	2.8%	
	1,101	16	0.6%	0.3%	<0.1%	0.4%	<0.1%	0.0%	1.1%	<0.1%	–	1.6%	

Note. Dashes indicate data not reported. AD-NOS = anxiety disorder not otherwise specified; AG = agoraphobia; Anx = anxiety; GAD = generalized anxiety disorder; N = number; OCD = obsessive-compulsive disorder; PD = panic disorder; PTSD = posttraumatic stress disorder; SAD = separation anxiety disorder; SOCP = social phobia; SPP = specific phobia.
[a]Severe impairment criteria not applied.

Table 5
Lifetime, 12-Month, and 3-Month Prevalence Estimates Grouped By Gender From Worldwide Studies of Anxiety Disorders

	N	Age	PD	AG	SPP	SOCP	OCD	PTSD	GAD	SAD	AD-NOS	Any anx	Country
Lifetime													
Essau et al. (2000)													Germany
Male	421	12–17	0.5%	2.9%	2.4%	1.0%	1.2%	1.4%	0.5%	–	9.5%	13.8%	
Female	614	12–17	0.5%	4.9%	4.2%	2.1%	1.3%	1.8%	0.3%	–	13.5%	21.8%	
Wittchen et al. (1998)													Germany
Male	1,493	14–24	0.8%	1.0%	1.2%	2.2%	0.5%	0.4%	0.8%	–	3.3%	8.3%	
Female	1,528	14–24	2.4%	4.2%	3.3%	4.8%	0.9%	2.3%	0.8%	–	7.0%	20.3%	
Merikangas, He, Burstein, et al. (2010)[a]													USA
Male	4,953	13–18	2.0%	1.4%	16.7%	7.0%	–	2.3%	1.5%	6.3%	–	26.1%	
Female	5,170	13–18	2.6%	3.4%	22.1%	11.2%	–	8.0%	3.0%	9.0%	–	38.0%	
12-month													
Merikangas, He, Brody, et al. (2010)													USA
Male	1,492	8–15	0.2%	–	–	–	–	–	0.3%	–	–	–	
Female	1,550	8–15	0.4%	–	–	–	–	–	0.1%	–	–	–	
Wittchen et al. (1998)													Germany
Male	1,493	14–24	0.4%	0.6%	1.0%	1.5%	0.4%	0.1%	0.5%	–	1.2%	4.7%	
Female	1,528	14–24	2.0%	2.6%	2.6%	3.7%	0.8%	1.3%	0.6%	–	4.1%	13.8%	

Table 5 continued

	N	Age	PD	AG	SPP	SOCP	OCD	PTSD	GAD	SAD	AD-NOS	Any anx	Country
3-month													
Costello et al. (2003)													USA
Male	3,669	9–16	0.1%	0.2%	0.2%	0.3%	0.2%	<0.1%	0.6%	1.0%	–	2.0%	
Female	3,005	9–16	0.3%	0.3%	0.2%	0.8%	0.1%	<0.1%	0.9%	1.0%	–	2.9%	
Angold et al. (2002)													USA
Male	482	9–17	0.2%	0.3%	0.0%	1.1%	0.1%	–	1.2%	2.5%	–	4.2%	
Female	438	9–17	2.1%	0.6%	0.8%	1.6%	0.4%	–	1.3%	3.4%	–	7.1%	

Note. Dashes indicate data not reported. AD-NOS = anxiety disorder not otherwise specified; AG = agoraphobia; Anx = anxiety; GAD = generalized anxiety disorder; N = number; OCD = obsessive-compulsive disorder; PD = panic disorder; PTSD = posttraumatic stress disorder; SAD = separation anxiety disorder; SOCP = social phobia; SPP = specific phobia.
[a]Severe impairment criteria not applied.

For example, lifetime and 12-month prevalence rates for OCD and GAD are more similar for boys and girls, while higher prevalence for females is more consistently reported with AG, SPP, SOCP, PTSD, and ADNOS diagnoses (rates for PD are inconsistent). Studies of 3-month prevalence reveal more variable findings but also include a greater age range which may further influence findings.

Inconclusive findings have emerged from the relatively small number of studies that have examined racial and ethnicity group distributions. For example, some studies have shown differences across ethnic groups, but findings have varied from noting lower overall ("any") anxiety disorder prevalence rates for African-American youths (Egger et al., 2006) to greater overall anxiety prevalence rates for African-American youths (Merikangas, He, Burstein, et al., 2010) to greater GAD prevalence rates among White youths (Kaplow et al., 2001). Moreover, still other studies have shown no evidence for ethnic group differences in child and adolescent samples (e.g., Angold et al., 2002; Kaplow et al., 2001; Lavigne, LeBailly, Hopkins, Gouze, & Binns, 2009; Merikangas, He, Brody, et al., 2010; Pina, Silverman, Fuentes, Kurtines, & Weems, 2003; Roberts & Roberts, 2007).

Inconclusive findings regarding racial/ethnicity differences and anxiety disorder prevalence rates in youths

1.4   Course and Prognosis

Although a subset of children appear to exhibit a continuous course of anxious tendencies (or behavioral inhibition) from infancy onward (e.g., Essex et al., 2010; Moehler et al., 2008), the majority of individuals report an onset in childhood or adolescence. Indeed, the median age of onset for anxiety disorders as a group has been reported to range from 6 to 11 years (Kessler et al., 2005; Merikangas, He, Burstein, et al., 2010). An example of this, as well as the varying onsets for the different disorders, is displayed below in Figure 1. Figure 1 shows data from the Great Smoky Mountains Study (Costello, Egger, & Angold, 2004) and illustrates the mean age of onset by age 16 and interquartile ranges for each of the anxiety disorders.

Age of onset for anxiety disorders is typically reported to be during childhood/adolescence (even in adult samples)

Somewhat surprisingly, inconsistent reports have emerged regarding the course of childhood anxiety disorders. For example, a handful of studies have shown promising outcomes for untreated anxious youths (e.g., Feng, Shaw, & Silk, 2008; Last, Hanson, & Francis, 1997). On the other hand, a large number of others have noted that, left untreated, anxious youths tend to remain anxious into adolescence and even adulthood (e.g., Bittner et al., 2007; Gregory et al., 2007; Hirshfeld-Becker, Micco, Simoes, & Henin, 2008; Woodward & Fergusson, 2001). Importantly, childhood anxiety disorders also tend to be associated with a variety of other psychological (e.g., depression, substance use), social (e.g., peer rejection, school avoidance and dropout, social incompetence), and emotional (e.g., low self-worth, poor self-concept, depression) difficulties (e.g., Beesdo, Knappe, & Pine, 2009; Costello et al., 2003; Gregory et al., 2007; Grills & Ollendick, 2002a; Woodward & Fergusson, 2001). Taken together, the overall picture for anxious youths appears to be one wherein the risk for some later anxious or related difficulty is high and supports the need for intervention and, whenever possible, prevention.

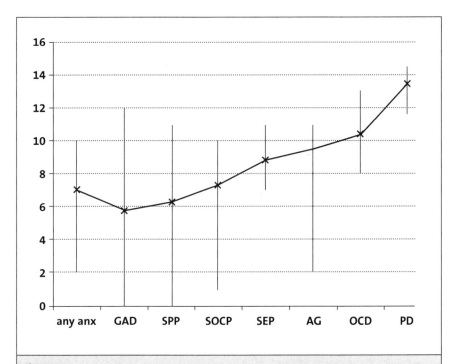

Figure 1
Xs mark the mean age of onset for each of the anxiety disorders noted, while solid vertical lines represent the interquartile ranges. Data from the Great Smoky Mountains Study. AG = agoraphobia; anx = anxiety; GAD = generalized anxiety disorder; OCD = obsessive-compulsive disorder; PD = panic disorder; SEP = separation anxiety disorder; SOCP = social phobia; SPP = specific phobia.
From "Developmental Epidemiology of Anxiety Disorders," by E. Costello, H. L. Egger, & A. Angold, in T. H. Ollendick & J. S. March, Eds., 2004, *Phobic and Anxiety Disorders in Children and Adolescents: A Clinician's Guide to Effective Psychosocial and Pharmacological Interventions*, p. 83. New York: Oxford University Press. © 2004 by Oxford University Press. Reprinted by permission of Oxford University Press.

Fortunately, treatment of childhood anxiety disorders has received a great deal of attention in the past several decades with many programs now showing quite favorable outcomes (e.g., Cartwright-Hatton, Roberts, Chitsabesan, Fothergill, & Harrington, 2004; Davis, May, & Whiting, 2011; Seligman & Ollendick, 2011). These treatments are detailed later in Chapter 4 of this book. What remains problematic, however, is how to reach youths in need of intervention for their anxiety. For example, in two recent reports, anxiety disorders were among the least likely areas for youths to have sought treatment (18% in Essau et al., 2000; and 34% in Merikangas, He, Brody, et al., 2010). Thus, a favorable prognosis is also limited by the fact that while effective treatments exist, most children with anxiety disorders will not receive them.

1.5   Differential Diagnosis

Several areas of differential diagnosis should be considered with childhood anxiety disorders. First, clinicians need to differentiate between normative versus pathological or clinically significant anxiety symptoms. Normative anxiety reactions tend to be milder in scope and response, are transitory and often follow a predictable developmental pattern (Bongers, Koot, van der Ende, & Verhulst, 2003; Ollendick, Grills, & Alexander, 2001; Van Oort et al., 2009). As an example, fears of the dark and parental separation are common in infants and young children, but would be concerning if they were causing excessive distress (child vomits when left at childcare) or interference (child does not sleep sufficiently because of fear of darkness). Likewise, fears of the dark or of parental separation would be a greater indicator of concern if expressed by a 15-year-old, as these are normatively outgrown by late childhood/early adolescence. Of course, normative fears and anxiety symptoms may also be subject to intervention; however, in these instances the clinician may focus on helping the child and his/her family cope with the transitory fears as well as providing anxiety prevention skills training.

Another major area of differentiation that often must occur is among the various anxiety disorder diagnoses. This can be accomplished by considering the primary stimuli feared and the reactions produced by those stimuli, and these are best differentiated through detailed investigation. As an illustration, a mother may bring her child for treatment reporting that he has excessive health concerns. With more information, the therapist can determine if these concerns are specific only to fear and avoidance of needles (SPP, blood-injection-injury subtype), represent a persistent concern with germs and contamination that is only alleviated with recurrent and time-consuming hand washing (obsessive-compulsive disorder), or is one of several uncontrollable worries expressed by the child that result in recurrent headaches and stomach aches (generalized anxiety disorder). PTSD, acute stress disorder, and adjustment disorders may also need differentiating; however, in these cases the timeline of symptoms following the stressor will most often guide the diagnosis. Table 2 provides brief descriptions of each of the anxiety disorder diagnoses that can be made in childhood, and it can be consulted when differentiating among these disorders.

Finally, anxiety disorders must be differentiated from other childhood disorders that have overlapping symptom presentations. For example, anxious children may appear inattentive/distracted or may behave in an oppositional way, especially when confronted by their fears. Given this, some children may present with a referral question pertaining to externalizing disorders, namely attention-deficit/hyperactivity disorder (ADHD) or oppositional defiant disorder (ODD). Similarly, anxious children often report physical symptoms of anxiety, such as stomach aches, sweating, or shaking, which may be confused with medical conditions or somatoform disorders such as hypochondriasis. Differentiating among these symptoms requires the clinician to discuss them carefully with the child's family and importantly, the child. Clinicians should focus on determining if a feared stimulus is present (e.g., tests at school, a bully, worries about family, germs) that accounts for these symptoms. In addition, clinicians should evaluate the pervasiveness and persistence of the symptoms across situations and over time. Finally, it is important for clinicians to

One problematic area is that anxious youth still rarely receive the treatment they need

When diagnosing an anxiety disorder, one needs to differentiate normal from clinical anxiety and anxiety from other disorders with overlapping symptoms

consider that, in some cases, multiple disorders may be present; an issue that is particularly important with anxiety disorders given the high rates of comorbidity found among them.

1.6   Comorbidities

Comorbidity is high, especially with other anxiety disorders, depression, externalizing, and substance use problems

Comorbidity (the co-occurrence of two or more disorders) is a substantial issue when examining the anxiety disorders, as both clinical and community studies have revealed significantly high rates. Other anxiety disorder diagnoses are typically the most frequently co-occurring, but comorbid depression, externalizing, and substance use disorders are also uniformly high. These areas are discussed below in turn. While these disorders are the most commonly comorbid, only a thorough assessment can determine the complete psychiatric profile.

Overall, anxiety–anxiety comorbidity rates in general population samples have been reported to be about 39% for children (Anderson, Williams, McGee, & Silva, 1987; Curry, March, & Hervey, 2004; Kashani & Orvaschel, 1990; Kendall et al., 2010) and about 14% for adolescents (Essau et al., 2000; Kashani & Orvaschel, 1988; McGee, Feehan, Williams, & Partridge, 1990). For specific disorders in epidemiological and clinical studies, these rates have been especially high for SOCP and SPP (~22–50% in Beidel, Turner, & Morris, 2000; Rao et al., 2007; Walkup et al., 2008), PD (63%–97% in Biederman et al., 1997; Doerfler, Connor, Volungis, & Toscano, 2007; Last, Perrin, Hersen, & Kazdin, 1992; Masi, Favilla, Mucci, & Millepiedi, 2000a), OCD (60% in Barrett, Healy-Farrell, Piacentini, & March, 2004; Last & Strauss, 1989) and OAD (over anxious disorder)/GAD (53–96% in Last et al., 1992; Masi, Mucci, Favilla, Romano, & Poli, 1999; Verduin & Kendall, 2003; Walkup et al., 2008).

Comorbid depression in children and adolescents with anxiety disorders is also extremely high, ranging from 17% to 69% in the general population and clinical samples (Biederman et al., 1997; Chavira, Garland, Daley, & Hough, 2008; Doerfler et al., 2007; Essau et al., 2000; Last et al., 1992; Masi et al., 1999, 2000b; Strauss, Last, Hersen, & Kazdin, 1988). Indeed, a review of studies on this issue reported that children with anxiety disorders were 8.2 times more likely to also have a depressive disorder than children without anxiety disorders (Angold et al., 1999). Identifying youths who are experiencing multiple anxiety disorders or comorbid anxiety and depressive disorders is particularly important as the combination of these disorders has been associated with increased psychopathology and severity of symptoms (e.g., Masi et al., 1999; Strauss et al., 1988; Viana, Rabian, & Beidel, 2008). For example, one longitudinal study found that the more adolescent anxiety diagnoses received, the greater the chance of having other comorbid disorders in adulthood, specifically anxiety, depression, suicidality, and substance dependence (Woodward & Fergusson, 2001).

Externalizing disorders are also frequently found to be comorbid with anxiety disorders (23–69% in Anderson et al., 1987; Biederman et al., 1997; Chavira et al., 2008; Doerfler et al., 2007). Specifically, comorbid rates with anxiety typically range from 5–50% for ADHD and 2–40% for ODD or conduct disorder (CD; Beidel, Turner, Young, et al., 2007; Doerfler et al., 2007; Marmorstein, 2006; Rao et al., 2007; Verduin & Kendall, 2003; Walkup et al., 2008; Wever & Rey, 1997). In a review of anxiety-externalizing disorder comorbidity, children with anxiety disorders were found to be 3.1 times more likely to have CD/ODD and 3.0 times more likely to have ADHD than those without an anxiety disorder (Angold et al., 1999). Although the impact of comorbid externalizing disorders is less clear than that with internalizing disorders, age patterns may emerge, with comorbid ADHD symptoms more common in childhood and comorbid ODD and/or CD more commonly comorbid in early and mid-adolescence (Ollendick, Hagopian, & King, 1997).

Substance use disorders have also been found to be comorbid with anxiety disorders in adolescence (e.g., 11–12% in Doerfler et al., 2007; Essau et al., 2000; McGee et al., 1990; Zimmermann et al., 2003), with research showing that anxiety precedes substance use in the majority of cases (see Brückl et al., 2007; Merikangas et al., 1998). Some have reported that substance use disorders are especially likely to be comorbid among those with particular anxiety disorders: namely, GAD (Bittner et al., 2007; Kaplow et al., 2001), SOCP, or PD/panic attacks (Zimmermann et al., 2003). In contrast, youths with SAD have been found to be less likely to engage in comorbid substance use (Bittner et al., 2007; Kaplow et al., 2001). Sex differences may also influence comorbidity with substance use. For example, two studies have reported that the link with substance use was only significant for anxious adolescent females (Bittner et al., 2007; Costello et al., 2003).

In addition to psychiatric disorders, anxious children have also been found to evidence other comorbid difficulties, such as in socioemotional/behavioral, academic, or medical domains, that may also warrant evaluation. In the academic domain, school refusal behaviors (Egger, Costello, & Angold, 2003), poorer academic achievement (Grills-Taquechel, Fletcher, Vaughn, & Stuebing, 2011; Ialongo, Edelsohn, Werthamer-Larsson, & Crockett, 1994; Woodward & Fergusson, 2001), and school dropout have been reported (Van Ameringen, Mancini, & Farvolden, 2003; Wittchen et al., 1998). Socioemotional and behavioral correlates commonly reported for anxious children include social incompetence and peer rejection/bullying (Carney, Hazler, Oh, Hibel, & Granger, 2010; Grills & Ollendick, 2002a; Strauss et al., 1988), feelings of loneliness (Løhre, Lydersen, & Vatten, 2010; Weeks, Coplan, & Kingsbury, 2009), poor self-concept or low self-worth (Grills & Ollendick, 2002a; La Greca & Fetter; 1995; Reijntjes et al., 2011), and sleep disturbances (e.g., Alfano, Ginsburg, & Kingery, 2007). Finally, children with several medical difficulties have been found to also experience anxiety disorders at disproportionately higher rates than expected or found in the general population. Two well-supported examples of these include recurrent abdominal pain (e.g., Campo et al., 2004; Dufton, Dunn, & Compas, 2009) and asthma (e.g., Katon et al., 2007; McQuaid, Kopel, & Nassau, 2001). In all, substantial comorbidity has been reported from research with anxious children and adolescents. These findings support the need for a thorough assessment, even when a child's initial presentation clearly supports an anxiety disorder diagnosis. Such an assessment may provide important information on other anxiety-related areas (e.g., social concerns) in need of intervention or indicate other diagnoses requiring primary intervention before the anxiety can be adequately addressed.

Anxiety disorders are also commonly associated with a variety of socioemotional, behavioral, academic, and medical difficulties

1.7   Future Diagnostic Considerations

As a final note, a new edition of the *Diagnostic and Statistical Manual of Mental Disorders* (DSM-5) is due to be published in May 2013. As DSM-5 remains in the development stage and far too many suggested alterations have been made to address here, only a few key issues will be noted. First, structurally, several considerations are being made to the "Anxiety Disorders" section of DSM-5. These include moving SAD into the anxiety disorders section, making selective mutism a specifier of SOCP, and making AG a separate diagnosis from PD. In addition, it has been proposed that OCD will be moved to a separate section (obsessive-compulsive and related disorders) and will be listed along with such conditions as skin picking, trichotillomania, hoarding, and body dysmorphic disorder. Likewise, PTSD, ASD, and adjustment disorders, along with several additional diagnoses (e.g., reactive attachment disorder, disinhibited social engagement disorder), are proposed for a separate section ("Trauma and Stressor Related Disorders") that would separate PTSD from PTSD in preschool children. Finally, mixed anxiety/depression is proposed to appear as a diagnosis in the depressive disorders section of DSM-5. Overall, attempts are also clearly being made to include more specific examples and clarifications with anxiety diagnostic criteria, and severity scales are being added to standardize measurement and enhance understanding of perceived distress. For more information or updates on DSM-5, the reader is referred to the Working Group website at http://www.dsm5.org.

2

Theories and Models of Phobic and Anxiety Disorders

Theoretical models of anxiety disorders have been continuously evolving over the last century. As a result, current theories tend to draw from several areas of research. For example, biopsychosocial and integrative models have evolved which commonly include the combination of biological, developmental, psychological, and social influences. Presenting the extensive research that has supported these theories is well beyond the scope of this chapter. Rather, brief mention will be given to each of these areas (see Table 6) and

Table 6
Common Risk and Maintenance Factors for Childhood Anxiety Disorders

Biological contributions	Child/developmental contributions	Psychosocial/environmental contributions
Genetics	Temperament – Behavioral inhibition – Negative emotionality	Direct exposure
Neurobiological influences	Poor attachment	Parental rearing behaviors – Rejection/criticism – Overcontrol
Medical conditions	Cognitive biases – Attention – Interpretation – Judgment – Memory	Parental modeling – Vicarious learning – Reinforcement – Information transfer
	Anxiety sensitivity	Peer relationships – Rejection/exclusion – Poor quality friendships
	Disgust sensitivity	Familial stressors – Parental divorce
	Emotion regulation/ dysregulation	– Parental loss – Parental/family conflict
	Control perceptions	– Abuse within family – Parental psychopathology – Low parental expectations
	Coping skills	Community stressors – Exposure to violence
	Social skills deficits	– Traumatic events

major areas of research focus within them, with references to pertinent work for interested readers. Greater focus is devoted to areas more directly relevant for assessment and treatment recommendations, and a final section provides a brief depiction of some of the contemporary integrated models of anxiety development.

2.1   Genetic/Biological Contributions

Anxiety disorders comprised both heritable and nonheritable (psychosocial/ environmental) components

Regarding biological contributions, it is now clear that anxiety disorders have a heritable component, as demonstrated by a growing body of genetic, familial, and twin research studies (see Arnold & Taillefer, 2011; Gregory & Eley, 2007; Hirshfeld-Becker, Micco, et al., 2008). From these studies, we know that higher concordance is found among identical versus fraternal twins, with reported heritability estimates typically in the range of .2 to .4. In addition, these studies have confirmed that there is a significantly greater risk of developing an anxiety disorder in children who have a parent with an anxiety disorder; though children are not predisposed to "inherit" the same disorder as their parent. Neurobiological research has also emerged, suggesting potentially important roles for the limbic and fear circuitry systems, especially the amygdala (e.g., De Bellis et al., 2000; Pine, 2009), frontal lobe asymmetry (see Forbes et al., 2006; Thibodeau, Jorgensen, & Kim, 2006), and neurotransmitter systems, such as those involving serotonin (see Arnold & Taillefer, 2011; Gregory & Eley, 2007). In short, findings from genetic and biologically oriented studies have provided substantial information regarding child anxiety disorders. However, this research only accounts for roughly one third to one half of cases, leaving a significant amount of influence to other areas. Of course even in those cases when genetics/biological contributions are present, they alone do not account for the development of anxiety disorders in young people, a fact that clearly illustrates the need to consider psychosocial/ environmental domains.

Nonetheless, it is important to recognize that given strong heritability rates, parents presenting with their anxious child may also be experiencing significant anxiety difficulties. In addition to any family history of mental health concerns, clinicians should consider incorporating a brief parent anxiety screener into their assessment battery for determining this. In such cases, for example, the therapist may also need to address the parents' anxiety (e.g., through referral for treatment or active participation in the child's treatment) to best intervene for the child and potentially decrease the chance of relapse.

2.2   Child/Developmental Characteristics

2.2.1   Early Behavioral Indicators

Several behaviors or traits of infants/young children have been linked with the later diagnosis of anxiety disorders. Among these, temperament has emerged as a robust and stable predictor, with both behavioral inhibition and negative affectivity or emotionality showing the strongest associations (see Degnan, Almas, & Fox, 2010; Feng, Shaw, & Silk, 2008; Hirshfeld-Becker, Micco, et al., 2008; Karevold, Røysamb, Ystrom, & Mathiesen, 2009; Muris, van Brakel, Arntz, & Schouten, 2011). Behavioral inhibition is present in about 10–15% of infants (Fox, Henderson, Marshall, Nichols, & Ghera, 2005). These infants typically experience physiological arousal and withdraw or show fear when exposed to unfamiliar situations. With advances in child development, the expression and developmental processes involved with behavioral inhibition tend to vary. Negative affectivity or emotionality refers to a pattern of negative mood and emotional reactions along with increased irritability and difficulty being soothed or comforted. Whereas behavioral inhibition has been specifically associated with anxiety disorders, negative emotionality has been associated with anxiety, mood, and internalizing symptoms, including depression and irritability.

> **Behavioral inhibition and negative affectivity, as well as poor attachment, are all strong predictors of later anxiety diagnoses**

Poor attachment patterns (insecure) with primary caregivers have also been linked with both behavioral inhibition and later anxiety disorders (e.g., Gar, Hudson, & Rapee, 2005; Manassis, 2001; Shamir-Essakow, Ungerer, & Rapee, 2005). Children with insecure attachments may show distress when separated from their primary caregiver or in new environments but also show little interest in receiving comfort from their caregiver. Insecure attachment is believed to influence the development of child anxiety, as the child may develop the sense of an unpredictable world and the lack of secure support from primary caregivers.

> **Most families will not present for treatment until the child is much older than when these characteristics are observed**

Although temperament and attachment have been well linked with the onset of child anxiety disorders, most often children will not present for treatment until several years beyond the development of these early behavioral indicators. That is, these two domains develop in infancy, and most children will not be brought for treatment of anxiety disorders until they are several years older. Still these early precursors are important as they may set the stage for the development of anxiety, and may inform treatment approaches insomuch as there may be a continuing negative pattern of parent–child interaction. For example, researchers have found that a transaction may occur in which children with behavioral inhibition elicit greater overprotection from their parents (e.g., Mills & Rubin, 1993). In such cases, it would be relevant for the clinician to be aware of this continued pattern, as it may serve as an additional target for intervention. Importantly, these early indicators may also represent identifiable areas to be modified in an attempt to prevent the onset of later anxiety disorders.

2.2.2 Cognitive and Emotional Contributions

Cognitive Biases

In terms of cognitive contributions, theorists have proposed several risk factors involving biases and misinterpretations, problem solving, and control. With regard to cognitive biases, four different areas are typically discussed (though varying terminology has been used), and these include attention bias, interpretation, judgment, and memory (Cowart & Ollendick, 2010; Vasey & MacLeod, 2001; Weems, Costa, Watts, Taylor, & Cannon, 2007).

> **Common cognitive biases of anxious youth include attention, interpretation, judgment, and memory**

Anxious children often have an attention bias toward things viewed as threatening and misinterpret ambiguous things as threatening

Numerous studies have shown that anxious children exhibit an attention bias toward perceived threatening stimuli, as well as an interpretation bias marked by misinterpretation of ambiguous aspects of their environment as threatening (e.g., Cannon & Weems, 2010; Creswell, Schniering, & Rapee, 2005; Hadwin & Field, 2010; Puliafico & Kendall, 2006). Attention bias toward threatening stimuli does not only appear to occur in anxious youths, however. Rather, this bias has been shown to occur in children more generally (e.g., Morren, Kindt, van den Hout, & van Kasteren, 2003; Waters, Lipp, & Spence, 2004) and to be present from early in infancy (Field & Lester, 2010). Interestingly, an attention bias has also been found to develop alongside increased fear in children who were given negative/fearful information about a novel stimulus (an unknown animal; Field, 2006). Thus, it may be that children with anxiety disorders have been provided fear information about a greater number of stimuli or have shown an increased tendency to generalize from specific fear stimuli to others, perhaps due to a predisposition for anxiety. Also remarkable, whereas in adults threat attention bias has been shown to dissipate following anxiety treatment using cognitive behavioral intervention (Mathews, Mogg, Kentish, & Eysenck, 1995; Mogg, Bradley, Millar, & White, 1995), this has not been replicated with children to date (Waters, Wharton, Zimmer-Gembeck, & Craske, 2008). Although replication of these findings is needed, it is likely the case that child anxiety treatments would benefit from more specifically addressing attention biases (Cowart & Ollendick, 2010; Puliafico & Kendall, 2006).

Interpretation bias reflects the tendency to view ambiguous stimuli as threatening. An example we commonly use to depict this for young people is the school cafeteria phenomenon:

> It is lunchtime, and you walk into the cafeteria and see your friends already sitting together. As you approach the table, they start laughing. Now how you interpret the situation will certainly influence how you feel. For example, if you think – wow my friends are having a great time, and I can't wait to join them, then you will probably feel happy and walk over to your friends; but, if you think – oh no, they are laughing at me, I probably have something on my face or said something stupid in class, then you will probably feel anxious and/or sad and leave the cafeteria.

Unfortunately, anxious children seem predisposed to adhere to interpretations such as the latter and respond with avoidance behaviors. For example, anxious and oppositional children have been found to differ from nonclinical children in that they both interpreted ambiguous situations as threatening and their responses also differed from one another, with the former responding with avoidance and the latter aggression (Barrett, Rapee, Dadds, & Ryan, 1996). Remarkably, research has shown that parents (mothers and fathers) of anxious children mirror these response patterns (Barrett, Rapee, et al., 1996; Chorpita, Albano, & Barlow, 1996; Creswell et al., 2005; Shortt, Barrett, & Fox, 2001) and that subsequent to discussions with their parents, children's avoidant responses increased (Barrett, Rapee, et al., 1996; Chorpita et al., 1996; Shortt et al., 2001). Moreover, a few studies have examined differences following cognitive behavior therapy (CBT) for anxiety and showed that threat interpretation biases decreased for children following CBT (Barrett, Dadds, & Rapee, 1996; Creswell et al., 2005; Waters et al., 2008). Given the associations between child and parent interpretation biases, it is not surprising that treatments that include parental components seem particularly beneficial. For example, one recent study showed decrements in both child and parent interpretation biases following a child/family anxiety treatment (Creswell et al., 2005), and another showed greater reductions in both the interpretation biases and avoidance plans of children whose parents were included in treatment compared with those whose parents were not and those who were not provided treatment (Barrett, Dadds, et al., 1996). Taken together, these findings suggest that parenting behaviors may serve to reinforce children's misinterpretations and avoidance of feared stimuli, a notion that will be further discussed in the parental behaviors section below (Section 2.3.1 Parenting Behaviors).

On a related note, it is believed that interpretation bias is fueled by children's use of cognitive distortions or errors (Cannon & Weems, 2010). Common cognitive distortions that have been linked with interpretation bias, and anxiety more generally, include catastrophizing (the tendency to expect the worst outcomes possible), overgeneralizing (generalizing from one event to all similar or future ones), personalizing (having an internal locus of control for negative events), and selective abstraction or filtering (seeing only the negative even when positives are overwhelmingly present in a situation) (Beck, 1976; Leitenberg, Yost, & Carroll-Wilson, 1986). Fortunately, the empirically supported child anxiety interventions detailed in Chapter 4 typically include a treatment component designed to address these cognitive biases.

Judgment biases reflect children's perceptions of their ability to cope and are considered to be poor among anxious youths. It has been specifically noted that, in children, these biases can "refer to lowered expectations of their ability to handle threatening situations or events" (Weems et al., 2007, p. 178). Thus, judgment biases encompass the role of perceived lack of control, where control is defined as "the ability to personally influence events and outcomes in one's environment, particularly those related to positive and negative reinforcement" (Chorpita & Barlow, 1998, p. 5). Early experiences with a lack of control can lead a child to more generally foresee outcomes as uncontrollable and aversive, feelings which in turn result in increased anxiety. Research has supported this notion, as anxious and nonanxious children have been found to differ in their levels of control beliefs and judgment biases (e.g., Cannon & Weems, 2010; Weems et al., 2007).

Judgment biases concern beliefs about your ability to cope, including perceived feelings of lack of control, and are considered to be poor among anxious youths

Memory biases reflect the selective recall of negative, fearful, or threatening information (Vasey & MacLeod, 2001). This could be considered a risk factor, as anxious children may be more likely to store and subsequently retrieve fear-congruent information. For example, SOCP symptoms may increase for a child who commits more negative (versus positive) experiences of social interactions into memory. Likewise, memory biases could serve to maintain anxiety as children may be more likely to recall negative information about feared situations. Although less research has been done in this area, studies do suggest that such memory biases are present in children with anxiety symptoms (e.g., Miles, MacLeod, & Pote, 2004; Watts & Weems, 2006), as well as in those with PTSD (Moradi, Taghavi, Neshat-Doost, Yule, & Dalgleish, 2000).

Memory biases reflect selective recall of information and can be characterized by negative, fearful, and threatening information for anxious children and adolescents

In summary, several cognitive biases have been noted to occur with greater frequency in anxious youths. While interrelated, each of these has been found to individually contribute to children's anxiety and distress levels (Watts & Weems, 2006; Weems et al., 2007). Given their potential influence on the maintenance of anxious symptoms, it would be beneficial for clinicians to explore these biases with children and their families as it may be beneficial to include extra emphasis on intervention modules addressing them during treatment.

Anxiety and Disgust Sensitivity

High anxiety sensitivity is associated with feelings that arousing situations are harmful and unpleasant and that anxious symptoms are something to fear

Anxiety and disgust sensitivity represent two additional areas that have received increased focus in terms of their role in the development and maintenance of child anxiety disorders. Anxiety sensitivity is conceptually similar to interpretation bias and refers to the degree to which an individual interprets arousing experiences in an anxious or apprehensive manner. For youths high in anxiety sensitivity, highly arousing situations are experienced as harmful and unpleasant, and anxiety symptoms themselves are highly feared, typically because of their perceived negative consequences (e.g., Reiss, 1991). To illustrate, a child who is high in anxiety sensitivity may become distressed after climbing a flight of stairs as he notices that he is sweating; a feared physical sign that the child misinterprets as meaning that he is going to pass out. Anxiety sensitivity has been linked with the development of child and adolescent anxiety disorders, and especially PD (e.g., Eley, Gregory, Clark, & Ehlers, 2007; Noël & Francis, 2011). Furthermore, a recent meta-analysis of child anxiety sensitivity findings revealed that it distinguishes between those with anxiety disorders and those without clinical diagnoses (Noël & Francis, 2011).

High disgust sensitivity is characterized by fear and avoidance of certain stimuli because of their association with contamination or disease

Disgust sensitivity represents the degree to which a child experiences generalized feelings of disgust toward a variety of stimuli; feelings which may subsequently increase avoidance behaviors of those highly "disgusted" stimuli (Deacon & Olatunji, 2007; McNally, 2002). The idea that disgust sensitivity may be involved with anxiety disorders has been derived from a connection with a disease-avoidance model (Matchett & Davey, 1991). Specifically, rather than the typical fear of harm associated with anxiety, with high disgust sensitivity stimuli are believed to be feared and avoided because of their association with contamination or disease. With adults, this has received greater attention and has been particularly associated with SPPs (i.e., blood-injection-injury and animals such as spiders or snakes) and OCD (e.g., Olatunji, Cisler, McKay, & Phillips, 2010; Olatunji & Deacon, 2008). Research with children has also been done by de Jong, Muris, and colleagues, and it appears that similar relations are present. Specifically, disgust sensitivity has been associated with various anxiety symptoms including phobias, separation anxiety, and OCD (Muris, Merckelbach, Schmidt, & Tierney, 1999; Muris, van der Heiden, & Rassin, 2008), differentiated between phobic and nonphobic youth (de Jong & Muris, 2002), and decreased in phobic girls following treatment (de Jong, Andrea, & Muris, 1997). In addition, disgust levels, fear beliefs, and avoidance behaviors have been shown to increase when children were told disgust-related information and decrease when they were told cleanliness-related information about an unknown animal (Muris, Huijding, et al., 2009; Muris, Mayer, Huijding, & Konings, 2008). While this remains a growing area of research, it presents an additional consideration when assessing and conceptualizing anxious cases.

Emotion Regulation/Dysregulation

Emotion regulation refers to an individual's goal-directed tendencies to modify their emotional states to best achieve social and biological adaptation (Eisenberg & Spinrad, 2004). Thus, in response to emotional arousal, attempts are made to efficiently regulate that emotion to a manageable level, and this can have clear implications for the child's personal and social experiences of emotions. For example, an angry child who turns red and begins throwing things is as likely to receive negative social feedback as a child who excessively celebrates when he gets a correct test answer. Further, in both instances, the child may experience an out-of-control feeling if the emotions cannot be modulated. Not surprisingly, anxious children are often characterized as experiencing greater emotion dysregulation (see Hannesdottir & Ollendick, 2007 for review). As examples, studies have revealed that anxious youths have poorer understanding and lower self-efficacy regarding emotions and how to modulate them to achieve interpersonal goals, as well as experiencing emotions with greater intensity (e.g., Southam-Gerow & Kendall, 2000; Suveg & Zeman, 2004). Together, these findings suggest that it may prove useful to incorporate into child anxiety treatments aspects such as psychoeducation on emotions and their influence on the experiences of self and others, as well as emotion regulation skills training (Hannesdottir & Ollendick, 2007).

> Anxious youths also appear to have poorer understanding about emotions and how to regulate them to achieve their goals

In short, several child characteristics have been implicated in the development of anxiety disorders, among which some of the most commonly purported and studied have included cognitive biases and distortions, anxiety and/or disgust sensitivities, and emotion dysregulation. Of course there are also numerous other domains, such as children's perceptions of control (e.g., Barlow, 2000; Chorpita & Barlow, 1998) and coping behaviors (e.g., Kendall, 1994), that may similarly be relevant to the development of anxiety. Further, because these areas are more likely to be present and/or emerging in youths presenting for treatment, it is pertinent for clinicians to understand their potential role in the development and maintenance of child anxiety. Clinicians might find it beneficial to screen for these areas, following up as necessary with more complete measures such as those detailed in Chapter 3, to assist with determining the etiology of a child's anxiety.

2.3   Environmental/Psychosocial Aspects

2.3.1   Parenting Behaviors

Among the varying lines of research on environmental/psychosocial influences on the development of child anxiety, parenting behaviors have received particular attention. In this domain, research has primarily focused on parental modeling of anxiety (see Beidel & Turner, 1998; Fisak & Grills-Taquechel, 2007) and parental rearing behaviors characterized by the dimensions of rejection/warmth and control/granting of autonomy (see DiBartolo & Helt, 2007; Rapee, 1997).

Parental Modeling

Learning experiences influence children's development in numerous ways. From an early age, children are like sponges absorbing information from those around them. Even young infants have been found to respond in anxious ways, for example, through a startle response to a loud noise or from observing a concerned expression on the face of a mother. In fact, children as young as 12 months have demonstrated fearful and avoidant behaviors toward a stranger that their mother had previously interacted anxiously with (de Rosnay, Cooper, Tsigaras, & Murray, 2006) and to a novel toy after their mothers reacted with negative facial expressions toward it (Gerull & Rapee, 2002). Indeed, it has long been known that children may learn to fear novel or familiar stimuli via the principles of conditioning. Certainly, a direct negative event may trigger fear; for example, a child bit by a dog develops a fear of dogs (Bouton, Mineka, & Barlow, 2001). However, children may also learn anxious behaviors from less direct processes. Specifically, research has shown that learning also occurs via transfer of information (e.g., a parent tells the child to watch out for bees because they can chase and sting you), observing others' behaviors (e.g., a spider phobic parent reacts by screaming and yelling for help when a spider is seen on the floor of the kitchen), and reinforcement of child anxious/ avoidant behaviors (e.g., providing excessive reassurance to a child when they show fearful behaviors, or removing the child from the situation). As parents/ primary caregivers typically provide the greatest amount of learning experiences during children's development, research has focused on their "teaching" of anxious and avoidant behaviors in these ways.

Vicarious learning or directly modeled parent behaviors have been among the most commonly investigated. Parents may model behaviors related to the development of anxiety in a number of ways, including expression of their own anxiety or anxious thoughts in front of their child, presenting as visibly anxious, and modeling avoidance behaviors. Studies have shown that children who report that their parents engage in anxious rearing behaviors such as these also tend to report greater symptoms of anxiety (e.g., Grüner, Muris, & Merckelbach, 1999; Roelofs, Meesters, Ter Huurne, Bamelis, & Muris, 2006) and worry (Muris, Meesters, Merckelbach, & Hülsenbeck, 2000). Similarly, parents who report expressing their fears and related behaviors more often in front of their children or who have been observed to display more anxious behaviors, have children who tend to report a greater number of fears (e.g., Buckley & Woodruff-Borden, 2006; Moore, Whaley, & Sigman, 2004). In addition, some disorder-specific findings have been noted. For example, studies have shown that adolescents and college students with greater social anxiety symptoms have recalled greater parental isolation, concern with other people's opinions, and shame, as well as less family sociability (e.g., Bruch & Heimberg, 1994; Spokas & Heimberg, 2009), while greater PD symptoms have been associated with greater recalled parental panic-related symptoms, anxiety sensitivity, and illness-related behaviors (Ehlers, 1993; Watt & Stewart, 2000).

Beyond modeling, the development of panic and anxiety has been associated with parental reinforcement of these symptoms in several retrospective studies (Ehlers, 1993; Watt & Stewart, 2000). For instance, a mother reinforces her son's fears by providing excessive comfort to him when he refuses to go in the water during swim class. In addition, research involving parent–child interactions has revealed that parents of anxious children may discourage brave behaviors and encourage avoidant and anxious ones (e.g., Barrett, Fox, & Farrell, 2005; Barrett, Rapee, et al., 1996; Dadds, Barrett, Rapee, & Ryan, 1996). For example, anxious, compared with nonanxious, children have been found to have parents who communicate more anxious messages (e.g., "be careful" and "don't climb too high") when they play (Beidel & Turner, 1998) and to reciprocate children's avoidant solutions to problems (Dadds et al., 1996).

Finally, information transfer pertains to messages given directly to children about such aspects as their safety, well-being, and situations or stimuli that should be avoided due to potential harm. Although the messages are intended to protect the child, the parent may be too frequently discussing these concerns with their child or communicating a level of danger that exceeds the actual threat from these situations. Studies asking children how their fears were acquired have found a particularly strong link with information transfer. For example, Ollendick and King (1991) and Muris, Merckelbach, and Meesters (2001) each found that information transfer (78–88%) was the most frequently reported mode of acquisition for children's fears as reported by children and their parents. Modeling (26–56%) and conditioning (13–36%) events were also reported but to much lesser extents. In the past decade, a series of fascinating studies have been completed by Andy Field and his colleagues supporting this pathway in the development of child anxiety, and particularly fears. Their work has repeatedly demonstrated that providing children with negative information about an unknown animal subsequently produces greater fear beliefs and avoidance of that creature (e.g., Field, 2006; Field & Lawson, 2003) that can persist over an extended period of time (Field, Lawson, & Banerjee, 2008).

Even providing negative information to a child can have a negative influence, resulting in greater fear beliefs and avoidance

Although in the studies by Field and colleagues, the source of information was not the child's parent, a recent study has shown that similar results emerge when parents are involved (Muris, Van Zwol, Huijding, & Mayer, 2010). Remarkably, this study showed that when parents were given negative information about an unknown animal, they tended to pass that onto their children, which in turn resulted in greater child fear beliefs. When parents were given ambiguous information about the animal, it was only the more anxious parents who tended to pass along negative information, again resulting in greater child fear beliefs. While these represent experimental research paradigms, it is clear that the potential impact of such parenting practices could be considerable.

Despite the fact that each of these parental modeling behaviors has been linked with child anxiety, it is important to note that anxious behaviors most likely develop and get maintained through a dynamic transaction between children and their parents. For instance, a young boy may begin showing fearful behaviors (e.g., freezing/whining) toward dogs after having one jumps and nips at him. His parents may then reinforce these anxious behaviors, even subtly – for instance, by expressing their own fear of dogs near their child or repeatedly telling him to be careful when dogs approach. Parents may also reinforce the child's avoidance of dogs by providing excessive reassurance or comfort, taking control of the situation for the child (e.g., telling the neighbor to put the dog inside), or by allowing the child to avoid dogs (e.g., by driving the child to the school bus instead of having him walk past homes that have dogs). These parental behaviors may then preclude the child from having to

Anxiety most likely develops and gets maintained through a dynamic transaction between children and their parents (or primary caregivers)

learn his own coping or problem-solving skills, as well as reinforce the child for displaying those fearful behaviors (Eisen, Brien, Bowers, & Strudler, 2001; Vasey & Ollendick, 2000). Such acts may also be reinforcing because of the relief experienced by the child when he is allowed to escape or avoid his fear (dogs). In addition, removing the child from the fear-inducing situation may also be reinforcing to the parent who is able to avoid their own distress and witnessing that of their child. Indeed, this may occur even for nonanxious parents, such that they allow their child to avoid feared stimuli because they do not wish to see him/her in distress. In turn, parental behaviors such as these may subsequently increase the child's anxiety resulting in more frequent or intense distress or avoidance when that stimulus (dog) is encountered again in the future.

Parental Rearing Behaviors

Two specific parental rearing dimensions have generally emerged as prominent in child anxiety research. The first dimension ranges from rejection and criticism to acceptance and warmth, while the second dimension ranges from extremes of control to autonomy granting. Since several reviews have provided extensive discussion of the role these parenting factors play in the development of anxiety (e.g., DiBartolo & Helt, 2007; Feng et al., 2008; McLeod, Wood, & Weisz, 2007; Rork & Morris, 2009; van der Bruggen, Stams, & Bögels, 2008; Wood, McLeod, Sigman, Hwang, & Chu, 2003), only a brief presentation of them follows.

Parenting behaviors marked by low warmth, high criticism, poor responsiveness, and overcontrol have been implicated in the development and maintenance of child anxiety

Regarding the first dimension, low warmth, high levels of criticism, and poor responsiveness from parents have been implicated in the development and maintenance of child anxiety. In general, it is believed that experiencing such behaviors results in the child's uncertainty about the self and the environment and that the child develops a view of the world as frightening and unpredictable (Wood, 2006; Wood et al., 2003). The second dimension includes acts such as manipulating the child's thoughts and feelings, as well as limiting the child's activities and regulating the child's actions (Wood et al., 2003). It is surmised that experiencing these behaviors inhibits the child's own exploration of their environment, the development of their own coping skills, and learning that the situation was not as bad as presumed (Hudson & Rapee, 2000, 2001; Moore et al., 2004), which in turn may make the child less convinced of their own self-efficacy and more dependent on their parent to assist them in the future (Wood, 2006). These sorts of influences on children's behaviors have been noted to result in increased anxiety (e.g., Chorpita & Barlow, 1998; Wood, 2006) using a variety of research paradigms. For example, when parents and children have interacted during completion of challenging tasks, anxious children have been less likely than their nonanxious peers to contribute when their parents were more controlling and negative in their feedback (Greco & Morris, 2002; Hummel & Gross, 2001). Similarly, when mothers assisted their children on a task and behaved in a more controlling manner, their children subsequently reported greater anxiety when asked to complete the task alone (de Wilde & Rapee, 2008). Interestingly, a recent review of research findings revealed that while child anxiety and parental control are well linked, parental control is not strongly associated with parental anxiety (van der Bruggen et al., 2008); that is, overly controlling behaviors may be demonstrated by both anxious and nonanxious parents.

Studies such as those described above, as well as numerous other observational, prospective, and retrospective studies, have supported the role that these negative parental styles (i.e., rejection and control) can play in the development and maintenance of child anxiety difficulties. Further, one recent review examined different combinations of these parenting dimensions and concluded that anxious children tended to have parents who were more controlling but not necessarily less warm, while anxious parents tended to be less warm toward their children but not necessarily overly controlling (DiBartolo & Helt, 2007). In addition, parental controlling behaviors have been associated with increasing anxiety during childhood and may be especially relevant in the middle-late childhood years, suggesting early childhood interventions that include a parenting component addressing parental control may be particularly beneficial (Feng et al., 2008).

Overall, the consistent findings for parental modeling and rearing behaviors suggest that clinicians may benefit from considering them in the assessment, case conceptualization, and treatment planning for anxious youths. To enhance treatment, clinicians may need to help parents recognize how they model and/or communicate anxiety-related messages, as well as how they reinforce anxious and/or avoidant behaviors in their children. Parents, themselves, may need treatment for their anxiety, or at least education, support, and coping skills to use when they see their child experience anxiety or distress. This would seem particularly important to accomplish prior to initiating child exposure exercises and homework assignments, as parental behaviors may interfere with the success of these important treatment components (Tiwari et al., 2008). Of course, other familial domains have also been discussed with regard to their influence on child anxiety. While less studied, the more common of these include family and community stressors, such as early childhood parental divorce, loss, conflict, or abuse (e.g., Allen, Rapee, & Sandberg, 2008; Chaffin, Silovsky, & Vaughn, 2005; Kroes et al., 2002; Spence, Najman, Bor, O'Callaghan, & Williams, 2002; Weich, Patterson, Shaw, & Stewart-Brown, 2009); negative or dysfunctional family environments (e.g., Grover, Ginsburg, & Ialongo, 2005; Pagani, Japel, Vaillancourt, Côté, & Tremblay, 2008; Shanahan et al., 2008); exposure to violence or traumatic events (e.g., Briggs-Gowan et al., 2010; Shanahan et al., 2008); and parental psychopathology (e.g., anxiety, depression, substance use) particularly in the child's early years (Karevold et al., 2009; Shanahan et al., 2008). Finally, parental expectations for how distressed their child will be or beliefs about how well the child can handle their anxiety and distress may also influence the development of anxiety in youth (e.g., Francis & Chorpita, 2011; Wheatcroft & Creswell, 2007).

Overall, findings support the importance of considering parental behaviors in the assessment, case conceptualization, and treatment planning of anxious youths

2.3.2   Peer Relationships

From an early age, children begin to spend a large part of their day surrounded by peers. From community to childcare to school to extracurricular activities/programs, youths are provided numerous opportunities to learn about social contexts and form relationships. Moreover, close peer relationships are important for healthy social and emotional development (Ladd, 2006; La Greca & Prinstein, 1999) and may serve a protective role against the development of psychosocial difficulties as friends can provide support, model appropriate coping behavior, promote self-esteem, and allow the practice of appropriate interactions (e.g., Campbell, Hansen, & Nangle, 2010; La Greca, 2001). Unfortunately, for anxious youths, peer relationships appear to be another common area of impairment and concern (see Kingery, Erdley, Marshall, Whitaker, & Reuter, 2010, for a review).

Anxious children often have difficult peer relationships as well, both in terms of quantity and quality

Several different areas of peer relationships have been linked with anxiety in samples of clinical and nonclinical/community children. Specifically, studies have shown that anxious children are more often rejected, less well liked, and excluded by peers (e.g., Erath, Flanagan, & Bierman, 2007; La Greca & Lopez, 1998; Oh et al., 2008; Verduin & Kendall, 2008). Not surprising then, anxious children have also been found to have fewer and/or poorer quality friendships (e.g., La Greca & Harrison, 2005; La Greca & Lopez, 1998; Schneider & Tessier, 2007; Shanahan, Copeland, Costello, & Angold, 2008) and fewer romantic relationships in adolescence (La Greca & Harrison, 2005; La Greca & Lopez, 1998). Thus, in addition to evaluating the number of friendships of anxious youths, it may also prove useful to specifically assess the quality of children's friendships. For instance, anxious children may report having friendships, but with further probing, clinicians may find that their quality is insufficient. As an example, Schneider and Tessier (2007) found that anxious 10- to 12-year-olds were more likely to identify circumstantial peers (e.g., classmates or neighbors) as friends and describe their interactions with a lack of familiarity, whereas their nonanxious peers described attributes that they enjoyed about their friends and activities they did together. Finally, in addition to peer relationship issues, anxious children often report social competency and skills deficits (e.g., Bosquet & Egeland, 2006; Chansky & Kendall, 1997; Grills, 2003; Rao et al., 2007; Strauss et al., 1988), which may be further exacerbated by low social self-efficacy beliefs (e.g., Kingery et al., 2010; Morgan & Banerjee, 2006).

Taken together, these studies provide clear evidence of peer relationship difficulties commonly reported for anxious youths. What has been less well articulated is the directionality of these associations. For example, anxiety has been hypothesized to result from negative peer experiences, as these may lead to greater levels of internal distress (feelings of loneliness or inadequacy), which may foster maladaptive behaviors such as anxiety (Kupersmidt, Coie, & Dodge, 1990). Alternatively, children who are not well liked by their peers may fail to obtain normative socialization experiences important for social, affective, and cognitive development (Kupersmidt et al., 1990; La Greca & Fetter, 1995). By missing out on these normative experiences, such children may develop socioemotional deficiencies which can then lead to later maladjustment, including anxiety disorders. Conversely, anxious children may have poorer peer relationships because other children find the behaviors of anxious children awkward or off-putting or because anxious children withdraw from social interactions/situations. Most likely, both of these hypotheses are true, and a negative cycle emerges wherein anxious behaviors and poor social experiences continue to negatively influence one another. Given this, it is important for clinicians to carefully evaluate the social lives and skills of anxious youths.

Many of the empirically supported treatments, especially those for SOCP, include some social skills components; however, it may prove beneficial to more specifically target these areas with other anxiety diagnoses as well.

Another important area to consider is that peers may model fearful behaviors in a similar manner to that previously discussed for parents. For instance, peers may demonstrate fearful behaviors or provide negative information that is then mimicked by another child, perhaps especially one with a preexisting anxious disposition. While limited research has been conducted in this area, Field and colleagues (Field & Lawson, 2003) have found that negative information from peers about public speaking was related to a significant increase in reported social fear beliefs, whereas peer input was not related to such an increase for the nonsocial experiments with unknown animals (Field, Argyris, & Knowles, 2001). Thus, the influence of peers may be particularly important for how children interpret their social environment.

Social skills may need to be specifically targeted with anxious children, especially for those with social phobia or school refusal

In summary, there is clearly a need to include environmental and psychosocial domains in the ongoing assessment and case conceptualization of anxious youths. While these areas have been well associated with the development of anxiety, which is pertinent for clinicians working with anxious children, these behaviors are also quite likely to be involved in the maintenance of anxious responses and therefore may need to be specifically targeted for intervention. Discussing parental/familial behaviors with parents and peer relationships with children can involve especially sensitive topics and should be addressed from a strong base of information. Fortunately, as presented in the next chapter, a variety of assessment techniques are available to assist with establishing such a basis. Moreover, when necessary, parental behavior should be integrated into treatment as early as possible, as these may be particularly counteractive against the child's progress (e.g., if a parent responds with anxious behavior when their child is attempting to complete an exposure task). In contrast, friendship and social skills building techniques may need to be addressed subsequent to the primary anxiety intervention, as children may not otherwise be able to adequately attempt or cope with these actions.

2.4 Integrative Models of Anxiety Disorder Development

As may be apparent, examining different combinations of these (and other) risk and maintenance factors for child anxiety disorders is a burgeoning area of research (e.g., Creswell & O'Connor, 2011; Degnan et al., 2010; Eley et al., 2007; Lonigan, Vasey, Phillips, & Hazen, 2004; Muris et al., 2011; Weems et al., 2007). Overall, these complex interrelations appear best encompassed by the developmental psychopathology model (e.g., Cicchetti & Rogosch, 1996; Ollendick, Grills, & King, 2001). Developmental psychopathology focuses on risk and protective factors that either increase or decrease the likelihood that an individual will develop a particular disorder. Two primary concepts often noted when discussing developmental psychopathology are: (1) *equifinality*, which refers to the notion that different processes or pathways may lead to the same outcome; and (2) *multifinality*, which refers to the notion that a par-

Integrative models incorporating the areas previously covered appear to best describe the development and maintenance of youth anxiety disorders

ticular risk factor or adverse event can lead to a number of potential outcomes (Cicchetti & Rogosch, 1996). Specific to anxiety disorders, it is clear that not one of the risk factors previously described accounts for 100% of cases. Rather, the same anxiety symptoms and disorders may result from numerous possible combinations of these risk factors (equifinality). Further, there are children who possess one or more of these risk factors and do not develop an anxiety disorder, but instead develop other childhood psychopathology (e.g., ODD) or no diagnosable condition.

Avoidance is another key component, especially for maintaining anxious symptoms, and requires specific intervention

Maintenance factors are also important to consider, and several of the above-described risk factors would similarly be considered maintenance factors (e.g., cognitive biases, parental behaviors, coping). In addition to these, avoidance is a key area that deserves mention. Avoidance plays a key role in the maintenance of anxiety, as it has long been known that avoiding feared stimuli creates a situation wherein the child is not able to appreciate that what they fear can be tolerated without harm. Moreover, the physical feelings experienced when anxious (e.g., racing heart, sweating) are typically perceived as averse and may further promote avoidance behaviors as the child discovers that leaving the situation reduces their physiological arousal. Finally, the bidirectional relationships among all these domains cannot be stressed enough. Interactions among children and others in their environment can become a negative feedback loop, with persisting or increasing child anxiety as the outcome. In addition, in some cases, parents or peers may take on an accommodating role for the anxious child, further enhancing or encouraging anxious behaviors. For example, with SM, siblings or peers may be entrusted by the child and may then speak to others on his/her behalf. Similarly, the parents of a child with OCD may return home so that the child can engage in checking rituals (e.g., checking that the door is locked).

Consistent with the above discussion, the most contemporary models of anxiety development are comprehensive in their inclusion of these different domains. Models such as these suggest that genetic influences and early childhood temperament and attachment patterns may interact and predispose a child to general fearfulness and behavioral inhibition. These behaviors, coupled with aspects of the developing child's environment – such as parenting behaviors, learning histories, and stressors – may result in the development of an anxiety disorder, with different combinations of these potentially resulting in the expression of different disorders. Several integrative models have been proposed that follow this general framework (e.g., Barlow, 2000; Chorpita et al., 1996; Lonigan et al., 2004; Rapee, 2001), a few of which will be highlighted below.

Consistent with a diathesis-stress view wherein predispositions can become activated in conjunction with stressors to result in psychopathology, Barlow (2000) has put forth a "triple vulnerability" model that involves the interactions of three main areas of vulnerability (see Figure 2 below). The first two vulnerabilities are considered generalized toward the development of negative affective states, including anxiety. These include: (1) a heritable vulnerability and (2) a psychological vulnerability "characterized by a diminished sense of control arising from early developmental experiences" (Suárez, Bennett, Goldstein, & Barlow, 2009, p. 156). The final vulnerability is considered a more specific psychological one, and focuses on the role of early learning experiences. The combination of the first two vulnerabilities is considered sufficient for developing a generalized anxious disposition, while the addition of the third vulnerability is considered key for the development of the other specific anxiety disorders. For example, in combination with the first two vulnerabilities, early learning marked by parental panic-related symptoms, anxiety sensitivity, and illness-related behaviors may lead to the development of PD; consistent with that described above regarding recalled parental behaviors of panic-disordered adults (e.g., Ehlers, 1993; Watt & Stewart, 2000).

Another integrative model of anxiety development has been proposed by Rapee and colleagues (Rapee, 2001; Rapee, Schniering, & Hudson, 2009). These authors have suggested that children's temperaments influence environmental interactions, including how caregivers respond to them, which then further influences their temperament. A transactional pattern is described in which a behaviorally inhibited child elicits comfort and protection from caregivers, who then attempt to keep the child from experiencing their fears in future encounters. These parental behaviors provide reinforcement for the child's fear response because of the positive interactions (comfort) they have with caregivers and perceived avoidance encouragement. That is, the child may become more fearful as they interpret the caregivers behavior as signaling that the stimuli should indeed be feared and/or avoided.

Finally, Vasey and Dadds (2001) have proposed an integrative model to account for both the onset and persistence of anxiety disorders (see Figure 3 below). In this model, risk (i.e., predisposing influences) and resiliency (i.e.,

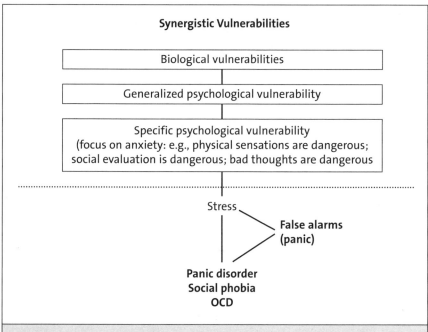

Figure 2
Example Integrative Model 1: The Triple Vulnerability Model.
OCD = obsessive-compulsive disorder.
From "Unraveling the Mysteries of Anxiety and Its Disorders From the Perspective of Emotion Theory," by D. H. Barlow, 2000, *American Psychologist, 55*, p. 1247–1263. © 2000 by D. H. Barlow. Reproduced with permission of the author.

protective influences) factors, such as those depicted in this chapter, continually interact with one another resulting in a cumulative risk factor for the development of an anxiety disorder. In addition to its direct path, the cumulative risk component is proposed to influence an anxiety disorder onset through its transactional relationship with precipitating influences; that is, cumulative risk may increase children's propensity for experiencing precipitating influences, which in turn results in the onset of an anxiety disorder. An additional risk by precipitating influence path (moderational) is proposed to be consistent with a diathesis-stress model, such that precipitating influences are more likely to result in an anxiety disorder when the cumulative risk component is high. A

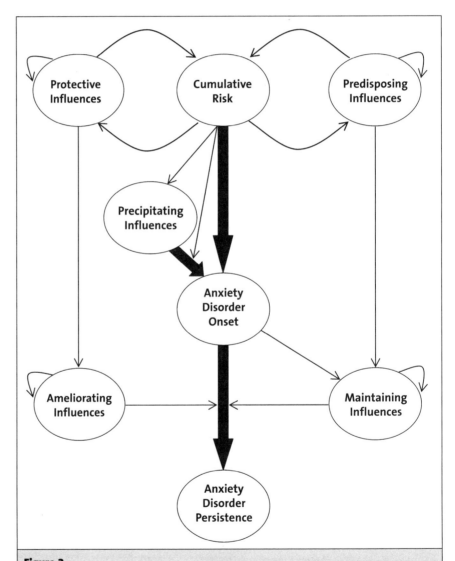

Figure 3
Example Integrative Model 2: Integrative Framework.
From *The Developmental Psychopathology of Anxiety*, by M. Vasey & M. Dadds, 2001, New York: Oxford University Press, p. 37. © 2001 Oxford University Press. Reprinted with permission.

direct path from precipitating influences to anxiety disorder onset is also present. Beyond the onset of an anxiety disorder as just described, this model also accounts for the persistence of an anxiety disorder. In this case, a direct path is suggested from onset to persistence, with several additional indirect paths. First, the risk/predisposing and protective influences are proposed to influence maintaining and ameliorating influences, respectively, which in turn, each influence the path from anxiety disorder onset to persistence. In addition, maintaining factors are also suggested to be involved in the persistence of anxiety as anxious children elicit responses from their environment that are consistent with their anxiety disorder. Suggested transactional relations are also put forth in this model that may help account for the maintenance, or conversely, remittance of an anxiety disorder following its onset.

As is apparent from integrative models, such as those described above, different ideas have emerged from the complex array of biological, environmen-

Table 7
Examples of Commonly Associated Anxiety-Related Domains and Sample Rating Scales Used to Assess Them

Child characteristics	Psychosocial/environmental characteristics

Comorbid conditions
  – Broad Rating Scales and Interviews (see Tables 8–9)
	Parental rearing behaviors
	  – Modified EMBU (My memories of upbringing)
	  – Parental Bonding Instrument

Coping
  – Children's Coping Strategies Checklist
  – How I Coped Under Pressure
	Parental modeling behaviors
	  – Parental Beliefs about Anxiety Questionnare
	  – Learing History Questionnare

Cognitive biases
  – Children's Negative Cognitive Error Questionnaire
  – Child Anxiety Control Questionnare
  – Negative Affectivity Self Statement Questionnaire
	Parental pschopathology
	  – Symptom Checklist-90-Revised
	  – Adult Self-Report

Anxiety sensitivity (see Table 11)	Family environment
	  – Family Environment Scale
	  – McMaster Family Assessment Device

Disgust sensitivity
  – Disgust Sensitivity Questionnaire
  – Disgust Scale
	Peer relationships
	  – Friendship Quality Questionnare
	  – Social Experience Questionnare
	  – Social Support Scale for Children/Adolescents
	  – Reynolds Bully-Victimization Scales

Control
  – Anxiety Control Questionnaire
  – Nowicki-Strickland Locus of Control Scale	

Social skills
  – Self Perception Profile for Children/Adolescents
  – Social Skills Rating System
	Stressors
	  – Children's Hassles Scale

Note. EMBU = "My Memories of Upbringing" (translated from Dutch acronym)

tal, and individual level contributions for the development of child anxiety. In addition, numerous variations of these themes have been proposed for specific individual anxiety disorders (e.g., model of GAD by Rapee, 2001, multifactorial model of SPPs by Muris & Merckelbach, 2001). Of course, clinically, cases will differ substantially with regard to how well the child and/or family can identify etiological information. While some families may detail a clear history leading to the child's symptoms, others may have more difficulty in doing so – for example, with parents reporting the child has "always" been a worrier. Further, although some of the anxiety disorders appear to be particularly linked with traumatic events (e.g., OCD, PTSD, and ADJs), cases may also present with these disorders and no identifiable triggers. The present chapter has described a number of different areas that can be considered for such cases where etiological information is unclear or unknown. In addition, a summary of these areas has been provided in Table 6, and Table 7 lists examples of measures for evaluating them. Overall, exploration of these domains should provide the clinician with a detailed etiological picture and case conceptualization, and help lead to the establishment of an appropriate treatment plan.

3

Diagnosis and Treatment Indications

3.1   General Information

A variety of assessment and diagnostic tools are available for evaluating child and adolescent anxiety. These range from child, parent, or teacher report forms, to structured and semistructured diagnostic interviews, to behavioral observations. As a general rule, it is advised that clinicians incorporate as many of these approaches from as many different informants as possible into their assessment, while also recognizing practical (e.g., time and money) constraints. Clinical judgment will be necessary for determining when enough objective information has been obtained to differentiate and support a diagnosis, as well as to sort out discrepancies in information obtained from these different sources and informants.

Multi-informant, multimethod assessments are recommended

Parents or primary caregivers are an important source of information and will most often be the party "presenting the child" for treatment. That is, children rarely seek treatment on their own accord and instead are usually brought in by concerned parents or caregivers, and oftentimes referred by pediatricians or the family doctor. As detailed below, a variety of assessment measures are available for parents or guardians to complete, pertaining to their child's anxiety. Some of these are specific to anxiety symptoms, some to DSM-IV anxiety disorders, and others for assessment of different disorders of childhood including anxiety.

In the very least, information should be obtained from the child and his/her primary caregivers

Despite past debate on the inclusion of young children in the assessment process, today it is well recognized that children of all ages should be involved, albeit to varying extents based on their developmental level. Even preschool-aged children may be able to answer simply worded questions (especially with pictorial aids) about their feelings. While young children may be most comfortable answering questions with a parent or caregiver present, adolescents may be more likely to divulge concerns in privacy. Details such as these will need to be determined on a case-by-case basis, taking developmentally appropriate considerations into account along with any information derived from prior screenings and developmental and medical history forms.

It can also be helpful to obtain information from teachers, particularly for issues that may occur in school or with peers. Aside from broad-based assessment scales, such as those described below, few standardized measures are available for teachers' ratings of child anxiety. Given this, clinicians may choose to use these measures along with (parent-sanctioned) interview or open-ended questionnaires specific to the child's anxiety concerns. Clinicians may also seek reports from medical professionals, such as the child's pediatrician or family doctor, particularly in cases where anxiety symptoms have a

It is common and acceptable for the information from different informants to vary; this in itself can be informative

strong physiological component (e.g., panic attacks, somatic complications). Oftentimes, parents will have already consulted with the child's pediatrician or family doctor; however, in those cases where this has not occurred, a physical examination and consultation can provide necessary rule-out information.

Clinicians should be aware that oftentimes informants, such as a child and his/her parent, will differ in their reports, sometimes substantially so. This has been found with both broad and anxiety-specific rating scales, as well as

Child Referred for Treatment
- History, medical, demographic, and broad rating scale forms are completed and returned (e.g., CBCL/YSR)
- Elevated anxiety scores noted as prominent

Prior to Initial Session
- Parent/child complete broad (multidimensional) anxiety scales (e.g., MASC, SCARED)
- Specific areas noted

Initial Session(s)
- Clinician administers semi-structured interview modules of significantly elevated areas to parent and child (e.g., ADIS-C/P)
- Differential diagnosis and comorbid disorder clarifications made through additional modules and/or unstructured interviewing

Subsequent Session(s)
- Diagnoses determined
- Case conceptualization identified with above assessments and a functional behavioral analysis of problem areas
- Additional discussion and rating scales completed by parents/children in line with anxiety-related areas identified (e.g., parent modeling and child negative self-statements scales)

Treatments Selected
- Primary Intervention based on primary diagnoses (e.g., Coping Cat)
- Additional treatment targets based on case conceptualization and comorbid conditions (e.g., Social skills training)
- Continued Symptom assessment

Figure 4
From assessment to intervention selection flowchart for child anxiety.
ADIS-C/P = Anxiety Disorders Interview Schedule Child/Parent; CBCL = Child Behavior Checklist; MASC = Multidimensional Anxiety Scale for Children; SCARED = Screen for Child Anxiety Related Emotional Disorders; YSR = Youth Self-Report.

structured diagnostic interviews. A number of individual, familial, and environmental reasons for these disagreements have been discussed by researchers (see De Los Reyes & Kazdin, 2005; Grills & Ollendick, 2002b; Karver, 2006); however, the overarching message has been to view each report as informative rather than attempting to select the "right" one.

Assessing anxiety in children should be done with full awareness of the differential diagnostic and comorbidity issues previously discussed. While clinicians will each have their own preferred approach, we present here the typical assessment strategy we use in our clinical practices. To begin, prior to meeting with the child and/or family, a basic history and an initial screen that broadly covers common child psychopathology can be completed by the child's primary caregiver. Information derived from this screen can then be pursued more fully in the initial meeting, targeting specific symptom areas reported by the caregivers. Clinicians can choose from among several assessment approaches, including structured or semistructured interviews, rating scales, functional behavioral assessments, and observations; however, of these, structured interviews are generally considered the gold standard approach as they ensure coverage of all key DSM diagnostic symptoms and disorders. While there is no one-size-fits-all approach for diagnosing child anxiety disorders, a combination of these assessment tools is recommended. Following is a brief description of each of these assessment approaches, and within each of these we also present some specific, commonly used, and research-supported examples. In addition, a flowchart is provided in Figure 4 for illustrative purposes.

3.2   Diagnostic Tools

3.2.1   Broad Screening Measures

Three of the more commonly used broad screening measures are summarized in Table 8 and include (1) the Achenbach System of Empirically Based Assessment (ASEBA; Achenbach, 2009), (2) the Behavior Assessment System for Children–Second Edition (BASC2; Reynolds & Kamphaus, 2004), and (3) the Conners Comprehensive Behavior Rating Scales (Conners, 2008). Each of these measures provides assessment of adaptive and maladaptive domains and takes approximately 15–20 min to complete. For each of these measures, several scales exist based on the child's age (e.g., preschool, school-age, adolescent, college-age) and informant (parent, teacher/caregiver, and child). Although these questionnaires differ in how items are combined (e.g., syndromes, problem scales, domain scores, DSM category scores, validity scales), each includes measurement of anxiety symptoms, as well as other internalizing (e.g., depression, withdrawal, somatic complaints), externalizing (e.g., aggression, attention problems, hyperactivity, conduct problems), academic (e.g., attitude toward school and teachers), and adaptive (e.g., interpersonal relations, social skills) problems or skills. A great deal of psychometric and normative research data has been collected on these scales and can be reviewed on their respective publisher websites (see Table 8).

Table 8
Examples of Commonly Used Broad-Based Measures of Adaptive and Maladaptive Child Behaviors

Measure	Author/website	Informants	Child age ranges assessed
Achenbach System of Empirically Based Assessment	Achenbach, 2009 http://www.aseba.org	Child (aged 11+) Parent Teacher/caregiver	Preschool versions (1.5–5 years) School age versions (6–18 years)
Behavior Assessment System for Children–2	Reynolds & Kamphaus, 2004 http://www.pearsonassessments.com/HAIWEB/Cultures/en-us/Productdetail.htm?Pid=PAa30000	Child (aged 6+) Parent Teacher	Preschool versions (2–5 years) Child versions (6–11 years) Adolescent versions (12–21 years)
Conners Comprehensive Behavior Rating Scales	Conners, 2008 http://www.mhs.com/product.aspx?gr=edu&prod=cbrs&id=overview	Child (aged 8+) Parent Teacher	Early childhood (2–6 years) Child/adolescent version (6–18 years)

3.2.2   Interviews

Structured or semistructured diagnostic interviews, or parts of them, are highly recommended for inclusion in the assessment process

All clinicians tend to use unstructured "clinical" interviews as part of the assessment process; however, structured diagnostic interviews can also be an important consideration and are highly recommended by us. Structured diagnostic interviews were designed to increase the reliability of diagnoses by standardizing the method used to elicit responses. This, in turn, is expected to have the effect of increasing the reliability of responses and eliminating potential biases (e.g., making decisions prior to the collection of all the information, only collecting confirming or disconfirming evidence) associated with clinical judgment (Angold, 2002). Structured interviews are generally geared toward gathering information about specific DSM criteria of various diagnoses and are therefore typically ideal for assessing psychiatric symptoms and formulating diagnoses. They are also frequently used for case conceptualization and treatment planning purposes. Table 9 provides basic descriptive information for seven of the more commonly used structured diagnostic interviews, and Table 10 indicates the different diagnoses covered by each of these interviews.

Table 9
Summary of Commonly Utilized Structured Diagnostic Interviews with Child and Parent Versions

Interview[a]	Type	~Length/ interview	Age range (versions)	Approximate cost range
Anxiety Disorders Interview Schedule	Semi-structured	2–3 hr	7–17 (child/ parent)	US $88 for manual, parent/ child interview
Child and Adolescent Psychiatric Assessment	Interviewer/ glossary-based	1.5 hr	9–18 (child/ parent)	US $2,650 for information packet/training
Children's Interview for Psychiatric Syndromes	Highly structured	0.5–1 hr	6–18 (child/ parent)	US $115
Diagnostic Interview for Children and Adolescents	Semi-structured	1–2 hr	6–12/13–18 (child/ adolescent) 6-18 (parent)	US $1,034 for computer version; paper/ pencil version costs vary
Diagnostic Interview Schedule for Children	Highly structured	1–2 hr	9–17 (child); 6–17 (parent)	US $150 to US $2,000
Interview Schedule for Children and Adolescents	Semi-structured	0.75–2.5 hr	8–17 (child/ parent)	Obtain from developer
Schedule for Affective Disorders and Schizophrenia for School Aged Children	Semi-structured	1.25–1.5 hr	6–18 (child/ parent)	Epidemiological – US $75; Present – Free; Present/Life-time – Online

Note. [a]Not an exhaustive list of interviews available.

All of the structured interviews are alike in that they are psychometrically strong and follow similar formats. For example, the interviews typically begin with screener questions for each disorder. When positive responses are given for screener questions, the interviewer continues to assess symptoms within that section as well as obtaining frequency, intensity, duration, and interference ratings when required. If the respondent responds negatively ("no") to screener questions, the interviewer can "skip out" of that section. With some variations, all of the structured interviews conclude with diagnoses being generated with predetermined algorithms or clinical judgment.

Given the similarities among the structured interviews, clinicians typically select among them based on personal preference. However, in some instances,

Table 10
Summary of Disorders Covered by the Structured Interviews Reviewed

	ADIS	CAPA	ChIPS	DICA	DISC	ISCA	K-SADS
Generalized anxiety disorder	Y	Y	Y	Y	Y	Y	Y
Separation anxiety disorder	Y	Y	Y	Y	Y	Y	Y
Obsessive-compulsive disorder	Y	Y	Y	Y	Y	Y	Y
Simple phobia	Y	Y	Y	Y	Y	Y	Y
Social phobia	Y	Y	Y	Y	Y	Y	Y
Agoraphobia	Y	N	N	N	Y	N	Y
Panic disorder	Y	Y	N	Y	Y	Y	Y
Selective mutism	Y[a]	Y	N	N	Y	N	Y
Posttraumatic stress disorder	Y	Y	Y	Y	Y	N	Y
Acute stress disorder	Y	–	Y	N	N	–	N
Adjustment disorder	N	Y	N	N	N	Y	N
Major depression	Y	Y	Y	Y	Y	Y	Y
Dysthymia	Y	Y	Y	Y	Y	Y	Y
Bipolar disorder	N	Y	Y	Y	Y	Y	Y
Mania	N	Y	Y	Y	Y	Y	Y
Hypomania	N	Y	Y	Y	Y	Y	Y
Cyclothymia	N	Y	N	N	N	Y	Y
Somatization disorder	Y[a]	Y	N	Y	N	Y	N
Attention-deficit/ hyperactivity disorder	Y	Y[b]	Y	Y	Y	Y	Y
Oppositional defiant disorder	Y[b]	Y	Y	Y	Y	Y	Y
Conduct disorder	Y[b]	Y	Y	Y	Y	Y	Y
Anorexia nervosa	Y[a]	Y	Y	Y	Y	Y	Y
Bulimia nervosa	Y[a]	Y	Y	Y	Y	Y	Y
Pica	N	N	N	N	Y	N	N
Enuresis	Y[b]	Y	Y	N	Y	Y	Y[c]
Encopresis	N	Y	Y	N	Y	Y	Y[c]
Sleep disorders	N	Y	N	N	N	Y	N
Tic disorders	N	Y	N	Y	Y	N	Y[c]

Table 10 continued

	ADIS	CAPA	ChIPS	DICA	DISC	ISCA	K-SADS
Trichotillomania	N	Y	N	N	Y	N	N
Schizophrenia	Y[a]	Y	Y	N	Y	N	Y
Schizoaffective	N	Y	N	N	N	N	Y
Delusional disorder	N	Y	N	N	Y	N	N
Substance disorders	Y[a]	Y	Y	Y	Y	Y	Y
Personality disorders	N	N	N	N	N	Y	Y
Gender identity disorder	N	N	N	Y	Y	N	N

Note. ADIS = Anxiety Disorders Interview Schedule; CAPA = Child and Adolescent Psychiatric Assessment; ChIPS = Children's Interview for Psychiatric Syndromes; DICA = Diagnostic Interview for Children and Adolescents; DISC = Diagnostic Interview Schedule for Children; ISCA = Interview Schedule for Children and Adolescents; K-SADS = Schedule for Affective Disorders and Schizophrenia for School Aged Children.
[a]Screens for these disorders only; [b]Parent version only; [c]K-SADS-E & K-SADS-P/L versions only.

clinicians may be guided by such issues as the presenting concerns in need of further assessment (see Table 10) or the sample type (e.g., clinical or research/ epidemiological, see Table 9). Related to sample type, clinicians may select an interview based on their interest in the time frame covered by the interview. For example, a whole life time frame is assessed with the Diagnostic Interview Schedule for Children (DISC; Shaffer, Fisher, Lucas, Dulcan, & Schwab-Stone, 2000), Diagnostic Interview for Children and Adolescents (DICA; Reich, 2000), Schedule for Affective Disorders and Schizophrenia for School Aged Children (K-SADS; Kaufman et al., 1997; Orvaschel, 1995), and Interview Schedule for Children and Adolescents (ISCA; Sherrill & Kovacs, 2000), but not the other interviews.

Clinicians may also consider the desired interview structure level. For instance, with highly structured interviews, clinicians are expected to ask questions and record responses in a specified manner and order, whereas semistructured interviews allow greater leeway and clinical flexibility. Of the interviews listed in Table 9, all but the DISC and the Children's Interview for Psychiatric Syndromes (Weller, Weller, Fristad, Rooney, & Schecter, 2000) are considered semistructured. In addition to interview structure, clinicians may consider administration format (paper/pencil versus computerized). For instance, some clinicians have incorporated computer-administered versions of structured interviews into their initial client appointments, as these can save time by being completed prior to session. These may be particularly useful for parents and adolescents, for example, as parents might complete the computerized assessment while the clinician meets with their child and vice versa; adolescents, on the other hand, might also feel more comfortable answering questions with a computer format than in person. Currently, there are computerized or Web-based versions of the present/lifetime version of the K-SADS, the DICA, the DISC, and the Child and Adolescent Psychiatric Assessment (CAPA; Angold & Costello, 2000).

Still another consideration may be the child's age, as only a couple of interviews are designed for children as young as 6. Moreover, with younger children, a semistructured approach is often preferable, as clinicians are more free to incorporate extra examples, clarifications, and visual/pictorial aids (Sattler & Hoge, 2006; Scott, Short, Singer, Russ, & Minnes, 2006). In fact, one research group has incorporated pictures into a structured interview for younger children (Valla, Bergeron, & Smolla, 2000). The Interactive Dominic Questionnaire for DSM-IV is a computerized interview for children aged 6–11 that utilizes cartoons designed to match children on gender and ethnicity (e.g., Hispanic, African-American, Asian, and White). An adolescent version is also available for youths aged 12–16 (see http://www.dominic-interactive.com). Symptom descriptions are read aloud by the computer and are accompanied by the cartoon figures engaged in representative situations. For example and as shown in Figure 5, "Do thunderstorms make you feel scared?" is accompanied by the image of one child looking frightened and another child sitting, neutral-faced, at a game while a storm occurs outside the window. Children are asked to respond in a yes/no format by clicking on a box on the screen. This interview provides assessment of SPP, SAD, GAD, MDD (major depressive

Figure 5
Sample Anxiety Item from the Dominic-Interactive Child Version.
From "The Dominic-R: A Pictorial Interview for 6- to 11-Year-Old Children," by J. Valla, L. Bergeron, & N. Smolla, 2000, *Journal of the American Academy of Child and Adolescent Psychiatry, 39,* 85–93. © 2000 by Jean-Pierre Valla. Reproduced with permission.

disorder), ADHD, ODD, and CD. However, frequency, duration, and onset questions are omitted, which precludes using the interview alone to determine diagnostic criteria. Nonetheless, research has supported use of this interview (e.g., Scott et al., 2006; Valla et al., 2000, 2002), and it may prove especially useful for improving younger children's comprehension of symptom questions, and subsequently, the reliability of their reports.

As previously noted, diagnostic interviews also tend to differ, albeit slightly, in the problem areas covered. Although several of the interviews presented in Tables 9 and 10 include assessment of the various childhood anxiety disorders, given its focus on this particular area relative to other interviews, the Anxiety Disorders Interview Schedule for DSM-IV Child/Parent version (ADIS-IV-C/P; Silverman & Albano, 1996) will be used as an illustration and described below in greater detail.

The ADIS-C/P has been used most frequently in the youth anxiety disorders research literature, including in randomized clinical trials. The current version, the ADIS-IV-C/P (for DSM-IV), contains modules that cover all of the anxiety disorders (except the ADJs with anxiety), as well as other prevalent childhood disorders. Additional questions are included that allow interviewers to obtain information about the history of the problem, as well as situational-contextual variables and cognitive factors influencing anxiety. Modules typically begin with screener questions and are followed by more detailed probing for instances where positive responses are made. Fear, avoidance, impairment, and interference ratings are made with the assistance of a feelings thermometer that ranges from 0 (no fear/distress/impairment) to 8 (very fearful/severely disturbing/impairing), and an individually customizable calendar is used to assist with timelines. Upon completion of the interview, clinicians consider information obtained from both the child and parent in assigning distress and interference ratings for each disorder where diagnostic symptom criteria are met. Clinicians use the same 0–8 rating scale, with those rated as a 4 (definitely disturbing/impairing) or higher considered to be at a clinical level. Figure 6 provides a sample of symptom (one of nine symptoms included) and interference questions, along with wording provided to assist the clinician in reviewing symptoms from the end of the Separation Anxiety Disorder module of the child version. As can be seen, symptoms are often assessed with multipart questions and include suggestions for the clinician, as well as instructions for evaluating symptoms and progressing. Psychometric details for the ADIS-IV-C/P, and other structured diagnostic interviews, can be reviewed in other recent publications (e.g., Grills-Taquechel & Ollendick, 2008; Silverman & Ollendick, 2008).

In summary, several structured interviews are available for clinicians to incorporate into their assessment process. While all clinicians will continue to use unstructured interviewing with their clients, and while relying on unstructured interviews may be acceptable for the most experienced clinicians (see Sattler & Hoge, 2006), we recommend that all clinicians use structured interviews whenever possible. However, in a typical practice setting, clinicians would be less likely to engage in a complete structured diagnostic interview due to issues such as cost, lengthiness, and relevance. Rather, based on their use of earlier screener measures, clinicians might instead select the most relevant modules of a structured interview to administer. Based on the outcome

Initial Inquiry

Some children (teenagers) worry a lot about being away from their parents or from home.

1a. **Do you feel really scared or worried when you are away from Mom or Dad and do you do whatever you can to be with them?** ☐ Yes ☐ No ☐ Other

1b. **Do you get very upset, cry, or beg your parents to stay home when they plan to go somewhere without you?** ☐ Yes ☐ No ☐ Other

1c. **When your parents leave you, do you cry or feel very bad because you miss them a lot?** ☐ Yes ☐ No ☐ Other

1d. **When you know that you are going to be away from home or your parents, do you get very upset and worry ahead of time?** ☐ Yes ☐ No ☐ Other

Count any "Yes" response to Questions 1a–1d as one symptom and place a check mark in the circle. **SYMPTOM**

Interference

Okay, I want to know how much you feel this problem has messed things up in your life. That is, how much has it messed things up for you with friends, in school, or at home? How much does it stop you from doing things you would like to do? Tell me how much by using the Feelings Thermometer we discussed earlier, okay? If necessary, explain the concept of interference with the child. Show the child the Feelings Thermometer (found on the back cover of the Clinician Manual) and obtain an overall rating of interference from the child. Record the number corresponding to the child's anchor response, 0–8.

Child's Rating

☐

If clinical interference is indicated (a rating of 4 or greater), place a check mark in the diamond. **CRITERIA**

If all three diamonds are checked, consider Separation Anxiety Disorder diagnosis and place a check mark in the star.

Figure 6
Sample item (1/9) and interference wording from the Anxiety Disorders Interview Schedule for DSM-IV, Child Version, Separation Anxiety Disorder section.
From *Anxiety Disorders Interview Schedule, Parent/Child Version*, by W. K. Silverman & A. M. Albano, 1996, New York: Oxford University Press. © 1996 by Oxford University Press. Reproduced with permission.

of those modules and clinical judgment, clinicians can then determine whether enough information has been obtained to proceed or whether additional modules should be administered.

3.2.3   Rating Scales

In contrast to the diagnostic interviews, rating scales offer the distinct advantage of being efficient and typically self-administered (see Appendix 2 for sample child anxiety self-report measures). Because of this, these scales are an invaluable part of the assessment process, as they can be completed between or before sessions and offer a way to easily track symptoms over time. In addition, rating scales can be used for conducting screenings of anxiety symptoms in larger groups, such as school-wide assessments conducted to identify children for prevention or intervention programs.

Several child self-report rating scales have been developed and are grouped below by the symptom areas they measure. The majority of these scales examines an array of anxiety symptoms, but do not necessarily match onto the DSM-IV anxiety disorder criteria. As listed in Table 11, some of the more well studied and commonly used general anxiety self-report rating scales include the Multidimensional Anxiety Scale for Children, the Revised Children's Manifest Anxiety Scale-2, Beck Anxiety Inventory for Youth, and the State-Trait Anxiety Scale for Children. In addition, there are three multidimensional measures that *do* provide scales that correspond with the DSM-IV anxiety disorders, and these are the Screen for Child Anxiety Related Emotional Disorders–Revised, Spence Children's Anxiety Scale (see Appendix 2), and Revised Child Anxiety and Depression Scale. Each of these assess symptoms that are consistent with diagnoses of SAD, GAD, SOCP, OCD, PD, while the

Rating scales are efficient tools for supporting diagnoses and case conceptualizations, and can be used to monitor change during treatment

Several measures of anxiety and related areas are recommended for inclusion in the assessment process

Table 11
Rating Scales by Anxiety Disorder Domain Assessed

Disorder / scales	Authors	Child/ adolescent ages evaluated	Informants
Global measures			
Beck Anxiety Inventory for Youth–II	Beck et al. (2005)	7+	Child
Multidimensional Anxiety Scale for Children	March et al. (1997)	8+	Child, Parent
Revised Child Anxiety and Depression Scale	Chorpita et al. (2000)	6+	Child, Parent
Revised Children's Manifest Anxiety Scale–2	Reynolds & Richmond (2008)	6+	Child
Revised Preschool Anxiety Scale	Edwards et al. (2010)	3–5	Parent
Screen for Child Anxiety Related Emotional Disorders	Birmaher et al. (1997)	8+	Child, Parent
Spence Children's Anxiety Scale	Spence (1998)	2.5+	Child, Parent
State-Trait Anxiety Scale for Children	Spielberger (1973)	9–12	Child, Parent
State-Trait Anxiety Scale		12+	Child, Parent

Table 11 continued

Disorder / scales	Authors	Child/ adolescent ages evaluated	Informants
Social phobia			
Social Anxiety Scale for Children/	La Greca & Stone (1993)	6–12	Child, Parent
Social Anxiety Scale for Adolescents	La Greca & Lopez (1998)	13+	Child, Parent
Liebowitz Social Anxiety Scale for Children and Adolescents	Masia-Warner et al. (2003)	7+	Child
Social Phobia and Anxiety Inventory for Children	Storch et al. (2006)	8–14	Child, Parent
Social Phobia and Anxiety Inventory	Beidel et al. (1995)	14+	Child, Parent
Social Worries Questionnaire	Spence (1995)	8-17	Child, Parent
Specific phobia			
Fear Survey Schedule for Children–Revised	Ollendick (1983)	3+	Child, Parent
Koala Fear Questionnaire	Muris et al. (2003)	4–12	Child
Panic symptoms			
Child Anxiety Sensitivity Index	Silverman et al. (1991)	7+	Child
Child Anxiety Sensitivity Index– Revised	Muris (2002)		Child
Generalized anxiety symptoms			
Penn State Worry Questionnaire for Children	Chorpita et al. (1997)	7+	Child
Posttraumatic stress disorder			
Trauma Symptom Checklist for Children	Briere (1996)	8–16	Child
Trauma Symptom Checklist for Young Children	Briere (2005)	3–12	Parent
Children's Impact of Traumatic Events Scale–II	Wolfe (2002)	8–16	Clinician administered
Child PTSD Symptom Scale	Foa et al. (2001)	8–18	Child
Obsessive compulsive disorder			
Children's Yale-Brown Obsessive Compulsive Scale	Scahill et al. (1997)	6–14	Clinician administered
Yale-Brown Obsessive Compulsive Scale		14+	Clinician administered
Children's Yale-Brown Obsessive Compulsive Scale – Self-Report	Storch et al. (2006)	6–14 14+	Child, Parent

Note. PTSD = posttraumatic stress disorder.

Screen for Child Anxiety Related Emotional Disorders–Revised alone also assesses symptoms of SPP and PTSD.

Child rating scales have also been developed to evaluate specific anxiety disorder symptoms. Examples of these are also presented by anxiety symptom type in Table 11, along with scale references, and the age range and rater information for each measure. In addition to these, other rating scales are commonly administered to evaluate anxiety-related difficulties or areas identified as part of the clinical case conceptualization (see Table 7). In Chapter 2, for instance, several child, psychosocial, and environmental characteristics were noted for their potential influence on the development and maintenance of anxiety symptoms. Thus, it may be pertinent for clinicians to include measures which assess these domains, to assist with the selection of the most appropriate treatment and any potential additional supplemental treatment components. For example, in cases where a primary caregiver indicates significant anxiety of his/her own, treatments that include parent education and involvement may be selected. Likewise, an adolescent who reports significant negative self-talk and poor coping skills may be especially likely to benefit from a treatment program that emphasizes both cognitive and behavioral components. It is also important to note that rating scales are useful for clinicians to use both in the initial assessment of symptoms, and as an indicator of treatment progress. This is true for monitoring anxiety symptom changes, but also for changes in these other areas (e.g., social support, parenting practices) as well.

3.2.4 Observational and Behavioral Assessments

Observation methods offer an additional way for clinicians to gather information about the child's anxiety. Observations are commonly made of children (and their families) in the waiting and therapy rooms. For example, a clinician may observe that a child is unwilling to allow her mother to separate from her to use the bathroom or to meet with the clinician alone. Observations can also be useful for directly witnessing behaviors that only occur outside the therapy context (e.g., compulsive ordering of personal objects in the home) or for determining the generalizability of anxious symptoms to settings wherein parents may be less knowledgeable, such as school or childcare. In addition, observational assessments can also be made by other informants (e.g., teachers, siblings) and across a variety of settings (e.g., home, classroom, playground). Standardized measures, such as the Test Observation Form (McConaughy & Achenbach, 2004) or the Student Observation System (Reynolds & Kamphaus, 2004) have been developed to record various behaviors (e.g., anxious, oppositional, attention); however, these are often designed for use at specific times (e.g., test taking). Alternatively, clinicians might create a list of symptoms or questions to complete during observation that are individualized to the particular client.

Behavioral avoidance tasks (also known as behavioral approach or assertiveness tests; BATs) are commonly used with anxious children in research settings or informally in clinical settings. These tasks ask children to engage in a feared and/or avoided behavior (see Beidel & Turner, 1998; DiBartolo &

Standardized and unstructured observational methods can also provide clinicians with important information for diagnostic and treatment decisions

Grills, 2006; Ollendick, Allen, Benoit, & Cowart, 2011, for examples). For instance, a socially anxious child may be asked to read aloud in front of a video camera, during which time the clinician can make observations of the child's distress as well as use child-reported ratings (e.g., on a 0–10 scale of how scared do you feel) or physiological measures (e.g., heart rate, heart rate variability). Similarly, an acrophobic child might be exposed to situations varying in height levels. BATs are often used to assist in diagnostic decision making and incorporated into treatment. Including observations such as those described above is recommended whenever time and feasibility permit, as they are a valuable way to gain insight into the client's behavior but also others' corresponding behaviors.

Conducting functional behavioral assessments are recommended to help determine the function anxiety serves for the child and to help identify targets for intervention

Finally, in addition to determining the specific symptoms and diagnostic criteria met for a particular anxiety disorder, it is important to conduct a functional behavioral assessment. That is, identifying the typical antecedents (i.e., settings and circumstances in which anxiety occurs) and consequences (i.e., what happens as a result of the anxious or avoidant behaviors) will provide clues to the function of the anxiety and help identify targets for intervention. This may be done via specific functional analysis interviews (e.g., Questions About Behavioral Function; Matson, Bamburg, Cherry, & Paclawskyj, 1999), unstructured interviewing, and/or through observations of the child. For example (see Table 12), through use of standardized assessment measures, a clinician may find that their 12-year-old client meets diagnostic criteria for a SPP of dogs which has inhibited his ability to walk to/from the school bus and play outside with friends. Using functional behavioral analysis, the clinician may find that the child's parents have supported his avoidance of dogs by driving him to/from the school bus and that they have been quick to soothe and comfort him when he has upset by dogs in the past. This additional information would help the clinician understand that including the child's parents in the treatment process would be critical for reducing avoidant behaviors and that increasing adaptive coping and self-soothing skills may be additional targets for therapy.

In conclusion, a number of assessment measure references have been provided in this chapter. It is important to note that this represents neither an exhaustive nor an inclusive list of those measures available. Moreover, information is commonly updated for these measures (e.g., when DSM cri-

Table 12
Examples of Findings From a Functional Behavioral Analysis

	Antecedent	Behavior	Consequence
Example 1	Child sees a dog while walking to the school bus	Child becomes scared, cries, and runs home	Parent comforts child and drives him to school, child's behaviors are reinforced
Example 2	Parent sees child running home and crying	Parent comforts child and agrees to drive him to school	Child calms down and parent distress is reduced

teria change or psychometric studies are conducted), and new measures are regularly developed. Nevertheless, those listed herein are among the most commonly used and evidence-based assessment tools available today and are provided to assist the reader in selecting appropriate tools for evaluating child anxiety and related difficulties.

4

Treatment

A simple Internet search reveals that a variety of treatments have been developed for childhood and youth disorders. Ranging from homeopathics to talk and play therapy to CBT, among the most important considerations in selecting a treatment is the evidence that it really works. The current chapter presents information on only those treatments which have been empirically supported, which in the case of child anxiety disorders translates to two main approaches: (1) behavior therapy and CBT and (2) psychopharmacology. In this chapter, the primary components of these treatments will be presented first, followed by specific examples of empirically supported child and youth anxiety disorder treatments, and then information regarding their efficacy.

> A variety of treatment approaches have been developed for child anxiety disorders

4.1 Methods of Treatment

Before presenting treatment programs for anxious children and youths, key terms and methods involved are briefly described.

Behavior therapy (BT) principles are largely drawn from learning theory (e.g., classical, operant, and vicarious conditioning) and have been used in the treatment of childhood fears and phobias for roughly a century now. A primary assumption of behavior therapy is that the proper subject matter is measurable or observable behavior itself rather than some hypothetical, underlying, intrapsychic process that is not available to scientific scrutiny. Common behavioral techniques employed in the treatment of anxiety include relaxation training, exposure, systematic desensitization, modeling, social skills training, and parent training. Each of these are briefly described below.

Cognitive behavior therapy (CBT) grew from behavior therapy but placed a greater emphasis on cognitive activity. Cognitions and cognitive activity are generally internal events that are more difficult to observe, and instead clinicians must rely on an individual's self-report. A central tenet with CBT is that thoughts, feelings, and behaviors continually and reciprocally influence one another, as depicted in Figure 7. It is critical that clients understand this model, and it is helpful to work through developmentally appropriate examples with children and their families. In addition to the techniques noted for BT, skills involving cognitive restructuring, positive self-talk/self-instruction training, and problem solving are typically included in CBT programs. As detailed below, the behavioral and cognitive behavioral interventions have been found to be a highly effective set of procedures for the treatment of anxiety and related difficulties.

> However, empirical support has only been shown for behavioral therapy and CBT, as well as psychopharmacology, at this time

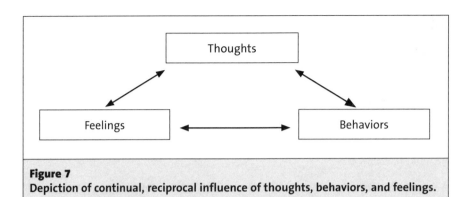

Figure 7
Depiction of continual, reciprocal influence of thoughts, behaviors, and feelings.

Psychopharmacology refers to the study of manufactured drugs (medications) that are presumed to effect change via alterations in the nervous system, typically the brain. The study of medications for childhood anxiety disorders has generally followed a downward extension from what has been shown with adults and, with a few notable exceptions, is generally *not* recommended as the first line of treatment. Exceptions would include severe forms of anxiety (e.g., intractable OCD), children who have not benefited from CBT/BT, and youths who may require an initial medication trial to assist them with overcoming their anxiety (e.g., PD with AG) so that they may subsequently receive greater benefit from CBT/BT. Nonetheless, several different medication classes have shown some efficacy in the treatment of youth anxiety (see Section 4.4), including selective serotonin reuptake inhibitors (SSRIs), benzodiazepines, and tricyclic antidepressants.

Psychoeducation is a broad term used to describe when clients are provided information, typically about areas such as diagnoses, treatment approaches, and therapeutic techniques. With children and adolescents, it is almost always advisable to provide psychoeducation to primary caregivers as well as the child. For instance, parents and children are often taught about the continuum of anxiety and that anxiety is a natural, normal, and generally harmless human experience (Mattis & Ollendick, 2002). Finally, many treatment programs also include psychoeducation about identifying different feelings, for example, using Jim Borgman's feelings cartoons like those depicted in Figure 8. In addition to teaching clients about these areas, psychoeducation often has the goal of normalizing the client's experiences and demystifying the disorder. For instance, a child who has had a panic attack may feel very frightened by that experience and may find some relief in learning that other children have had similar experiences and that they can be controlled.

Relaxation training is employed to teach children a skill that can be applied at any point when they might feel tense or anxious. Relaxation can be achieved in a number of ways, and a variety of techniques exist, including progressive muscle relaxation, positive imagery, autogenic training, and diaphragmatic breathing. With any of these, children are typically encouraged to find a comfortable position, close their eyes, and follow the verbal instructions of the therapist (or recording). Progressive muscle relaxation involves the tensing and relaxing of various major muscle groups. For adolescents, basic relaxation instructions can be used (e.g., "Make a fist and hold it tight, now release

Figure 8
Examples of feelings/emotion education tools: Jim Borgman Cartoons (Anxious/Angry).
From *Mood Swings: Show 'Em How You're Feeling!* by Jim Borgman, 2001, text and illustrations by CTA, Inc., © 2001; compilation by Karen Dreyfuss 2001; easel display format by Price Stern Sloan, 2001. Used by permission of Price Stern & Sloan, A Division of Penguin Young Readers Group, A Member of Penguin Group (USA) Inc., 345 Hudson Street, New York, NY 10014. All rights reserved.

it"), while for younger children, increased use of imaginative descriptions is helpful (e.g., "Pretend you are a furry, lazy cat. You want to stretch. Stretch your arms out in front of you...."). A sample relaxation script for children is included in the resources section (Appendices 3 and 4) at the end of this book. Diaphragmatic breathing can be taught by having the child place one hand (or a plastic cup) on their stomach and the other on their chest. Children can then watch/feel their hands move as they learn to "belly breathe," as opposed to taking typical shallow chest breaths. Positive imagery involves providing vivid descriptions of something the child finds especially calm and relaxing. For example, the therapist may describe a family day playing at the beach (e.g., "It is a warm sunny day, and the seagulls are flying over the blue water. There are little waves making splashing sounds as they roll up the shore. You have lots of sand toys with you and are building a castle with your best friend...."). Finally, autogenic training involves the combination of controlled breathing and heart rate with descriptions of feelings of warmth and heaviness throughout the body. Clearly the child's developmental and comfort levels will need to be considered when deciding on a relaxation approach, and oftentimes, younger children prefer to have their parents remain with them during relaxation training. This can also be beneficial, as parents can take on the role of "therapist-coach" outside of sessions and help the child with relaxation. Depending on the age of the child and technique used, relaxation sessions typically last anywhere from 5 to 20 min.

Exposure is a general term used to refer to the process of presenting the child with that which is feared by him/her. Exposures can be done live in person (i.e., in vivo) or imaginally via vivid sensory descriptions. Although in vivo exposure to items is preferred, in some cases imaginal exposures may be necessary – either because in vivo confrontation would be too logistically difficult (e.g., airline travel) or because the child is not yet ready for in vivo exposure. For example, a dog phobic child may eventually be exposed to live dogs of varying sizes but may initially begin by looking at pictures of dogs or listening to dogs barking. In some cases, the dog phobic child might also benefit from simply imagining a dog and interactions with it. *Exposure with response prevention* is another term commonly used, most often with regard to CBT for OCD, and describes the procedure of exposing a child to a feared stimulus while not allowing engagement of avoidance behaviors. For instance, a child who compulsively washes his hands because of contamination fears might be asked to hold onto a door knob or place his hands in dirt and then not allowed to engage in washing rituals afterwards. The primary purpose of exposure is for children to develop confidence in their ability to engage feared stimuli without their perceived negative consequences. However, exposure is not typically used alone but rather in combination with relaxation and modeling approaches as described in the sections below.

Systematic desensitization was derived from classical conditioning principles as an attempt to disrupt a conditioned response to a feared stimulus. One of the main underlying assumptions of systematic desensitization is called reciprocal inhibition (or counterconditioning) – that is pairing an anxiety-provoking stimulus (e.g., a spider) with a response (e.g., a relaxed state) that is incompatible with the anxiety response (e.g., a tense or flight state). This has been proposed to block the anxious response from occurring as such opposing emotional states cannot occur at the same time (Wolpe, 1958). Relaxation, as described above, is the most commonly used incompatible response, though others have been successfully employed as well (e.g., eating, singing, playing games, imagery). With systematic desensitization, once a child has become relaxed, the clinician and child confront items from a preconstructed anxiety hierarchy list. Table 13 presents an example of a hierarchy list as might be constructed for a child with a SPP of spiders. As depicted in this example, items are arranged based on the amount of fear they induce in the child (therapists generally use a 0–10 scale to assist with child ratings), with anywhere from 10 to 20 items considered ideal for most hierarchies. It is imperative that clinicians include the child and his/her family in the creation of the hierarchy, as children themselves best know how fearful they may be in each situation and may also try to avoid by not sharing their most feared items. Clinicians begin with the easiest item on the list, and in our experience, it is best to have such an item be one that the child can definitely accomplish. This provides the child with an initial success and allows a "practice round" before moving on to more difficult items on the list. Once the child has shown that she or he is able to remain relaxed while confronting a hierarchy item, progression can be made to the next item on the list. This approach has been used with children of all ages and with a variety of fear-producing stimuli, including animals, situations (e.g., stage fright), tests and academic evaluations, and interpersonal sensitivities (e.g., weight gain).

Table 13
Sample Anxiety Hierarchy for a Child With a Spider Phobia

	Feared stimulus/situation	Fear rating
1	Letting a spider crawl on my hand and arm for more than 10 s	10
2	Having a spider in my hands	10
3	Touching a spider someone else is handling	10
4	Being in the same room as a spider that is not in an enclosed setting (i.e., a cage or box)	10
5	Putting my hand near a spider in an enclosed setting for more than 10 s	9
6	Putting my finger near a spider in an enclosed setting	8
7	Holding the jar without a cover on it	7
8	Watching someone else handle a spider	6
9	Covering and lifting the jar and releasing the spider	6
10	Capturing a spider by covering it with a jar	5
11	Sitting next to a spider in an enclosed setting	4
12	Being in the same room with a spider in an enclosed setting	3
13	Closely watching a spider outside and describing it	2
14	Talking about a spider	1
15	Seeing a picture of a spider	1

Participant modeling is derived from the fact that, as described in Chapter 2, modeling or vicarious conditioning has been associated with the development and maintenance of anxiety in children. Conversely, modeling has also been used in the treatment of anxiety disorders, particularly SPP, SOCP, and OCD. That is, just as a child may learn negative behaviors from others, so might they learn nonfearful behaviors. For example, a snake phobic girl who observes her older brother engage in nonfearful interactions with his friend's pet snake may disinhibit her avoidant responses and subsequently engage in approach behaviors; especially if positively reinforced for doing so. With fearful children, this disinhibiting effect is believed to play a particularly critical role. While other forms of modeling may also be used (e.g., watching videotaped modeling of another child or observing live modeling by another individual), participant modeling has shown the greatest success for treating childhood fears and phobias (e.g., Ollendick & Cerny, 1981). With participant modeling, a fear hierarchy is typically constructed and then followed through four stages of progressively greater exposure for the child with the active participation of the therapist. First, the child observes a live model complete the hierarchy tasks, using positive verbalizations. Next, the child is asked to place his hand on the therapist's shoulder and then hand, while the therapist interacts with the feared object. Then the therapist assists the child through the tasks, for example, by standing beside him. Finally, the child progresses to completing the tasks alone. Throughout these procedures the child is reinforced profusely and praised for initiating nonfearful approach and imitation behaviors. These stages are illustrated below with the Case Example for Grace.

Parent training is an approach that has been largely adapted from programs using behavior modification for children with externalizing (e.g., oppositional) behaviors. The general idea is that parents are incorporated into treatment to improve their relationship with the child and to provide them training in positive parenting practices that can serve the purpose of increasing positive and decreasing negative child behaviors. To accomplish this, McNeil and Ware (2003) note that parents are taught "to alter the antecedents and consequences of their child's behavior" and "to strengthen the parent-child relationship, placing particular emphasis on effective communication skills" (p. 443). Because children and their parents are often asked to continue therapeutic techniques between sessions, parent training can be especially useful for assisting parents in learning the skills needed to be an effective "parent-therapist," by modeling and praising positive approach behaviors to the feared stimulus.

Case example: Grace, age 3, and her parents presented for treatment of a SPP–animal type (bugs). It was presumed that Grace had developed this fear through the combination of two main events. Although she had not previously exhibited fearful behaviors around bugs, she first expressed some concern about them after observing classmates scream and cry when bugs approached them on the playground at childcare. Her fear then escalated significantly after an incident when a mosquito buzzed around her head while she was strapped into her car seat. At that time, she tried to get her father's attention and when he did not respond she cried, screamed, and began to hyperventilate. Although the bug was subsequently removed, and Grace was calmed, she rapidly began evidencing fearful behaviors around bugs and anything resembling bugs (e.g., lint, fur, dirt). Grace was treated using the combination of parent training, systematic desensitization, and participant modeling with reinforcement. Grace's parents were first provided with psychoeducation about phobias and behavior therapy, and were then given specific examples of how to examine antecedents, behaviors, and consequences related to their daughter's specific phobia. In addition, they were taught how to reinforce and encourage her approach behaviors. Given Grace's young age, her parents were also enlisted to serve as participant models, and a small hierarchy list was created with their input. The hierarchy included approaching an area with bugs, sitting on the ground next to the bugs, putting a hand by the bugs, picking up a bug on a stick, and letting a bug crawl on her. Since Grace was too young to teach relaxation, her favorite candy treat was given to her during these exercises, and rewards of exuberant praise and "high-fives" were used to reinforce her. Grace was given her candies to eat while sitting outside with her parents and the therapist. It was decided that Grace's parents would slowly use participant modeling, only progressing to subsequent actions from their hierarchy and stages when Grace was relaxed and showing nonfearful behaviors (e.g., not clinging, crying, or hiding). Grace first watched as her mother and father took turns progressively moving closer to a bug, putting their hand next to it, and then letting it crawl onto them. Grace's parents were coached to make positive verbalizations, such as, "see how the bug just runs on my hand – he tickles me!" and to smile and laugh while they interacted with the bug. In the second stage, Grace's mother first held her while her father again demonstrated approaching and letting a bug crawl on him. Grace's mother slowly moved closer and closer while this occurred, praising Grace for being brave while her father continued to remark about how nice (and silly) the bug was. Grace was then held by her father while he went through the same procedures of gradually approaching and handling a bug. Finally, Grace's parents asked her to let a bug tickle her hand, first by placing it on the ground near the bug, then by holding a stick with a bug on it, and finally by letting her father pass one to her from his hand. Grace was able to move through all of these tasks in a 2-hr session, and her parents were given the homework of continuing to practice every day until their next session.

Cognitive restructuring and positive self-talk: Cognitive restructuring refers to the process of helping children to identify and alter cognitive biases, first in general with psychoeducation, and subsequently as they personally experience them. Children are then encouraged to embark on experimental tests of their negative cognitions. Often linked with cognitive restructuring is positive self-talk, which refers to teaching children alternatives to the negative cognitions that they report. Basically the children are taught to self-instruct themselves in how to deal with the situation. For example, a child who reports telling herself that she cannot eat in the cafeteria, because all the other children will laugh at her, would first be guided toward recognizing the negativity and bias in these cognitions (e.g., all-or-none thinking, catastrophizing) and then would be prompted to identify alternative thoughts (e.g., "Just because other kids are laughing doesn't mean they are laughing at me" or "I do not really know what other kids will do, so I could try eating something small in the cafeteria today").

Social skills and/or social problem solving training: As previously described, social skills and problem solving deficits are often thought to contribute to the onset and maintenance of childhood anxiety disorders. For instance, anxious children are often depicted as shy from an early age and are frequently rejected or ignored by peers. Improving these areas for anxious children may provide them with additional tools for coping with anxiety (i.e., supportive friends), as well as increase their feelings of social competency. The main goal of social skills training is introducing and reviewing techniques that will assist children in the initiation and maintenance of positive peer relationships. La Greca and Fetter (1995) have identified several skills important for positive peer interactions, which clinicians can evaluate (i.e., showing enjoyment of interactions, greeting, joining, inviting, conversation, sharing/cooperation, complimenting/giving positive feedback, and conflict resolution). In addition, as noted in Chapters 2 and 3, several rating scales are available for assessing social skills as part of broader measures (e.g., Child Behavior Checklist) or on separate scales (e.g., Social Skills Rating System). Modeling, coaching, role plays, outside practice (homework), feedback, and reinforcement are typically the methods used by clinicians to address social skills deficits (e.g., Gresham, 2002), while with social problem solving, children are typically taught a series of steps to take when evaluating ambiguous or anxiety-provoking situations. A standard problem solving approach is to have children (1) identify the problem, (2) brainstorm diverse solutions, (3) weigh the pros/cons of each solution, (4) select and implement a solution, and (5) evaluate the chosen solution and outcome (Spence, 2003). This can be an especially helpful technique for children who have become "stuck" in their assessment of social situations. For example, with SOCP, children often misinterpret ambiguous situations in a negative manner which can result in increased distress and avoidance. For such children, social problem solving may serve as a tool for helping the child slow down and evaluate the situation more fully before responding (e.g., leaving) or thinking (e.g., they are staring at me) in what may have become an automatic way.

Although a number of different techniques have been successfully used in the treatment of anxious youths, interventions should be individually tailored

In summary, a variety of methods for working with anxious children and adolescents have been described and found to have strong empirical support. In addition to these commonly employed strategies, it is not uncommon that other approaches also need to be invoked. For example, it has been suggested that emotion regulation training needs to take a more prominent role in anxious youth treatment programs (Hannesdottir & Ollendick, 2007). Such programs may help deal with basic emotion recognition and regulation strategies. Moreover, when stressors are present as with PTSD, ADJ, and anxiety disorder, it may be important to reduce the stressor as much as possible as the first line of treatment, and subsequently target the anxiety using programs such as those previously described with adaptations made as necessary. Likewise, with substance-induced anxiety disorders, there is oftentimes the need to address the substance issues at the forefront. With general medical conditions, referrals to appropriate medical professionals to assist with management of that condition may be necessary. Finally, as we have discussed elsewhere (Ollendick et al., 2001), considerations should always be given to the developmental level of the child, with accommodations made to CBT/BT procedures as necessary. What is evident here is that the treatment must be individually tailored to the given child and her family and that the treatment must be implemented in a flexible yet evidence-based way.

4.2   Mechanisms of Action

Remarkably, little is currently known about the mechanisms of action involved in the treatment of anxiety disorders. While it is presumed that acquiring and completing the skills and techniques described above are critical, this has not been well studied to date. Since CBT approaches have been shown to be superior to waiting-list control groups (discussed below), it is clear that something is resulting in effective treatment gains; however, it is less clear what that is. For example, homework is generally considered a critical aspect of CBT programs, facilitating between-session practice and allowing children greater opportunities for success and competency development; however, in the only known study to examine it, therapist-reported child homework compliance was not found to predict treatment outcome (Hughes & Kendall, 2007).

4.2.1   Psychotherapy

The therapeutic relationship and working alliance have been proposed to be critical factors for not only CBT, but also for the efficacy of most psychotherapy programs (see Karver, Handelsman, Fields, & Bickman, 2006). Interestingly, for child anxiety disorder treatments, inconsistent findings appear regarding the therapeutic relationship, based on the informant. For example, while children who have received CBT for anxiety disorders retrospectively recalled the therapeutic relationship to be among the most important treatment factors (Kendall & Southam-Gerow, 1996), prospective child ratings of the therapeutic relationship have not been found to predict treatment outcome (Fjermestad et al., 2009; Kendall, 1994; Kendall et al., 1997). Conversely, therapist perceptions of the therapeutic relationships have been found to predict improved anxiety treatment outcomes at both posttreatment and 1-year follow-up (Hughes & Kendall, 2007). Contrasting findings have also been revealed when observers have provided ratings of the therapeutic alliance. That is, more positive child–therapist and parent–therapist alliances have predicted greater reductions in posttreatment child anxiety in one study (McLeod & Weisz, 2005), but not in others (Chiu et al., 2009: Liber et al., 2010). Remarkably, session-by-session analysis of the child–therapist alliance (based on therapist, child, mother, and father reports) has shown an increasingly positive relation that tends to level off over time and that has been associated with more positive treatment outcomes (Chiu et al., 2009; Chu et al., 2004). Further, this pattern has been found regardless of whether the child received exposure as part of their treatment (Kendall et al., 2009). The last represents an especially important finding, as concerns have previously been raised about the intensity and content of exposure sessions and their potential to disrupt the therapeutic alliance and relationships. Notwithstanding these findings, what may also be important is the level of child engagement in therapy immediately prior to the initiation of exposure sessions. For example, several studies have found that more positive child engagements or child–therapist alliances assessed just prior to the start of in vivo exposures predicted improved diagnostic outcomes (e.g., Chu & Kendall, 2004, 2009; Karver et al., 2006). Thus, child investment and commitment to therapy, as well as his or her trust in the therapist may be crucial for producing the most beneficial effects from exposure exercises. Overall, findings such as these support clinical lore recognizing the importance of early child and parent engagement for successful therapy continuation and participation, as well as preliminarily dispelling concerns that participating in exposure exercises may irreparably damage the therapeutic alliance and adversely affect treatment outcome (Kendall et al., 2009).

> There is a general support for the therapeutic relationship and working alliance in the therapy process

Others have argued that the simple act of attending to the child and his/her needs along with the aforementioned positive therapeutic alliance may be the active ingredients of effective therapy. For example, several studies have shown comparable anxiety treatment efficacy rates among CBT and active control groups that included components such as psychoeducation and support (Last, Hansen, & Franco, 1997; Silverman et al., 1999); however, Kendall, Hudson, Gosch, Flannery-Schroeder, and Suveg (2008) examined this more carefully and reported that control groups tend to be quite similar to CBT programs with approximately 65% of their content considered to overlap. Following up on these findings, Hudson et al. (2009) compared a CBT (with family involvement) program with a carefully selected supportive attention control group that did not consist of such overlap, and in this instance the CBT program showed superiority (69% versus 45% diagnosis-free at posttreatment). Similarly, another recent study demonstrated that CBT treatment was superior to an attention control group in the treatment of specific phobias (Ollendick et al., 2009).

A mechanism of action is the successful confrontation of that which is feared and coping with the anxiety that results

Although findings have suggested a role for the therapeutic alliance and relationship, findings are not conclusive and indicate that there are additionally important components that make up CBT programs. The exposure exercises involved in BT/CBT programs are commonly believed to be such a key component and have been shown to be such in several recent investigations (e.g., King, Heyne, & Ollendick, 2005; Nakamura, Pestle, & Chorpita, 2009). That is, researchers have often suggested that the main mechanism of action pertains to the act of directly confronting anxiety provoking stimuli and the consequences that result from such successful encounters. That is, children learn that such confrontations do not result in feared outcomes and that their dreaded thoughts are not confirmed. It is further hypothesized that a sense of self-efficacy or mastery develops from such experiences (Ollendick et al., 2009).

Still, a second mechanism of action is the reduction in negative anxious self-talk

Self-talk has also been proposed to be a crucial component of CBT programs, and studies investigating this have provided preliminary support for decreasing anxious self-talk. For instance, negative anxious self-statements have been found to predict posttreatment anxiety disorder severity and have also been shown to decrease in unison with treatment gains (e.g., Kendall & Treadwell, 2007; Muris, Mayer, den Adel, Roos, & van Wamelen, 2009). Moreover, anxious cognitions, as well as anxious coping behaviors, have been found to mediate treatment outcome (Chu & Harrison, 2007; Lau, Chan, Li, & Au, 2010). In contrast, positive and depressive self-statements were found to be unrelated to anxiety outcomes in these studies, highlighting the specific role of anxious cognitions (Kendall & Treadwell, 2007).

In summary, several mechanisms of action for CBT efficacy have been proposed, with varying levels of support found for each of them. Unfortunately, only a handful of studies have examined these important issues, and findings may well indeed vary by anxiety diagnosis. For example, psychoeducation and cognitive restructuring were reported to be important components of an adolescent treatment for PD (Micco, Choate-Summers, Ehrenreich, Pincus, & Mattis, 2007), while decreases in loneliness and increases in social effectiveness predicted posttreatment change in SOCP symptoms (Alfano et al., 2009). Furthermore, specific parent training tools have been found to predict improvements in child functioning following CBT with family involvement for a variety of anxiety disorders (Khanna & Kendall, 2009; Wood, McLeod, Piacentini, & Sigman, 2009). Thus, despite several advances in this domain, what constitutes the "active ingredients" making CBT effective in the treatment of child anxiety seems to remain largely unknown and is a critical area for future research (Seligman & Ollendick, 2011).

The mechanism of action for psycho-pharmacological treatments pertain to the manner with which they influence the nervous system

4.2.2   Psychopharmacology

In contrast to psychotherapy studies that have contained a certain amount of guesswork in their analysis, mechanisms of action for pharmacological treatments are presumed to depend on the particular psychotropic medication used and their known influence on the nervous system. For example, SSRIs are presumed to inhibit the absorption of the neurotransmitter serotonin after its release, thus allowing more of it to remain active in the synaptic cleft. Benzodiazepines, which are also commonly associated with the pharmacological treatment of anxiety, operate on another neurotransmitter system, gamma-aminobutyric acid (GABA). Thus, for psychopharmacological treatments of anxiety disorders, the particular mechanism of action involved depends on the medication selected. However, since these result in only temporary alterations to neurotransmitter systems, it is not surprising, then, that positive effects are typically restricted to periods of active treatment, with relapse seen upon medication discontinuation.

4.3   Variations and Combinations of Methods

A number of multicomponent behavior and cognitive behavior programs have been created for the treatment of child/adolescent anxiety disorders, and similarly, several studies of varying complexity have been conducted with potential pharmacological treatments. A complete review of these would be well beyond the scope of this text, indeed entire volumes have been dedicated to each of the childhood anxiety disorders and their treatments. Instead, we focus on a selection of those treatments that have received the most empirical attention.

Before beginning, some commonalities among the BT/CBT approaches are important to note. First, these represent short-term interventions, usually between 10 and 20 sessions, though as few as one session can be involved, and oftentimes booster sessions are held on a varying and infrequent basis for several months posttreatment. While the main focus of these approaches is on skill building and anxiety reduction, a strong, supportive therapeutic relationship is also considered imperative (see above). Moreover, treatments tend to vary on what specific skills are taught (e.g., deep breathing versus imagery) and who is included in the treatment. Regarding the latter, treatments are referred to as individual (ICBT) when only the anxious child is included, group (GCBT) when several anxious children are included, and child plus family (CBT+F) when the anxious child and his or her family are included.

CBT/BT programs share several commonalities, but specific interventions have been developed and empirically supported for the different child anxiety diagnoses (detailed by diagnosis below)

4.3.1   Multiple Anxiety Diagnoses

One of the first and best-studied treatments for child anxiety disorders is the Coping Cat (cf. Kendall, 1990). Originally examined in youth with diagnoses of SAD and the precursors to GAD (i.e., overanxious disorder) and SOCP (i.e., avoidant disorder), the Coping Cat has subsequently been examined by multiple research groups around the world (with such name changes as the Coping Koala in Australia and the Coping Bear in Canada) and with individual, group, and family adaptations. In the most basic form, the Coping Cat (child version, ages 7–13; Kendall & Hedtke, 2006) and C.A.T. Project (adolescent version, ages 14–17; Kendall, Choudhury, Hudson, & Webb, 2002) typically lasts 16 sessions (with booster sessions added as necessary). Early sessions focus on rapport building and information gathering, and are followed by skills building sessions (e.g., recognition of emotions, relaxation, cognitive restructuring). The second part of treatment focuses on exposure exercises along with profuse reinforcement for engaging in those exposure exercises, with approximately six sessions conducted before one final session dedicated to review and termination issues. During the course of treatment, parents are generally included in two sessions – one that introduces the treatment skills and the other prior to the exposure components. To assist in coping and problem solving throughout, children are taught the acronym FEAR (*F*eeling frightened, *E*xpecting bad things to happen, *A*ttitudes/actions that will help, *R*esults and rewards), and homework assignments are referred to as STIC tasks ("Show That I Can") to avoid negative connotations children may associate with the term *homework* from school. In addition to the individual programs, a manual and workbook are available for a parent/family-based version, and a separate manual is available for adapting the Coping Cat for a group approach. Training materials for therapists and a recently developed computer-assisted version (Camp Cope) are also available for purchase (see Table 14).

The FRIENDS for Life Program (Barrett, 2004) is a GCBT+F program comprising 10 sessions for children (child version, aged 7–11) or adolescents (youth version, aged 12–16) and their families, which was developed from an adaptation of the ICBT Coping Cat program (the Coping Koala). Variations of the FRIENDS program have also been studied in youth with various anxiety disorder diagnoses (GAD, SOCP, SAD, and SPP; Pahl & Barrett, 2010), as well as those at risk for or with subclinical anxiety (Dadds, Spence, Holland, Barrett, & Laurens, 1997). The basic protocol consists of 10 weekly group sessions for children along with two booster sessions occurring approximately one and

Table 14
Commonly Utilized CBT Programs for Anxious Children and Youths

Program	Available from
Coping Cat CAT Project (and others)	http://www.workbookpublishing.com/anxiety.html
FRIENDS for Life	https://www.australianacademicpress.com.au/friends
Timid to Tiger	Cartwright-Hatton et al. (2011)
SET-C	http://www.mhs.com/product.aspx?gr=edu&prod=setc&id=overview
PCT-A	http://www.us.oup.com/us/catalog/general/subject/Psychology/PractitionerClientGuides/?view=usa&ci=9780195335804
FOCUS	http://www.pathwayshrc.com.au/for-kids-4-12/focus-program/
TF-CBT	http://www.guilford.com/cgi-bin/cartscript.cgi?page=pr/cohen.htm&dir=pp/taptsd&cart_id=

Note. CBT = cognitive behavior therapy; FOCUS = Freedom from Obsessions and Compulsions Using Cognitive-Behavioral Strategies; PCT-A = Panic Control Treatment for Adolescents (Mastery of Anxiety and Panic for Adolescents: Riding the Wave); SET-C = Social Effectiveness Therapy for Children and Adolescents; TF-CBT = trauma-focused CBT.

three months posttreatment. In addition, group parent sessions (4 hr) are part of the program and can be flexibly divided into a different number of sessions; though family members are also commonly involved at the end of each session for review and reinforcement. Child sessions include psychoeducation, relaxation, exposure, problem solving, cognitive restructuring, and social support components, while parent sessions consist primarily of psychoeducation, parenting skills, and reinforcement approaches to use with their children (Barrett, Farrell, Ollendick, & Dadds, 2006). Thus, aligning with the primary skills taught in the program, FRIENDS is an acronym for the program treatment sessions: *F*eelings, *R*emember to Relax, *I* can do it, *E*xplore solutions and coping step plans, *N*ow reward yourself, *D*on't forget to practice, *S*mile and Stay calm for life! (Pahl & Barrett, 2010). In addition, a newer program, Fun Friends (Barrett, 2007), has been developmentally adapted for younger children (aged 4–6) and shortens the FRIENDS acronym accordingly (*F*eelings, *R*elax, *I* can try, *E*ncourage, *N*urture, *D*on't forget to be brave, *S*tay happy). The program has been successfully used as a universal, school-based early intervention by several research groups in different countries (e.g., Germany, United Kingdom, South Africa, and Australia). Importantly, this program has also been used as a prevention program with positive outcomes (e.g., higher self-esteem, lower anxiety) revealed at posttreatment and over time (see Barrett & Turner, 2004).

While much of the early work on multicomponent CBT programs for youths with various anxiety diagnoses, such as those noted above, focused on older children and adolescents, programs have begun to emerge that are designed to reach younger children – typically by working with their families. For example, the Timid to Tiger program (Cartwright-Hatton et al., 2011) is a 10-session parent-only group intervention for anxious children aged 9 and under. Cotherapists run each 2-hr session, with the first hour dedicated to reviewing homework and practice from the previous session and the second hour on teaching new skills. Focus is placed on psychoeducation, teaching positive parenting skills (e.g., ignoring, limit setting, reinforcement of confident/brave behaviors), as well as teaching parents CBT approaches (e.g., problem-solving skills, exposure) to use in managing their child's anxiety. Other newly developed programs that similarly target younger children, in addition to the Fun Friends program noted above, include Being Brave – A Program for Coping With Anxiety for Young Children and Their Parents (Hirshfeld-Becker et al., 2010) and Taming "Sneaky Fears" (Monga, Young, & Owens, 2009).

Several new CBT programs have recently emerged that specifically target younger youths suffering from anxiety

4.3.2 Social Phobia

Two multicomponent GCBT programs have been studied that utilize the same CBT components as the previously described ICBT programs, while adding greater emphasis on the social concerns inherent in this disorder (Albano & Barlow, 1996; Spence, Donovan, & Brechman-Toussaint, 2000). For example, the exposure exercises in these treatments are conducted on social fears, and addressing social skills (friendship building, problem solving, assertiveness training, etc.) is of primary importance. Thus far demonstrating the most success in treating SOCP, however, is Social Effectiveness Therapy for Children (Beidel et al., 2000). This program comprises social skills training, peer generalization, and in vivo social exposures, along with parent psychoeducation and reinforcement. Following an initial joint parent–child psychoeducation session, children attend 12 weekly group and individual sessions each lasting about an hour. Groups typically consist of 4–6 similarly aged socially phobic children; however, nonanxious peers also join the group to practice social skills during developmentally appropriate peer interaction activities (e.g., bowling, eating in a cafeteria). As discussed later in this chapter, this program has shown positive posttreatment and long-term outcomes and manual/treatment kits are available for purchase by qualified practitioners (see Table 14).

4.3.3   Separation Anxiety Disorder

Pincus and colleagues (2008) have recently Adapted Parent–Child Interaction Training, an intervention with proven efficacy in treating various child behavior difficulties (see Callahan, Stevens, & Eyberg, 2010, for a review), to target SAD. This program is also designed for younger children (4–8 years), which is important given the common younger age of children presenting with this disorder. Following the standard protocols for parent- and child-directed interactions, a third component (bravery-directed interaction) was added to more specifically address SAD concerns, with parents provided psychoeducation and reinforcement/reward techniques to use with their children as they complete separation exposures (using a fear hierarchy). Also in line with standard parent–child interaction training, parents receive training (psychoeducation and skill building) and coaching sessions, with the latter involving the parent implementing the learned skills with their child with the aid of therapist coaching (e.g., bug in ear).

4.3.4   Specific Phobia

A combination of cognitive and behavioral procedures are used in the treatment of SPPs in children. In recent years, these procedures have been folded into what is referred to as a "one-session treatment." Although originally developed by Lars-Goran Öst (1989, 1997) as an intervention with adults, its use with children and adolescents has progressed substantially in the last decade or so. One-session treatment is a massed CBT that is delivered in the course of a single 3-hr session. Typically used in outpatient settings, the 3-hr session is conducted a few days or 1 week, following a functional assessment of the child's phobia. Conducting successful one-session treatment depends on the clinician's ability to adequately plan for the massed session and anticipate the stimuli needed for the session, as well as the child's likely response at each step in the graduated hierarchy of exposure. Above all, it is necessary for the clinician to be able to judge and range the intensity of exposure the child can tolerate during the session – not making exposure steps too easy or too hard, but rather getting the exposure "just right" (i.e., challenging but acceptable to the child). As a result, a detailed functional assessment (see Section 3.2.4) is a crucial initial step in preparing for the massed one-session treatment (Davis, Ollendick, & Öst, 2009). During the 3-hr session, the clinician combines several evidence-based techniques together: exposure, cognitive challenges, participant modeling, reinforcement, psychoeducation, and skills training (Davis et al., 2009). Quite frequently, the combination of these techniques can be used with children in a fun turn-taking approach – as both clinician and child take turns suggesting behavioral experiment ideas once the overall treatment format and pace are established. In general, the session begins with a review of the rationale for treatment and a description of the process to be used for conducting exposure (labeled as "behavioral experiments") with the child. The clinician should emphasize that nothing will be done to surprise or shock the child, rather the session will be completed with the child and clinician working as a team with the goal of overcoming the child's phobia. A detailed manual for the implementation of this procedure is available (Ollendick et al., 2009).

4.3.5 Panic Disorder

Ollendick (1995) first demonstrated the efficacy of CBT techniques in the treatment of youths with PD and AG. The approach used combined psychoeducation, relaxation training, cognitive restructuring, problem solving, parent training, and exposures for feared situations, and resulted in successful treatment of four adolescents after 10–12 weeks. Subsequently, a similar, manualized approach that was a downward extension of a successful adult treatment emerged that added interoceptive exposures to the techniques used by Ollendick. *Interoceptive exposures* refers to exposure to the panic symptoms themselves – for example, exposure to rapid heartbeat by having the child run up stairs. Panic Control Treatment for Adolescents (PCT-A; Hoffman & Mattis, 2000; Mattis & Ollendick, 2002) is an 11-session program primarily for adolescents but also includes parents by providing them psychoeducation materials and having them attend the end of four treatment sessions. A therapist manual and adolescent workbook are also now available for this program (Mastery of Anxiety and Panic for Adolescents: Riding the Wave; see Table 14).

4.3.6 Obsessive-Compulsive Disorder

Perhaps the best-known CBT program for childhood OCD has been How I Ran OCD Off My Land, which was more recently revised as *OCD in Children and Adolescents: A Cognitive-Behavioral Treatment Manual* (March & Mulle, 1998). This primarily ICBT program is typically completed in 12–20 sessions, but also explicitly includes parents in four sessions spaced throughout the treatment as well as at the beginning and end of each session (March & Mulle, 1998). Four main components make up this program. First is psychoeducation, with particular emphasis on a medical comparison model of OCD and separating the child from the disorder (externalizing it). The second component is cognitive restructuring and coping skills training that the child can apply during exposures. The third component is referred to as "Mapping OCD" and includes functional behavioral analysis of the specifics for the individual child's symptoms, as well as hierarchy building and pictorial representations of the child's progress combating the disorder. The final component includes therapist-assisted, graded exposures with response prevention and varies in length depending on the child and his or her symptoms. In addition, two final treatment sessions are dedicated to relapse prevention once successful treatment gains have been made.

Adding greater parent/family involvement, the Freedom from Obsessions and Compulsions Using Cognitive-Behavioral Strategies (FOCUS) program (Barrett, Healy-Farrell, & March, 2004) was derived from How I Ran OCD Off My Land. The FOCUS program consists of 12–14 weekly sessions, as well as 2–4 posttreatment booster sessions, and can be administered in an individual or small group format (Barrett, Healy-Farrell, & March, 2004; Barrett, Healy-Farrell, Piacentini, & March, 2004). Family sessions are conducted with all family members at the beginning and toward the end of the program, while all other sessions include separate child (e.g., 50-min), family (e.g., parent and/ or sibling, 30-min), and joint (e.g., 10-min) components. The child sessions follow the same general approach as that described above for the original ICBT program (see Barrett, Healy-Farrell, Piacentini, et al., 2004, for session outlines). The family sessions are intended for parents *and* siblings and primarily cover psychoeducation, problem-solving skills, and reinforcement/support for the anxious child's approach behaviors, along with disengaging from any accommodating or avoidance-supporting behaviors.

With slight variations, other similar individual- and family-based OCD treatment programs have also been developed (e.g., Freeman et al., 2008; Ginsburg et al., 2011; Lewin et al., 2005). As discussed in Section 4.4, results from these studies have been uniformly positive, showing significant symptom reduction in children as young as 3 years.

4.3.7   Posttraumatic Stress Disorder

Trauma-focused CBT (TF-CBT) has emerged as the treatment of choice for youths with PTSD. TF-CBT is a flexible program that often lasts from 8–20 sessions and ideally includes parallel and joint child and parent sessions (though it can be adapted to include only children when necessary; Cohen, Mannarino, & Deblinger, 2010). The program comprises components that are similar to the other evidence-based anxiety treatment programs previously reviewed (e.g., psychoeducation, relaxation, cognitive-restructuring and coping skills, exposure, and parent training); however, focus is directed at the source of the trauma, with some modifications made as necessary. For example, emotion recognition and regulation, trauma narratives, and safety planning are additional key components of TF-CBT, as is a separate section on healthy sexuality for child sexual abuse survivors. A thorough description of this program is available elsewhere (e.g., Cohen, Mannarino, & Deblinger, 2006), and an online training program and additional resources are currently available at http://tfcbt.musc.edu/. Positive outcomes have been shown using individual and group TF-CBT for youths experiencing PTSD following such sexual abuse, physical abuse, witnesses violence, and disasters.

4.3.8   Additional Comments

As previously noted, the above examples represent only a subset of those behavior and cognitive behavior programs available for the treatment of childhood and youth anxiety disorders. Indeed, programs with greater emphasis on the cognitive factors presumed to be involved in the development and maintenance of anxiety disorders have also been receiving attention. For example, studies have been published in just the past year examining programs with more cognitive therapy components for childhood SOCP (Melfsen et al., 2011), GAD (Payne, Bolton, & Perrin, 2011), and OCD (Williams et al., 2010). Promising studies have also emerged on anxiety-related areas, such as attention modification training (Rozenman, Weersing, & Amir, 2011), and the combination of evidence-based treatments to address commonly comorbid conditions. For example, a multicomponent CBT+F program has recently been developed for child maltreatment victims, which combines empirically supported aspects of PTSD and substance use treatments (Danielson et al., 2010). With advances in technology have also come changes to treatment implementation. For example, several bibliotherapy and computerized treatment programs are currently under investigation (e.g., Cunningham et al., 2009; Rapee, Abbott, & Lyneham, 2006; Spence et al., 2011), and technology may be increasingly used to provide training or assistance to therapists providing treatment for anxious children or youths. For instance, treatment developers may soon be able to utilize web-based programs to interact with therapists (e.g., video chats or Q&A sessions, video supervision for training or fidelity), thus potentially improving transportability of their programs from research labs to community practices.

> **Other interventions have also received support, including those with a prevention focus and those using a stepped-care approach**

With advances in child anxiety interventions have also come important movements for early intervention and prevention studies, with some clear successes demonstrated. In general, these efforts have tended to focus on universal and broadly targeted approaches. For example, prevention studies have targeted entire school grades or in some cases have even been conducted school-wide (see Barrett & Turner, 2004, for a detailed review of prevention work), while early intervention studies have selected children considered "at risk" for anxiety disorders for inclusion. In the latter case, children have been selected based on high scores on anxiety screening measures or on identification of other risk factors, such as having an anxious parent.

The previously described FRIENDS program (see Section 4.3.1) has been the most investigated early intervention/prevention program to date. Although the program requires extensive training, it has been successfully implemented by trained school personnel (e.g., trained teachers and school nurses). The same 10 child (1 hr each) plus three parent and two booster session format is used, with a number of researchers showing positive outcomes (see Briesch, Sanetti, & Briesch, 2010). In a first examination of FRIENDS as a universal prevention program, the efficacy of teacher-led or therapist-led intervention groups was compared with class as usual across 10 Australian elementary schools (Barrett & Turner, 2001). Both prevention groups showed greater improvements than class as usual for areas such as anxiety symptoms and self-esteem; findings that have subsequently been replicated in several additional studies (e.g., Stallard et al., 2005; Stopa, Barrett, & Golingi, 2010). In addition, researchers have found that these intervention gains have been maintained over time (e.g., Barrett et al., 2006; Stallard, Simpson, Anderson, Hibbert, & Osborn, 2007; Stopa et al., 2010). While positive outcomes such as these have often been reported, others have failed to replicate them, and effects have often varied substantially by study, informant, or child age (see Briesch et al., 2010).

Early intervention school-based studies using FRIENDS and other similar CBT programs have similarly demonstrated significant decreases in anxiety for children receiving the intervention as compared with those who did not (Dadds et al., 1997; Shortt et al., 2001). As an example, another intervention recently targeted children considered at risk for anxiety disorders, because of having a parent with an anxiety disorder, and found significant benefit for a family-based CBT program, particularly over time (Ginsburg, 2009). The intervention lasted 8 weeks and was followed by 3 monthly booster sessions. Children who received the family-based program, as compared with a waiting-list control group of children, showed significantly lower clinician severity ratings of anxiety both 6 and 12 months following treatment. Child and parent ratings were more variable, with children reporting no significant changes at either time point, and parent reports of their child's anxiety significantly different only at the 12-month follow-up. Importantly, while none of the children had an anxiety disorder at pretreatment, differences had emerged between the intervention and nonintervention groups over time. Specifically, none of the children whose families received the intervention developed an anxiety disorder during the course of the study, whereas an anxiety disorder diagnosis was present in three (out of 20) children from the waiting-list group by the postintervention assessment and six children by the 12-month follow-up assessment (Ginsburg, 2009).

Early intervention and prevention programs such as these offer important advances for potentially improving children's mental health and quality of life. Universal, school-based, approaches also offer the advantage of being cost-effective means of reaching a large number of children. They can also potentially remove barriers to accessing treatment that might exist for some children (e.g., those without insurance or whose families may be unable or unwilling to access services). Moreover, if children who are prone to experience anxiety can be taught coping skills before these symptoms escalate, subsequent interventions may be unnecessary or may be shortened in duration and/or intensity. Related to this notion, are the multitiered or stepped treatment approaches that have been increasingly recommended for anxious youths (e.g., Ronan, Finnis, & Johnston, 2006; Salloum, 2010; van der Leeden et al., 2011). Such approaches generally consist of systematic assessment of symptoms with increasingly tailored interventions for treatment of nonresponders (e.g., from GCBT to ICBT). As an illustration, a recent study examined a stepped care approach with 133 children and their parents, beginning with the FRIENDS program and followed by two ICBT phases that included increasingly greater intervention for parents (van der Leeden et al., 2011). Seventy children participated in the first intervention phase only, while 38 participated in Phases 1 and 2, and 24 in all three phases. In total, 74% of children no longer met criteria for an anxiety disorder at the end of the program, with 45% responding to Phase 1 and an additional 17% and 11% responding following Phases 2 and 3 (van der Leeden et al., 2011).

Finally, as is discussed more thoroughly below, psychopharmacological approaches have also been used alone and in combination with CBT programs. Among these, SSRIs are considered first-line medications and have been recommended for all anxiety disorders except SPP. Benzodiazepines are also often prescribed, but are typically used for short-term management of anxiety symptoms. Tricyclic antidepressants, on the other hand, are generally recommended as second-line medications given the increased side effects and monitoring required with them (Kratochvil, Kutcher, Reiter, & March, 1999). In general, psychopharmacology alone results in remission rates comparable to or somewhat less than CBT alone, while the combination of these approaches tends to result in slightly improved remission rates over either individual approach (see below). However, two important caveats to psychopharmacological approaches have led to the recommendation that CBT remain the first-line treatment for childhood anxiety disorders (e.g., Baldwin et al., 2005; March et al., 1997; Vitiello & Waslick, 2010). First, every medication comes with potential side effects (e.g., gastrointestinal problems, agitation, sleep disruptions, suicidal ideation; see Ellis & Singh, 1999; Pliszka, 2011), and several of those commonly used medications have not received sufficient empirical study with child samples, especially in terms of their long-term impact on children's development (Mancuso, Faro, Joshi, & Geller, 2010; Rynn et al., 2011). Moreover, with the exception of those for OCD, none of the commonly studied and prescribed medications, including SSRIs, have been approved by the US Food and Drug Administration for the treatment of child anxiety disorders (Vitiello & Waslick, 2010). Second, while psychopharmacological treatments often result in positive remission rates, relapse is typical upon their discontinuation (Mancuso et al., 2010), and thus long-term treatment is often involved (e.g., it has been recommended that treatment continue for 12 months following remission; see Mancuso et al., 2010; Vitiello & Waslick, 2010).

Although psychopharmacological treatments have shown promise, CBT is still recommended as the first-line of treatment for child anxiety disorders

4.4   Efficacy

As previously noted, one of the most critical aspects for selecting a treatment should be its demonstrated efficacy. One of the strongest ways to demonstrate efficacy for a treatment is by conducting a randomized controlled trial (RCTs). RCTs are more powerful than experimental or open trial studies in that subjects are randomly allocated to treatments and waiting-list control or other control conditions for comparison. Oftentimes, the comparison is simply one of treatment versus no treatment; however, other studies utilize an active control group that receives another treatment that is presumed to differ from the one of interest (e.g., a psychoeducation or support group condition). While all studies are important for establishing a base for treatment efficacy, given the wealth of studies on childhood anxiety disorders and the strength of RCTs in demonstrating potential treatment differences, the latter will be focused on in this chapter.

4.4.1   CBT/BT Efficacy Studies

Numerous RCTs using BT and CBT have now been conducted with children diagnosed with anxiety disorders. Studies tend to be of the same combined

RCTs of CBT/BT have shown that roughly 2/3 of youths no longer meet criteria for their primary anxiety diagnosis at posttreatment

cluster of anxiety disorders (GAD, SAD, SOCP, and maybe SPP/PD), or less commonly of one of these alone, as well as of individual diagnoses of SPP, PTSD, and OCD. A comprehensive review of each of 78 identified RCTs conducted for child/adolescent anxiety disorders has recently been reported by Grills-Taquechel and Ollendick (2012), which is summarized below and in Tables 15 and 16. Overall, posttreatment and follow-up assessments typically show that better than two thirds of children no longer meet criteria for their primary anxiety diagnosis. In fact, several research groups have recently reviewed RCTs of child anxiety disorders and concluded that approximately 56–68% of children or youths treated with CBT were classified as remitted following treatment, compared with 21–35% of children or youths in control groups (Cartwright-Hatton et al., 2004; James, Soler, & Weatherall, 2005; Silverman, Pina, & Viswesvaran, 2008).

The most RCTs have been published on the combined group of anxiety disorders (i.e., children or youths diagnosed with GAD, SAD, SOCP, or SPP) and have shown significant improvements at posttreatment and long-term follow-ups (from 3 months up to 13 years). Moreover, these studies have ranged from including children only, to parents only, to all family members, with varying degrees, and have been conducted in both individual and group formats. Overall, posttreatment response rates (typically defined as the percentage of children no longer meeting criteria for their principal anxiety disorder diagnosis) have ranged from 33% to 88% for those in CBT/BT programs, as compared with 0 to 38% for those in waiting-list groups.

When response rates have been reported, considerably more children receiving treatment show a favorable response when compared with those in waiting-list conditions

Remarkably, consistent findings have also been revealed for the RCTs conducted with singular diagnoses (see Tables 15 and 16). For example, posttreatment response rates of 39–88% and 60–92%, compared with 0–4% and 20–42% for waiting-list comparison groups were reported for CBT/BT approaches with OCD and PTSD, respectively. Likewise, single diagnosis studies that have been conducted with children diagnosed with SPP and SOCP have revealed posttreatment response rates of 53–55% and 27–88% in those receiving treatment. While only two studies each reported response rates for diagnoses of SPP and PTSD, other findings further support the efficacy of

Table 15
Summary of CBT/BT Versus Waiting-List: Response Rates by Disorder

Diagnosis (no. of studies)	CBT/BT response rate ranges	Waiting-list response rate ranges
Combined anxiety (30)	33–88%	0–38%
SPP (2)	53–55%	2–50%
SOCP (9)	27–88%	0–16%
PTSD (2)	60–92%	20–42%
OCD (5)	39–88%	0–4%

Note. Not all studies represented above, as some did not report response rates. Combined anxiety group includes studies of children with varied anxiety diagnoses (i.e., GAD, SOCP, SAD, or SPP). BT = behavior therapy; CBT = cognitive behavior therapy; GAD = generalized anxiety disorder; OCD = obsessive-compulsive disorder; PTSD = posttraumatic stress disorder; SAD = separation anxiety disorder; SOCP = social phobia; SPP = specific phobia.

Table 16
Summary of CBT/BT Follow-up Study Response Rates

Diagnosis	Follow-up time frame	Response rates (and study types)
Combined anxiety group	6 month	75% (GCBT+F) and 86% (GCBT)
	1 year	83% (GCBT+F) and 92% (GCBT)
	1 year	78% (GCBT) and 81% (ICBT)
	1 year	50% (ICBT) and 78% (CBT+F)
	3 years	70% (GCBT) and 93% (GCBT+F)
	3.35 years (ave)	71% (ICBT)
	6 years	86% (ICBT) and 86% (CBT+F)
	7.4 years (ave)	81–93% (ICBT)
	8–13 years	96% (ICBT) and 100% (GCBT)
SOCP	1 year	25–61% (GCBT)
	3 years	72% (ICBT)
	5 years	43–50% (GCBT)
	5 years	81% (ICBT)
OCD	1 year	70% (ICBT) and 84% (GCBT)
	1.5 years	70% (ICBT) and 84% (GCBT)
	7 years	95% (ICBT) and 79% (GCBT)

Note. Not all studies represented above, as some did not report response rates. Combined anxiety group includes studies of children with varied anxiety diagnoses (i.e., GAD, SOCP, SAD, or SPP). ave = average (mean); BT = behavior therapy; CBT = cognitive behavior therapy; CBT+F = cognitive behavior therapy with family components; GAD = generalized anxiety disorder; GCBT = group cognitive behavior therapy; GCBT+F = group cognitive behavior therapy with family components; ICBT = individual cognitive behavior therapy; OCD = obsessive-compulsive disorder; SAD = separation anxiety disorder; SOCP = social phobia; SPP = specific phobia.

CBT/BT approaches with these. For example, four additional studies with children diagnosed with SPPs reported significant benefits for BT over waiting-list, computer-assisted BT, and other psychological interventions (Cornwall et al., 1996; Dewis et al., 2001; Muris et al., 1998; Öst et al., 2001). Similarly, numerous studies have documented the significant benefits for children receiving CBT for PTSD and related symptoms (see Silverman et al., 2008). Overall, these programs have consistently demonstrated superiority over such comparison groups as usual care, waiting lists, and nondirective supportive therapy for varied traumatic experiences (e.g., sexual abuse, violence, disasters; see Silverman et al., 2008), particularly for the reduction of internalizing and total problems scores on the CBCL – Child Behavior Checklist (Kowalik, Weller, Venter, & Drachman, 2011). Positive posttreatment findings from these studies also tend to be maintained at long-term follow-up (e.g., Cohen Mannarino, & Knudsen, 2005; Deblinger, Steer, & Lippmann, 1999).

Taken together, follow-up studies also show that these anxiety treatments are durable, with treatment gains generally maintained

Therapy format (e.g., individual, group, or family-included) does not appear to substantially influence the positive outcome findings reported

Importantly, CBT approaches for child and youth anxiety disorders are also durable, with studies demonstrating that treatment gains are maintained over long-term follow-up periods (from 3 months up to 13 years). Table 16 summarizes findings from the follow-up reports from RCTs of anxiety disorders including multiple diagnoses, OCD, and SOCP. In all cases, overall, treatment gains have been maintained or improved upon in the follow-up period.

Overall, therapy format appears to have little influence on treatment outcomes for children or youths receiving CBT for anxiety disorders. For example, studies that included children with varied anxiety diagnoses revealed posttreatment response rates for individual CBT (ICBT) ranging from 33% to 88%, group CBT (GCBT) ranging from 47% to 82%, and CBT with family involvement (CBT+F) ranging from 42% to 84%. Similarly, the follow-up studies reported in Table 16 also showed remarkably consistent response rates across treatment modalities. These ranges, too, are consistent with other recent reviews summarizing treatment outcomes by modality and reporting nonsignificant differences across ICBT, GCBT, and CBT+F (54%, 57%, and 67%, respectively, in James et al., 2005; and 59%, 62%, and 68%, respectively, in Silverman et al., 2008).

While these findings are clearly impressive, it is important to note that these are simply the overall highlights and that considerable variability exists in the findings of individual studies. For instance, some studies comparing individual and family-involved CBT have shown one to be superior to the other (e.g., Barrett, Dadds, & Rapee, 1996; Bodden et al., 2008), whereas others have shown statistically nonsignificant differences but improved response rates for one or other group (e.g., Wood, Piacentini, Southam-Gerow, Chu, & Sigman, 2006). In addition, when other outcome measures are examined – for example, rating scales – different studies have reported varying improvements based on different informants' ratings (e.g., child, parent, therapist), with some favoring individual and others family-included therapies. Interestingly, Wood et al. (2009) suggested that differences in the way parents are included in CBT+F may account for some of these diverse findings. That is, they noted that some programs had shared parent and child therapists while others had different therapists and group formats, with potential benefits and better findings for the former. Findings such as these are clearly in need of further exploration but also highlight the fact that there is much still to uncover about the details of CBT treatments. Moreover, research is yet to clearly specify when and if there may be instances where one treatment modality is preferable over another. For instance, given that studies have found large percentages of parent(s) who present with an anxious child and also have an anxiety disorder, it may be particularly valuable to include such families in CBT+F programs, as the parent may be able to apply learned information to themselves and/or learn techniques for controlling their own anxious behaviors in the presence of their child. Indeed, a recent study that included mothers in treatment as supportive and modeling agents for their anxious children showed a potentially positive benefit for the mothers (as well as children); such that, 60% of mothers had a pretreatment anxiety disorder diagnosis but only 39% did at posttreatment (Gar & Hudson, 2009).

A few additional points are important to note. First, differences often emerge between intention-to-treat and treatment-completer analyses, with poorer response rates often noted when children and/or families do not complete the majority of "prescribed" treatment sessions. Second, response rates, like those summarized in Tables 15 and 16, generally reflect those for principal diagnoses; however, given substantial comorbidity with youth anxiety disorders, it is also important to consider secondary diagnoses, especially any secondary anxiety diagnoses. Nonetheless, many of the studies summarized have provided information on primary and secondary diagnoses with similar patterns reported. That is, most studies report only slightly fewer responders (typically 10–20%) when considering remission rates across all secondary (or secondary anxiety) diagnoses. Finally, response rates tend to vary both within and across studies when different informant reports are considered. For example, when parent, child, and/or clinician rating scales are compared, findings regarding treatment outcomes tend to vary, oftentimes with the most minimal changes noted by children.

> Varying success shown with psycho-pharmacological agents, although far fewer studies have been conducted with them

4.4.2   Psychopharmacology Efficacy Studies

Psychopharmacological trials have also demonstrated varying success in treating child and youth anxiety disorders, both in terms of the different medications and disorders studied. Table 17 provides a summary of the most commonly used psychopharmacological agents for child and youth anxiety disorders. Among the child anxiety disorders, OCD has been the most frequently examined, with some medications evaluated in two different RCTs. In contrast, for all other anxiety disorders, each medication has been studied in only one trial that included children/adolescents.

With regard to OCD, the tricyclic antidepressant, clomipramine, and four different SSRIs (i.e., fluoxetine, sertraline, fluvoxamine, and paroxetine) have demonstrated efficacy over placebo controls. Specifically, the following response rates have been reported: 49–57% for fluoxetine (placebo 25–32%; Geller et al., 2001; Liebowitz et al., 2002), 21–53% for sertraline (placebo 4–37%; March et al., 1998; Pediatric OCD Treatment Study Team [POTS], 2004), 42% for fluvoxamine (placebo 26%; Riddle et al., 2001), and 65% for paroxetine (placebo 41%; Geller et al., 2004). Moreover, a meta-analysis concluded that none of these SSRIs were superior to the others, with pooled treat-

Table 17
Commonly Studied Psychopharmacological Agents for Childhood and Youth Anxiety Disorders

Selective serotonin reuptake inhibitors ("first-line" medications)

| Fluoxetine | Sertraline | Fluvoxamine | Paroxetine |

Tricyclic antidepressants

| Clomipramine | Imipramine | Desipramine (not effective) |

Recent additions
Serotonin-norepinephrine reuptake inhibitors (e.g., venlafaxine)
N-Methyl-D-aspartate agonists (e.g., D-cycloserine)

ment response rates of 52% for the SSRIs and 32% for placebo reported (Geller et al., 2003). While clomipramine was found to be superior to the SSRIs in the same meta-analysis (i.e., clomipramine effect sizes = .8–1.0 and .85 overall versus SSRI effect sizes = .2–.27 and .46 overall; Geller et al., 2003; Watson & Rees, 2008), the SSRIs remained recommended as "first-line" treatments because they have fewer adverse side effects and monitoring concerns (Geller et al., 2003; Vitiello & Waslick, 2010).

Another tricyclic antidepressant, imipramine, as well as benzodiazepines (alprazolam, clonazepam) and several of the above-noted SSRIs have also been studied for the treatment of non-OCD anxiety disorders of youth. Findings for imipramine have varied, with mixed findings for school-refusing children with anxiety and depressive disorders (Bernstein et al., 2000) versus no improvement with its inclusion in a BT treatment for SAD (Klein, Koplewicz, & Kanner, 1992). The two benzodiazepines did not show clinically significant benefit over placebo (Graae, Milner, Rizzotto, & Klein, 1994; Simeon, Ferguson, Knott, & Roberts, 1992). In contrast, the SSRIs have demonstrated efficacy for the treatment of several additional child anxiety disorders. For GAD, sertraline has shown superiority over placebo (90% versus 10%; Rynn, Siqueland, & Rickels, 2001), while paroxetine has been shown to be superior to placebo (78% versus 38%; Wagner et al., 2004) for SOCP. In addition, studies including children with multiple anxiety disorders (e.g., GAD, SAD, SOCP) have shown similarly positive outcomes with fluoxetine (61% versus 35%; Birmaher et al., 2003), sertraline (55% versus 24%; Walkup et al., 2008), and fluvoxamine, (76% versus 29%; Walkup et al., 2001). Finally, an additional medication, venlafaxine, has also recently received some support for treating non-OCD anxiety disorders. Venlafaxine is classified as a serotonin-norepinephrine reuptake inhibitor and has been shown to be superior to placebo in the treatment of children with GAD (69% versus 48% response rates; Rynn, Riddle, Yeung, & Kunz, 2007) and SOCP (56% versus 37% response rates; March, Entusah, Rynn, Albano, & Tourian, 2007).

In addition to addressing the treatment of anxiety disorders, recent advances have also suggested potential treatment augmentation using psychopharmacology. For example, several drugs proposed to operate on the N-methyl-D-aspartate (NMDA) system have received attention for their potential benefits during exposure sessions (see Rynn et al., 2011). Perhaps the most studied among these has been D-cycloserine, which has demonstrated enhanced treatment efficacy with animal and adult samples (see Norberg, Krystal, & Tolin, 2008, for review) and is currently being investigated in a sample of children with OCD (Storch et al., 2010).

4.4.3   CBT/BT and Psychopharmacology Combination Efficacy Studies

Notably, rates of improvement with psychopharmacological treatments typically remain lower than or equal to those found with CBT; a finding that has been most clearly demonstrated in several studies that have conducted head-to-head comparisons of these treatment approaches. Results from these studies have varied somewhat but generally show greater success for BT/CBTapproaches compared with tricyclic antidepressants, equivalent success for SSRIs and BT/CBT approaches, and the greatest success for SSRI and CBT combination approaches. For childhood OCD, comparative studies have shown better response rates for behavior therapy over clomipramine (De Haan, Hoogduin, Buitelaar, & Keijsers, 1998) and equal responsiveness for GCBT and Setraline (Asbahr et al., 2005). In a more detailed investigation, the combination of CBT and sertraline was found to offer improved remission rates over either approach alone, and all were superior to placebo (POTS, 2004). The same pattern of results was also demonstrated for CBT and sertraline in a recent study including children with various anxiety disorders (GAD, SOCP, and SAD; Walkup et al., 2008). However, the addition of sertraline to TF-CBT was not found to improve outcomes for children with PTSD (Cohen, Mannarino, Perel, & Staron, 2007), and likewise, the addition of imipramine to a BT program was not found to improve outcomes for children with SAD (Klein et al., 1992). As previously noted, mixed findings emerged with the combination of imipramine with a CBT program for school-refusing children and adolescents who also had anxiety and depressive disorders, with improvements shown in the combination group for school attendance but not for anxiety ratings (Bernstein et al., 2000). Finally, while both CBT and fluoxetine demonstrated better response rates than placebo for SOCP, the CBT group was also superior to fluoxetine, with approximately double the percentage of children responding (53%, 21%, and 3%; Beidel, Turner, Sallee, et al., 2007; Beidel, Turner, Young, et al., 2007).

Overall, this basic review has depicted the fact that psychopharmacological approaches, particularly the SSRIs, have shown efficacy in the treatment of several childhood anxiety disorders. For a more thorough review of these studies and others, along with information on medication dosage levels, tolerability, and side effects, the reader is referred to several recent child anxiety psychopharmacology reviews (e.g., Rynn et al., 2011; Vitiello & Waslick, 2010). Additional high-quality (RCT) studies appear warranted, however, as replication is needed for many of the findings noted, and still other child anxiety disorders that are commonly treated with psychopharmacology (e.g., PD) have not been sufficiently studied at all. Moreover, it is apparent from response rate/effect size comparisons and combination studies that, when selected, psychopharmacological treatments should be accompanied by CBT/BT. While across-study comparisons are difficult, as psychopharmacology trials tend to employ less rigorous diagnostic and outcome methodology, some support can be provided for this assertion. For instance, on the whole, CBT/BT tends to evidence improved outcomes and in no cases has a pharmacological treatment been found to be superior to CBT, while the combination of these approaches has evidenced some improvements over either alone. It is also important to note that long-term differences between psychopharmacological and cognitive behavior treatments have also favored the latter. For example, Asbahr et al. (2005) found similar response rates for sertraline and GCBT in youths with OCD; however posttreatment, relapse rates significantly differed, with 50% of those from the sertraline group relapsing versus only 5% from the GCBT group. Finally, computed effect sizes are also typically better for CBT programs. Effect sizes are often used to describe treatment outcomes or differences between treatment groups and are often categorized as small, medium, or large. On the whole, effect sizes from randomized clinical trials

Studies that have compared CBT/BT and psychopharmacological treatments have shown equivalent or better outcomes for the former and the greatest success for the combination of these approaches

Although some psychopharmacological treatments show favorable outcomes, it is recommended that they always be accompanied by CBT/BT as well

of CBT programs tend to be medium to large (e.g., Chorpita et al., 2011; Chu & Harrison, 2007; Ishikawa et al., 2007; James et al., 2005), while effect sizes from psychopharmacology studies tend to be small to medium (Geller et al., 2003; Watson & Rees, 2008). As a whole, these findings illustrate the superiority of CBT/BT programs. Although there may be instances where psychopharmacological treatments are called for, these findings also support recommendations that CBT/BT programs be used as a first-line treatment either alone or in combination with psychopharmacological treatment.

4.4.4   Evidence-Based Treatments

Using varying criteria, treatments have also been classified into different levels of support based on their accumulated evidence base and procedures

There are a variety of ways to examine the efficacy of treatment programs. In fact, in this chapter alone we have already described several of them (e.g., response/remission rates, effect sizes). Recognizing this and, in an attempt to draw conclusions more broadly about different treatments, various teams have organized and set forth criteria for what have since been termed *evidence-based treatments, empirically supported treatments,* and *empirically validated treatments.* The first set of these criteria sets appeared with a 1995 report by the Society of Clinical Psychology Task Force on Promotion and Dissemination of Psychological Procedures which focused on identifying different levels of support for psychological treatments, based on their accumulated evidence base and procedures (see Chambless & Ollendick, 2001). Since then, several similar groups / task forces (e.g., the Evidence Based Mental Health Movement) have gathered with the purpose of evaluating and classifying treatment programs for youths, as well as adults. Several different guidelines have now been put forth, with slight variations in their criteria and classification sets (see Chambless & Ollendick, 2001; Chorpita & Daleiden, 2009, Davis, May, & Whiting, 2011). While well-intentioned, the overall outcome of these varied criteria sets has been a return to the lack of descriptive consistency for studies and treatments that it was the initial goal of this movement to overcome. Further, it seems that, in the excitement to ride the empirically supported treatment wave, some have become focused on a race to best and/or most quickly classify treatments, resulting in inconsistent listings, frequent misuse of terms like *evidence-based,* and a general sense of confusion among laypersons and mental health professionals alike.

Despite the varied criteria and terminology used, the various guidelines have in common a series of categories that, at the lowest level includes treatments with little or no evidence supporting their efficacy and, at the highest level, treatments that have shown efficacy in multiple studies (by different research teams) using stringent criteria (e.g., randomized clinical trials, including treatment manuals). Although any one of these guidelines could be used to illustrate the current status of treatments for child anxiety disorders, those put forth by Chorpita and colleagues have been selected by us based on their comprehensiveness and contemporariness. The criteria used to classify treatments are summarized below in Table 18. Further information on this approach has been reported in a recent review (Chorpita et al., 2011), and a database of studies used to inform classification is regularly updated (http://www.practicewise.com).

4.4.5   Variables Which May Influence Treatment Efficacy

Following promising efficacy findings, a number of researchers have also examined conditions which may positively or negatively influence treatment outcomes. As previously noted, treatment modality (individual or group) and individuals involved in treatment (child or family) have generally not been found to influence outcomes. Although not often specifically studied, demographic variables, such as child gender, age, and ethnicity have also typically been unrelated to treatment efficacy or have shown mixed findings. For example, one study found that older youths responded more poorly to an ICBT treatment (Southam-Gerow, Kendall, & Weesing, 2001), whereas several others reported no age differences (e.g., Ginsburg et al., 2008; Kendall et al., 1997; Suveg et al., 2009). Still another study suggested interactions among child characteristics and treatment modality such that younger children (aged 7–10) and girls were more likely to respond to CBT+F than ICBT, whereas for adolescents and boys outcomes for these two approaches were equivalent (Barrett et al., 1996). Regarding ethnicity group comparisons, few studies have examined the issue directly or had large enough sample sizes to conduct formal comparisons. Nonetheless, in the handful of studies that have, no treatment outcome differences have been reported between Latino and European Americans (Pina et al., 2003) or African and European Americans (Ferrell, Beidel, & Turner, 2004). Nonetheless, it may prove beneficial to adapt treatment protocols to different groups (e.g., ethnic, racial, and religious) to best incorporate beliefs and practices into interventions with the goal of more successful outcomes; an area of work that has begun to be studied (e.g., Berger & Gelkopf, 2009; Pina, Villalta, & Zerr, 2009).

Treatment modality, family member inclusion, and comorbidity have generally not been found to influence outcomes for children treated for anxiety disorders

In contrast, socio-demographics (such as age, sex, and ethnicity) have shown more varied findings

Perhaps the most consistently found influence on treatment outcomes following treatment for child anxiety disorders pertains to parent psychopathology or family dysfunction. Indeed, a number of findings have cited the moderating role of these family variables (e.g., Barrington, Prior, Richardson, & Allen, 2005; Ginsburg et al., 2008; Southam-Gerow et al., 2001). Specific to parental anxiety, several investigators have actually found a pattern of initial negative influence on children's treatment outcomes that is ameliorated by follow-up. For instance, Gar and Hudson (2009) examined outcomes following a CBT program in anxious children with anxious mothers versus those without anxious mothers. At posttreatment, older children (10–14 years) with an anxious mother had less favorable response rates than those with nonanxious mothers; however, this difference had dissipated at a 12-month follow-up assessment. This pattern was also replicated by two other research teams (Bodden et al., 2008; Cobham, Dadds, Spence, & McDermott, 2010).

Parent psychopathology and/or family dysfunction has been consistently linked with adverse treatment outcomes for anxious youths

Because comorbidity is common for children with anxiety disorders, concern has been raised that the presence of multiple disorders may negatively influence treatment efficacy. Remarkably, a recent review of CBT/BT for childhood disorders found that the addition of comorbid disorders in the diagnostic profile of anxious children did not typically have a significant influence on their treatment outcomes (Ollendick, Jarrett, Grills-Taquechel, Hovey, & Wolff, 2008). A few additional areas have been associated with treatment outcomes (e.g., symptom severity); however, this largely remains an area in need of future study As research continues to address questions

Table 18
Example Criteria for Classifying Evidence-Based Treatments: 5-Level Approach

Level 1: Best support

I. At least two randomized trials demonstrating efficacy in one or more of the following ways:
    a. Superior to pill placebo, psychological placebo, or another treatment.
    b. Equivalent to all other groups representing at least one Level 1 or Level 2 treatment in a study with adequate statistical power (30 participants per group on average; cf. Kazdin & Bass, 1989) and that showed significant pre-post change in the Index group as well as the group(s) being tied. Ties of treatments that have previously qualified only through ties are ineligible.

II. Experiments must be conducted with treatment manuals.

III. Effects must have been demonstrated by at least two different investigator teams.

Level 2: Good support

I. Two experiments showing the treatment is (statistically significantly) superior to a waiting-list or no-treatment control group. Manuals, specification of sample, and independent investigators are not required.

OR

II. One between-group design experiment with clear specification of group, use of manuals, and demonstrating efficacy by either:
    a. Superior to pill placebo, psychological placebo, or another treatment.
    b. Equivalent to an established treatment (see qualifying tie definition above).

Level 3: Moderate support

One between-group design experiment with clear specification of group and treatment approach and demonstrating efficacy by either:
    a. Superior to pill placebo, psychological placebo, or another treatment.
    b. Equivalent to an already established treatment in experiments with adequate statistical power (30 participants per group on average).

Level 4: Minimal support

One experiment showing the treatment is (statistically significantly) superior to a waiting-list or no-treatment control group. Manuals, specification of sample, and independent investigators are not required.

Level 5: No support

The treatment has been tested in at least one study, but has failed to meet criteria for Levels 1 through 4.

Note. From "Evidence-Based Treatments for Children and Adolescents: An Updated Review of Indicators of Efficacy and Effectiveness," by B. F. Chorpita et al., 2011, *Clinical Psychology: Science and Practice, 18*, p. 154–172. ©2011 by John Wiley. Reproduced with permission.

of mechanisms of action, as well as mediators and moderators of treatment outcomes, intervention programs and their effectiveness will also progress, potentially closing the gaps in the successful treatment of children and youths with anxiety disorders.

4.5   Problems in Carrying Out the Treatments

Perhaps the greatest concern about carrying out treatments for anxious youth pertains to transportability. That is, transporting "laboratory-based" treatments to the real world – the world of clinical practice, also referred to as effectiveness research. Although a recent review of youth anxiety disorder treatment studies suggested significantly larger effect sizes for university and hospital clinic studies than other settings (e.g., schools, community; ds = .77 and .37, respectively; Ishikawa et al., 2007); overall, consensus appears to support the transportability of cognitive behavior treatments to clinical settings, albeit with slightly lowered effect sizes / remission rates reported (e.g., Barrington et al., 2005; Bodden et al., 2008; Williams et al., 2010). Effectiveness of CBT interventions has also been demonstrated by the varied school-based programs studied which are conducted with trained school personnel as "therapists" (e.g., Barrett & Turner, 2001; Berger & Gelkopf, 2009; Ginsburg et al., 2008; Rolfsnes & Idsoe, 2011; Stallard et al., 2005). As described in previous sections, school-based programs have successfully been used in the treatment of anxiety disorders (e.g., SOCP, SAD, and GAD) and related symptoms (e.g., peer problems and self-esteem), and have also been used in universal prevention and targeted intervention efforts. In addition to those previously noted, school-based interventions for PTSD symptoms have been conducted following a variety of traumatic events (e.g., major national disasters and exposure to terrorism; see Rolfsnes & Idsoe, 2011, for review), typically by teachers or other nonclinical research personnel, with an overall medium-large effect size found (d = .68, Rolfsnes & Idsoe, 2011). Finally, in an attempt to improve therapist training, competence, and ultimately effectiveness in delivering evidence-based treatments in standard clinical practices, a protocol of competencies needed for delivering empirically supported anxiety treatments has recently been developed (Sburlati, Schniering, Lyneham, & Rapee, 2011). Including training programs, adherence procedures, and competency protocols like these in future effectiveness trials may further bridge the gap between research and clinical practice outcomes. Still, although much remains to be done, our armamentarium for addressing the anxiety disorders of childhood and adolescence has burgeoned in recent years, and we have a solid empirical base from which to move forward.

Transportability of treatments to real-world settings remains an area of concern

5

Case Vignettes

Case Vignette 1: Nicolo

Nicolo Girardi was a 9-year-old, third-grade white boy from Providence, Rhode Island. Nicolo lived at home with his mother (Mia, 36), father (John, 40), and sister (Giulia, 15) and was referred by his pediatrician. Mrs. Girardi presented with concerns regarding Nicolo's worries, somatic anxiety symptoms (e.g., feeling that he could not breathe, ringing in his ears, extremity tingling/numbness), difficulties sleeping, and poor school attendance. Nicolo reported being most bothered by the feeling that his throat was closing or that he had "pins and needles," and that this had happened both during the day and at night. Regarding his sleep difficulties, Nicolo reported having trouble falling asleep at night because of worries that his throat would close when he was lying down. He reported an easier time falling asleep when his mother sat with him or if he was propped up with pillows in bed. Mrs. Girardi reported that Nicolo also frequently slept in her room and that he had tantrums when she did not allow this. These problems had begun approximately five months prior to their first appointment and had developed suddenly. The only known changes at the time symptoms began were the commencement of school and an incident at the beach during summer vacation. Nicolo reported that he had been pulled under by a riptide at the ocean that summer and that the lifeguards saved him from drowning by swimming him back to shore. He had swallowed some water that made him feel sick, but he had required no medical attention following the incident. He reported being fearful that something like this would happen again and that he did not want to be in any water (e.g., shower, bath, pool) anymore for fear he would drown. Mrs. Girardi indicated that Nicolo had seen his pediatrician several times over the past few months and that he had found no medical basis to Nicolo's complaints (throat tightness, stomachaches, pins and needles).

Prior to these difficulties, Nicolo's mother reported a normal developmental and medical history. He had not previously received psychological treatment and had no family history of psychological disorders aside from a maternal aunt with depression. Nicolo's social and academic histories had also been unremarkable until that academic year. His teacher, Ms. Jones, reported that his grades were incomplete because of excessive absences and that he was no longer attending gym class for fear of losing his breath while exercising. Nicolo's mother reported that her son typically attended school in the morning but then called her reporting somatic complaints or stress about his throat closing by lunch. She reported that she would try to calm him down and tell him to stay at school but that the school usually insisted she pick him up because of behavior problems (tantrums) that would occur if she did not.

Nicolo's attitude and mood varied during therapy sessions. Initially he had presented as relaxed and pleasant, but became argumentative in the first session when the therapist asked to speak with him and his mother separately. Despite his mother's attempts to calm him, he quickly became visibly anxious and ran from the therapy room to his sister in the waiting area. Nicolo's sister came to the therapy room several minutes later and stated that Nicolo insisted they leave, a request that his mother apologetically complied with.

Self-report measures completed by Nicolo, his parents, and his teacher confirmed significant elevations on anxiety and school refusal, as well as oppositional/defiant, scales. The ADIS-IV-C/P was given and resulted in clinician severity ratings indicative of a primary diagnosis of panic disorder, as well as secondary diagnoses of specific phobia (water) and oppositional defiant disorder. These diagnoses appeared linked, as Nicolo's panic and phobia symptoms had developed after a near-drowning experience. In addition, Nicolo appeared to behave oppositionally almost exclusively when anxious and unable to avoid/ escape the situation. Nicolo's panic attacks were especially likely to be triggered by feelings or thoughts of his throat closing or of numbness, which were also symptoms he had reported experiencing during his water rescue. Nicolo was extremely preoccupied with his concern about having additional panic attacks, particularly in school, which had led to his attempts to avoid school. He tried to avoid anything that made him experience the feeling of tightness in his throat, including lying flat on his back and exercising. In addition, his anxiety appeared to be maintained, in part, by the successful avoidance behaviors he engaged in by behaving in an oppositional manner. For example, at home and school, he had been able to successfully avoid anxiety-provoking situations (sleeping alone, gym class, attending school) by throwing tantrums and giving commands to his mother. Nicolo's mother and school administrators had been generally compliant with his demands because they were worried his somatic symptoms were serious and that his anxiety would overwhelm him. Similarly, Nicolo's water phobia appeared to be partially maintained by his mother's concern with upsetting him and enabling him to continue avoiding water (e.g., by allowing him to take sponge baths).

The primary goals of therapy for Nicolo were to address his significant anxiety concerns and to have him attend and remain in school on a regular basis. Nicolo's oppositional behaviors were presumed to decrease alongside successful treatment of his anxiety; however, parent training was included in the treatment plan to further address this area as well. Specifically, empirically supported treatments for panic disorder (panic control therapy) and anxiety (cognitive behavior family therapy for anxious children; Howard et al., 2000) were integrated and combined with targeted intervention at Nicolo's school. In addition, a one-session phobia treatment protocol (Ollendick et al., 2009) was initiated to address Nicolo's water phobia approximately midway through his other therapy programs. To specifically address his school refusal behaviors, the therapist established a meeting with Nicolo's mother and school administrators to create an attendance plan for him. At that meeting, the therapist provided psychoeducation for his teacher, school nurse, and principal, and it was decided that Nicolo could visit the school nurse's office for assistance using his new anxiety reduction skills, but that he could no longer call his mother or depart school early. His principal also agreed to allow Nicolo to "cool off" in his office when tantrums occurred at school rather than insist that his mother pick him up. Nicolo was provided information on the plan and allowed input in so much as that he selected the school nurse's office (with her prior consent) as he had reported having a positive relationship with her. A reward chart was initiated by his mother to support Nicolo's successful attendance at school, lack of tantrums when redirected, and remaining within his own classroom. At the same time, Nicolo's parents began a parent training group to assist them with addressing his oppositional behaviors.

Case Vignette 2: Meredith

Meredith (not her real name), a 10-year-old African-American girl, lived with her parents and 6-year-old brother. Her mother (age 38) was a business woman, and her father (age 40) a skilled craftsman. Meredith was referred to our clinic for a phobia of dogs. Although she appeared physically normal and healthy for her age, she was shy and seemed somewhat lethargic and "depressed" during the assessment session. Based on her parents' report, Meredith's fear of dogs interfered significantly with her own and their lives. Her mother reported that whenever she had to take her daughter to school, she had to avoid driving in neighborhoods where dogs might be present; if she did not do so, Meredith would panic and become so upset that she refused to get out of the car and go into school. On one school day, she refused to go to school even before leaving home because everyone was supposed to bring their pets and she was afraid that her classmates would bring their dogs. Her fear had become worse in recent months, precipitating her appointment, after their neighbor bought a dog. Meredith refused to go outside to play in her own yard and asked her parents to keep the doors to their home locked to make sure the dog could not get into their house. Her parents indicated they tried to listen to their daughter's complaints and concerns but they had become increasingly frustrated with her. They also indicated they tried to make her "happy" by avoiding situations where dogs might be present.

A comprehensive assessment was undertaken. Two separate clinicians interviewed Meredith and her parents simultaneously using the Anxiety Disorders Interview Schedule for DSM-IV Child/Parent version (ADIS-IV-C/P). Her parents indicated that Meredith's fear started when she was 5 years of age and the family lived in a nearby neighborhood where a neighbor had a "really mean-looking dog" penned in the backyard. However, they could not recall any incident in which Meredith was hurt or attacked by the dog, nor, to their knowledge, did Meredith ever witness anyone else being hurt or attacked by this dog or any other dog. The parents did report, however, that the neighbor's dog often barked and growled at children and others when they passed the home. In a separate interview, Meredith reported very similar concerns. She noted that she was "petrified" by dogs and just did not like them or the way they looked, especially their "big teeth and how they growl." Based on the separate diagnostic interviews, Meredith was diagnosed with a specific phobia of dogs with a clinician severity rating (CSR) of 8 (maximum score on a scale from 0 to 8). Additionally, Meredith endorsed criteria for a diagnosis of social phobia (a clinical severity rating of 4) whereas her parents also raised concerns about her social interactions and social fears but at a subclinical level of a 3. Meredith and her parents both indicated subclinical levels of a diagnosis of major depressive disorder (CSR of 3). Meredith's fear of dogs was most pronounced and troubling and was viewed as the primary diagnosis.

A behavioral avoidance task (BAT) was administered in which Meredith was asked to enter a room where a dog was being held on a leash by an assistant and to pet the dog for 10 s. She refused to enter the room and reported her subjective anxiety to be an 8 (on a scale ranging from 0 to 8). Throughout this task, her heart rate was monitored. Although her heart rate had been relatively stable prior to this task (beats per minute [BPM] = 76), it rose dramatically to 119 BPM while standing outside the door of the room where the dog was located. While standing in front of the closed door, she became extremely agitated, stating "I cannot go into the room … no way … the dog might jump on me and hurt me. It will bite me."

Upon further questioning, she indicated that she feared any and all dogs and that if her family was watching a program on TV and a dog appeared she would ask them to turn the TV off immediately. She also indicated that she checks the doors at home throughout the day to see if they are locked and shuts the blinds on the windows to avoid seeing their neighbor's new dog. When asked if the fear of dogs prevented her from doing things she wanted to do, she indicated she was okay as long as her parents did not make her go outside or do things where dogs might be present. She had a good awareness of her fears and their impact upon her.

On a fear hierarchy, Meredith stated that seeing a dog on the street or in a park without a leash would result in a fear level of 8 (0–8 scale) and that seeing a dog being walked on the street with a leash would be a fear level of 7. Looking at a dog from her home or some other safe place would result in a fear level of 6, and just seeing a dog on TV would produce a fear level of 5. Even just looking at pictures of dogs would increase her fear level to a 3. Writing the word "dog" and spelling it out loud were indicated to present a level of fear at a 1. Various steps in between these were also determined to construct a full fear hierarchy that could be used in therapy.

Meredith's phobia of dogs was severe. The origin of her fear could not be clearly identified, but was seemingly related to experiences that occurred while she lived in the neighborhood, near a "vicious-looking dog." We hypothesized that she learned over time that dogs might be dangerous; moreover, her avoidance appeared to be reinforced and maintained by her mother's overprotective parenting style and her father's reluctance to become involved in parenting with her. Behaviorally, she appeared to be a somewhat introverted and inhibited child. She was also socially phobic and subclinically depressed. It was hypothesized that the social phobia and depression were at least partially associated with her longstanding fear level and isolation from peers. Her motivation for treatment appeared reduced, likely because of the family's accommodation of her avoidance behavior. Her parents, however, expressed interest in helping her, and Meredith was willing to come in for the treatment because of the disruption her fear was causing her. Even though her parents expressed interest in helping their daughter, they did not seem to know how to do so.

Treatment followed the format of one-session treatment (3 hr of gradual exposure, modeling, reinforcement of approach behavior, and testing of faulty cognitions; see Ollendick et al., 2009). Meredith was seen alone, and her parents were not directly involved in treatment. Initially, Meredith was reluctant to talk about dogs or to look at pictures of dogs in a colorful book. After repeated encouragement, however, she agreed to talk and to look at the pictures. The therapist provided information about dogs and their behavior (e.g., why they bark, why and when they wag their tails, how to approach them, etc.). Next, Meredith was asked to watch a brief videotape depicting the information provided by the therapist. While watching the videotape, Meredith initially indicated that her fear level was a 7 (on a 0 to 8 scale). She learned, however, that she could be exposed to a dog on the video screen without developing a panic attack. This exercise, as with other exercises, was repeated three times. Following the third viewing, her fear level had dropped to a level of 2. After talking more about dogs and their behavior, she agreed to look outside the clinic window at a dog held on a leash by an assistant. Again, after the third trial, her fear had dropped from an 8 to a 3. Gradually, over the course of 3 hr, she was asked to do the following activities: allow the dog that was outside the clinic to be brought into the clinic waiting room and to look at it from the hallway, have the dog brought into the far end of the therapy room and then to increasingly approach the dog, feed it some dog biscuits, and then pet it on the head for a few seconds. Throughout, her faulty cognitions were tested and disconfirmed, and she practiced her skills about approaching and interacting with dogs. The therapist engaged in extensive modeling (demonstrating the various steps), participant modeling (having Meredith touch his shoulder, then arm, and then hand while interacting with the dog), and profuse praise (for approaching the dog with the therapist slightly behind her). A playful, supportive, and trusting relationship was developed. Although considerable progress was made during the session, Meredith still displayed some fear and reticence to interact more "naturally" with the dog. Meredith and her parents were informed that if the treatment were to work fully, it would be important for them to continue exposure activities outside therapy for the next month. Weekly phone calls were arranged to check in with them on the progress that she was making.

Upon posttesting a week later, her CSR ratings on the ADIS-IV-C/P were a 2, and in the behavioral task she opened the door, looked inside the room, saw the dog, approached it and petted it for about 10 s. Moreover, her catastrophic cognitions were now nonexistent (rating of 0, with a statement of "who would ever think that"), and her heart rate was 78 BPM. In addition, a CSR of 4 (still clinical) on the ADIS-IV-C/P Social Phobia module and a CSR of 1 on the Major Depression module were obtained. One month later, she was reevaluated one more time. Her ADIS-IV-C/P CSR rating for a specific phobia of dogs was a 0, for social phobia a 3, and for major depression a 0. During the behavioral test, she approached and petted the dog and even requested to take it on a walk. Her formerly catastrophic cognitions remained at a 0, and her heart rate during the exposure task was now 76 BPM. At this time, Meredith and her parents were requested to return 6 months later for an extended follow-up session to let us know how they were doing. They did so, and by all indications Meredith continued to have little or no fear of dogs and to be more socially engaged. Her parents said she seemed "like a different child."

6

Further Reading

Barrett, P. M., & Ollendick, T. H. (Eds.). (2004). *Handbook of interventions that work with children and adolescents: Prevention and treatment*. New York: John Wiley
An edited text with contributions by world-wide experts on youth psychopathology, this book provides detailed descriptions of evidence-based practice in terms of basic research foundations and is issued for "competent clinical and research practice" and intervention/prevention programs for specific youth disorders (including anxiety disorders).

Cohen, J. A., Mannarino, A. P., & Deblinger, E. (2006). *Treating trauma and traumatic grief in children and adolescents*. New York: Guilford Press.
Provides coverage of child trauma and grief issues with a thorough depiction of the trauma-focused cognitive behavior therapy model and its implementation.

Hadwin, J. A., & Field, A. P. (Eds.). (2010). *Information processing biases and anxiety: A developmental perspective*. Oxford, UK: Wiley-Blackwell.
This recently published edited book adapts a developmental perspective and provides in-depth information on issues from etiology to treatment for the information processing model of anxiety disorders.

Huebner, D. (2005). *What to do when you worry too much: A kid's guide to overcoming anxiety*. Washington DC: Magination Press.
This self-help book is written for anxious children (ages 6 and older) and their families and provides kid-friendly descriptions of symptoms and treatment components in a manner that encourages them to challenge and overcome their anxiety.

Last, C. G. (2006). *Help for worried kids: How your child can conquer anxiety and fear.* New York: Guilford Press.
Clinician- and parent-friendly, this book is an exceptional self-help tool for families. Information is delivered on topics including differentiating normal and atypical levels of anxiety and worries and helping families understand the development and treatments of anxiety. In addition, an excellent resources section is included at the end of the book.

McKay, D., & Storch, E. (Eds.). (2011). *Handbook of child and adolescent anxiety disorders*. New York: Springer.
This comprehensive, research-focused handbook details youth anxiety from etiology through treatment and includes information on emerging areas of research interest.

Wood, J. J., & McLeod, B. D. (2008). *Child anxiety disorders: A family-based treatment manual for practitioners*. New York: W. W. Norton.
A clinician-focused book with basic information on etiological and assessment practices, followed by detailed description of a family-focused cognitive behavior therapy for child anxiety. Worksheets and handouts to accompany the depicted treatment are also included.

7

References

Achenbach, T. M. (2009). *The Achenbach System of Empirically Based Assessment (ASEBA): Development, findings, theory, and applications*. Burlington, VT: University of Vermont Research Center for Children, Youth and Families.

Albano, A., & Barlow, D. H. (1996). Breaking the vicious cycle: Cognitive-behavioral group treatment for socially anxious youth. In E. D. Hibbs & P. S. Jensen (Eds.), *Psychosocial treatments for child and adolescent disorders: Empirically based strategies for clinical practice* (pp. 43–62). Washington, DC: American Psychological Association.

Alfano, C., Ginsburg, G., & Kingery, J. (2007). Sleep-related problems among children and adolescents with anxiety disorders. *Journal of the American Academy of Child and Adolescent Psychiatry, 46*, 224–232.

Alfano, C. A., Pina, A. A., Villalta, I. K., Beidel, D. C., Ammerman, R. T., & Crosby, L. E. (2009). Mediators and moderators of outcome in the behavioral treatment of childhood social phobia. *Journal of the American Academy of Child and Adolescent Psychiatry, 48*, 945–953.

Allen, J. L., Rapee, R. M., & Sandberg, S. (2008). Severe life events and chronic adversities as antecedents to anxiety in children: A matched control study. *Journal of Abnormal Child Psychology, 36*, 1047–1056.

American Psychiatric Association. (2000). *Diagnostic and statistical manual of mental disorders* (4th ed., text revision). Washington, DC: Author.

Anderson, J. C., Williams, S. M., McGee, R., & Silva, P. A. (1987). DSM-III disorders in preadolescent children: Prevalence in a large sample from the general population. *Archives of General Psychiatry, 44*, 69–76.

Angold, A. (2002). Diagnostic interviews with parents and children. In M. Rutter & E. Taylor (Eds.), *Child and adolescent psychiatry: Modern approaches* (4th ed., pp. 32–51). Oxford, UK: Blackwell.

Angold, A., & Costello, E. (2000). The Child and Adolescent Psychiatric Assessment (CAPA). *Journal of the American Academy of Child and Adolescent Psychiatry, 39*, 39–48.

Angold, A., Costello, E. J., & Erkanli, A. (1999). Comorbidity. *Journal of Child Psychology and Psychiatry and Allied Disciplines, 40*, 57–87.

Angold, A., Erkanli, A., Farmer, E. Z., Fairbank, J. A., Burns, B. J., Keeler, G., & Costello, E. (2002). Psychiatric disorder, impairment, and service use in rural African American and White youth. *Archives of General Psychiatry, 59*, 893–904.

Arnold, P. D., & Taillefer, S. (2011). Genetics of childhood and adolescent anxiety. In D. McKay & E. A. Storch (Eds.), *Handbook of child and adolescent anxiety disorders* (pp. 49–73). New York: Springer Science + Business Media.

Asbahr, F., Castillo, A., Ito, L., Latorre, M., Moreira, M., & Lotufo-Neto, F. (2005). Group cognitive-behavioral therapy versus sertraline for the treatment of children and adolescents with obsessive-compulsive disorder. *Journal of the American Academy of Child and Adolescent Psychiatry, 44*, 1128–1136.

Baldwin, D., Anderson, I., Nutt, D., Bandelow, B., Bond, A., Davidson, J., ... Wittchen, H. (2005). Evidence-based guidelines for the pharmacological treatment of anxiety disorders: Recommendations from the British Association for Psychopharmacology. *Journal of Psychopharmacology (Oxford, England), 19*, 567–596.

Barlow, D. H. (2000). Unraveling the mysteries of anxiety and its disorders from the perspective of emotion theory. *American Psychologist, 55,* 1247–1263.

Barrett, P. M. (2004). *Friends for Life: Group leader's manual for children* (4th ed.). Brisbane, Australia: Australian Academic Press.

Barrett, P. M. (2007). *Fun Friends. The teaching and training manual for group leaders.* Brisbane, Australia: Fun Friends.

Barrett, P. M., Dadds, M. R., & Rapee, R. M. (1996). Family treatment of childhood anxiety: A controlled trial. *Journal of Consulting and Clinical Psychology, 64,* 333–342.

Barrett, P. M., Farrell, L. J., Ollendick, T. H., & Dadds, M. (2006). Long-term outcomes of an Australian universal prevention trial of anxiety and depression symptoms in children and youth: An evaluation of the friends program. *Journal of Clinical Child and Adolescent Psychology, 35,* 403–411.

Barrett, P. M., Fox, T., & Farrell, F. (2005). Parent-child interactions with anxious children and with their siblings: An observational study. *Behaviour Change, 22,* 220–235.

Barrett, P., Healy-Farrell, L., & March, J. S. (2004). Cognitive-behavioral family treatment of childhood obsessive-compulsive disorder: A controlled trial. *Journal of the American Academy of Child and Adolescent Psychiatry, 43,* 46–62.

Barrett, P. M., Healy-Farrell, L., Piacentini, J., & March, J. (2004). Obsessive-compulsive disorder in childhood and adolescence: Description and treatment. In P. M. Barrett & T. H. Ollendick (Eds.), *Handbook of interventions that work with children and adolescents: Prevention and treatment* (pp. 187–216). New York: John Wiley.

Barrett, P., Rapee, R., Dadds, M., & Ryan, S. (1996). Family enhancement of cognitive style in anxious and aggressive children. *Journal of Abnormal Child Psychology, 24,* 187–203.

Barrett, P., & Turner, C. (2001). Prevention of anxiety symptoms in primary school children: Preliminary results from a universal school-based trial. *British Journal of Clinical Psychology, 40,* 399–410.

Barrett, P. M., & Turner, C. M. (2004). Prevention of childhood anxiety and depression. In P. M. Barrett & T. H. Ollendick (Eds.), *Handbook of interventions that work with children and adolescents: Prevention and treatment* (pp. 429–474). New York: John Wiley.

Barrington, J., Prior, M., Richardson, M., & Allen, K. (2005). Effectiveness of CBT versus standard treatment for childhood anxiety disorders in a community clinic setting. *Behaviour Change, 22,* 29–43.

Beck, A. T. (1976). *Cognitive therapies and emotional disorders.* New York: New American Library.

Beck, J. S., Beck, A. T., Jolly, J. B., & Steer, R. A. (2005). *The Beck Youth Inventories* (2nd ed.). San Antonio, TX: Psychological Corporation.

Beesdo, K., Knappe, S., & Pine, D. (2009). Anxiety and anxiety disorders in children and adolescents: developmental issues and implications for DSM-V. *Psychiatric Clinics of North America, 32,* 483–524.

Beidel, D. C., & Turner, S. M. (1998). *Shy children, phobic adults: Nature and treatment of social phobia.* Washington, DC: American Psychological Association.

Beidel, D. C., Turner, S. M., & Morris, T. L. (1995). A new inventory to assess social phobia in children: The Social Phobia and Anxiety Inventory for Children. *Psychological Assessment, 7,* 73–79.

Beidel, D. C., Turner, S. M., & Morris, T. L. (2000). Behavioral treatment of childhood social phobia. *Journal of Consulting and Clinical Psychology, 68,* 1072–1080.

Beidel, D. C., Turner, S. M., Sallee, F. R., Ammerman, R. T., Crosby, L. A., & Pathak, S. (2007). SET-C versus fluoxetine in the treatment of childhood social phobia. *Journal of the American Academy of Child and Adolescent Psychiatry, 46,* 1622–1632.

Beidel, D. C., Turner, S. M., Young, B. J., Ammerman, R. T., Sallee, F. R., & Crosby, L. (2007). Psychopathology of adolescent social phobia. *Journal of Psychopathology and Behavioral Assessment, 29,* 47–54.

Berger, R. & Gelkopf, M. (2009). School-based intervention for the treatment of tsunami-related distress in children: A quasi-randomized controlled trial. *Psychotherapy and Psychosomatics, 78*(6) 364–371.

Bernstein, G. A. (1991). Comorbidity and severity of anxiety and depressive disorders in a clinic sample. *Journal of the American Academy of Child and Adolescent Psychiatry, 30*, 43–50.

Bernstein, G. A., Borchardt, C. M., Perwien, A. R., Crosby, R. D., Kushner, M. G., Thuras, P. D., & Last, C. G. (2000). Imipramine plus cognitive-behavioral therapy in the treatment of school refusal. *Journal of the American Academy of Child and Adolescent Psychiatry, 39*, 276–283.

Bernstein, G. A., & Garfinkel, B. D. (1986). School phobia: The overlap of affective and anxiety disorders. *Journal of the American Academy of Child Psychiatry, 25*, 235–241.

Bernstein, G. A., Victor, A. M., Pipal, A. J., & Williams, K. A. (2010). Comparison of clinical characteristics of pediatric autoimmune neuropsychiatric disorders associated with streptococcal infections and childhood obsessive-compulsive disorder. *Journal of Child and Adolescent Psychopharmacology, 20*, 333–340.

Biederman, J., Faraone, S. V., Marrs, A., & Moore, P. (1997). Panic disorder and agoraphobia in consecutively referred children and adolescents. *Journal of the American Academy of Child and Adolescent Psychiatry, 36*, 214–223.

Biederman, J., Newcorn, J., & Sprich, S. (1991). Comorbidity of attention deficit hyperactivity disorder with conduct, depressive, anxiety, and other disorders. *American Journal of Psychiatry, 148*, 564–577.

Birmaher, B., Axelson, D. A., Monk, K., Kalas, C., Clark, D. B., Ehmann, M., ... Brent, D. A. (2003). Fluoxetine for the treatment of childhood anxiety disorders. *Journal of the American Academy of Child and Adolescent Psychiatry, 42*, 415–423.

Birmaher, B., Khetarpal, S., Brent, D., Cully, M., Balach, L., Kaufman, J., & Neer, S. M. (1997). The Screen for Child Anxiety Related Emotional Disorders (SCARED): Scale construction and psychometric characteristics. *Journal of the American Academy of Child and Adolescent Psychiatry, 36,* 545–553.

Bittner, A., Egger, H. L., Erkanli, A., Costello, E., Foley, D. L., & Angold, A. (2007). What do childhood anxiety disorders predict? *Journal of Child Psychology and Psychiatry, 48*, 1174–1183.

Bodden, D. M., Bögels, S. M., Nauta, M. H., De Haan, E., Ringrose, J., Appelboom, C., ... Appelboom-Geerts, K. J. (2008). Child versus family cognitive-behavioral therapy in clinically anxious youth: An efficacy and partial effectiveness study. *Journal of the American Academy of Child and Adolescent Psychiatry, 47,* 1384–1394.

Bongers, I. L., Koot, H. M., van der Ende, J., & Verhulst, F. C. (2003). The normative development of child and adolescent problem behavior. *Journal of Abnormal Psychology, 112*, 179–192.

Bosquet, M., & Egeland, B. (2006). The development and maintenance of anxiety symptoms from infancy through adolescence in a longitudinal sample. *Development and Psychopathology, 18*, 517–550.

Bouton, M., Mineka, S., & Barlow, D. (2001). A modern learning theory perspective on the etiology of panic disorder. *Psychological Review, 108*, 4–32.

Briere, J. (1996). *Trauma Symptom Checklist for Children (TSCC) professional manual.* Odessa, FL: Psychological Assessment Resources.

Briere, J. (2005). *Trauma Symptom Checklist for Young Children (TSCYC): Professional Manual.* Odessa, FL: Psychological Assessment Resources.

Briesch, A. M., Sanetti, L., & Briesch, J. M. (2010). Reducing the prevalence of anxiety in children and adolescents: An evaluation of the evidence base for the FRIENDS for Life program. *School Mental Health, 2*, 155–165.

Briggs-Gowan, M. J., Carter, A. S., Clark, R., Augustyn, M., McCarthy, K. J., & Ford, J. D. (2010). Exposure to potentially traumatic events in early childhood: Differential links to emergent psychopathology. *Journal of Child Psychology and Psychiatry, 51*, 1132–1140.

Briggs-Gowan, M. J., Horwitz, S. M., Schwab-Stone, M., Leventhal, J. M., & Leaf, P. J. (2000). Mental health in pediatric settings: Distribution of disorders and factors related to service use. *Journal of the American Academy of Child and Adolescent Psychiatry, 39*, 841–849.

Bruch, M. A., & Heimberg, R. G. (1994). Differences in perceptions of parental and personal characteristics between generalized and nongeneralized social phobics. *Journal of Anxiety, 8,* 155–168.

Brückl, T., Wittchen, H., Höfler, M., Pfister, H., Schneider, S., & Lieb, R. (2007). Childhood separation anxiety and the risk of subsequent psychopathology: Results from a community study. *Psychotherapy and Psychosomatics, 76,* 47–56.

Buckley, A., & Woodruff-Borden, J. (2006). Parental modeling of coping: Relation to child anxiety. *Child and Family Behavior Therapy, 28,* 59–80.

Callahan, C. L., Stevens, M. L., & Eyberg, S. (2010). Parent-child interaction therapy. In C. E. Schaefer (Ed.), *Play therapy for preschool children* (pp. 199–221). Washington, DC: American Psychological Association.

Campbell, C., Hansen, D. J., & Nangle, D. W. (2010). Social skills and psychological adjustment. In D. W. Nangle, D. J. Hansen, C. A. Erdley, & P. J. Norton (Eds.), *Practitioner's guide to empirically based measures of social skills* (pp. 51–67). New York,: Springer.

Campo, J., Bridge, J., Ehmann, M., Altman, S., Lucas, A., Birmaher, B., ... Brent, D. (2004). Recurrent abdominal pain, anxiety, and depression in primary care. *Pediatrics, 113,* 817–824.

Canino, G., Shrout, P. E., Rubio-Stipec, M., Bird, H. R., Bravo, M., Ramirez, R., . . . Martinez-Taboas, A. (2004). The DSM-IV rates of child and adolescent disorders in Puerto Rico: Prevalence, correlates, service use, and the effects of impairment. *Archives of General Psychiatry, 61,* 85–93.

Cannon, M. F., & Weems, C. F. (2010). Cognitive biases in childhood anxiety disorders: Do interpretive and judgment biases distinguish anxious youth from their non-anxious peers? *Journal of Anxiety Disorders, 24,* 751–758.

Carney, J. V., Hazler, R. J., Oh, I., Hibel, L. C., & Granger, D. A. (2010). The relations between bullying exposures in middle childhood, anxiety, and adrenocortical activity. *Journal of School Violence, 9,* 194–211.

Cartwright-Hatton, S., McNally, D., Field, A. P., Rust, S., Laskey, B., Dixon, C., ... Woodham, A. (2011). A new parenting-based group intervention for young anxious children: Results of a randomized controlled trial. *Journal of the American Academy of Child and Adolescent Psychiatry, 50,* 242–251.

Cartwright-Hatton, S., McNicol, K., & Doubleday, E. (2006). Anxiety in a neglected population: Prevalence of anxiety disorders in pre-adolescent children. *Clinical Psychology Review, 26,* 817–833.

Cartwright-Hatton, S., Roberts, C., Chitsabesan, P., Fothergill, C., & Harrington, R. (2004). Systematic review of the efficacy of cognitive behaviour therapies for childhood and adolescent anxiety disorders. *British Journal of Clinical Psychology, 43,* 421–436.

Chaffin, M., Silovsky, J. F., & Vaughn, C. (2005). Temporal concordance of anxiety disorders and child sexual abuse: Implications for direct versus artifactual effects of sexual abuse. *Journal of Clinical Child and Adolescent Psychology, 34,* 210–222.

Chambless, D. L., & Ollendick, T. H. (2001). Empirically supported psychological interventions: Controversies and evidence. *Annual Review of Psychology, 52,* 685–716.

Chansky, T., & Kendall, P. C. (1997). Social expectancies and self-perceptions in anxiety-disordered children. *Journal of Anxiety Disorders, 11,* 347–363.

Chavira, D. A., Garland, A. F., Daley, S., & Hough, R. (2008). The impact of medical comorbidity on mental health and functional health outcomes among children with anxiety disorders. *Journal of Developmental and Behavioral Pediatrics, 29,* 394–402.

Chiu, A. J., McLeod, B. D., Har, K., & Wood, J. J. (2009). Child–therapist alliance and clinical outcomes in cognitive behavioral therapy for child anxiety disorders. *Journal of Child Psychology and Psychiatry, 50,* 751–758.

Chorpita, B. F., Albano, A., & Barlow, D. H. (1996). Cognitive processing in children: Relation to anxiety and family influences. *Journal of Clinical Child Psychology, 25,* 170–176.

Chorpita, B. F., & Barlow, D. H. (1998). The development of anxiety: The role of control in the early environment. *Psychological Bulletin, 124,* 3–21.

Chorpita, B. F., & Daleiden, E. L. (2009). Mapping evidence-based treatments for children and adolescents: Application of the distillation and matching model to 615 treatments from 322 randomized trials. *Journal of Consulting and Clinical Psychology, 77,* 566–579.

Chorpita, B. F., Daleiden, E. L., Ebesutani, C., Young, J., Becker, K. D., Nakamura, B. J., ... Starace, N. (2011). Evidence-based treatments for children and adolescents: An updated review of indicators of efficacy and effectiveness. *Clinical Psychology: Science and Practice, 18,* 154–172.

Chorpita, B. F., Tracey, S. A., Brown, T. A., Collica, T. J., & Barlow, D. H. (1997). Assessment of worry in children and adolescents: An adaptation of the Penn State Worry Questionnaire. *Behaviour Research and Therapy, 35,* 569–581.

Chorpita, B. F., Yim, L., Moffitt, C., Umemoto, L. A., & Francis, S. E. (2000). Assessment of symptoms of DSM-IV anxiety and depression in children: A revised child anxiety and depression scale. *Behaviour Research and Therapy, 38,* 835–855.

Chu, B. C., Choudhury, M. S., Shortt, A. L., Pincus, D. B., Creed, T. A., & Kendall, P. C. (2004). Alliance, technology, and outcome in the treatment of anxious youth. *Cognitive and Behavioral Practice, 11,* 44–55.

Chu, B. C., & Harrison, T. L. (2007). Disorder-specific effects of CBT for anxious and depressed youth: A meta-analysis of candidate mediators of change. *Clinical Child and Family Psychology Review, 10,* 352–372.

Chu, B. C., & Kendall, P. C. (2004). Positive association of child involvement and treatment outcome within a manual-based cognitive-behavioral treatment for children with anxiety. *Journal of Consulting and Clinical Psychology, 72,* 821–829.

Chu, B. C., & Kendall, P. C. (2009). Therapist responsiveness to child engagement: Flexibility within manual-based CBT for anxious youth. *Journal of Clinical Psychology, 65,* 736–754.

Cicchetti, D., & Rogosch, F. A. (1996). Equifinality and multifinality in developmental psychopathology. *Development and Psychopathology, 8,* 597–600.

Clark, L. A., Watson, D., & Mineka, S. (1994). Temperament, personality, and the mood and anxiety disorders. *Journal of Abnormal Psychology, 103,* 103–116.

Cobham, V. E., Dadds, M. R., Spence, S. H., & McDermott, B. (2010). Parental anxiety in the treatment of childhood anxiety: A different story three years later. *Journal of Clinical Child and Adolescent Psychology, 39,* 410–420.

Cohen, J. A., Mannarino, A. P., & Deblinger, E. (2006). *Treating trauma and traumatic grief in children and adolescents.* New York: Guilford Press.

Cohen, J. A., Mannarino, A. P., & Deblinger, E. (2010). Trauma-focused cognitive-behavioral therapy for traumatized children. In J. R. Weisz & A. E. Kazdin (Eds.), *Evidence-based psychotherapies for children and adolescents* (2nd ed., pp. 295–311). New York: Guilford Press.

Cohen, J. A., Mannarino, A. P., & Knudsen, K. (2005). Treating sexually abused children: 1 year follow-up of a randomized controlled trial. *Child Abuse and Neglect, 29,* 135–145.

Cohen, J., Mannarino, A., Perel, J., & Staron, V. (2007). A pilot randomized controlled trial of combined trauma-focused CBT and sertraline for childhood PTSD symptoms. *Journal of the American Academy of Child and Adolescent Psychiatry, 46,* 811–819.

Cohen, P., Cohen, J., Kasen, S., & Velez, C. N. (1993). An epidemiological study of disorders in late childhood and adolescence: Part I: Age- and gender-specific prevalence. *Journal of Child Psychology and Psychiatry, 34,* 851–867.

Conners, C. K. (2008). *Conners Comprehensive Behavior Rating Scale Manual.* Toronto, Ontario: Multi-Health Systems.

Cornwall, E., Spence, S. H., & Schotte, D. (1996). The effectiveness of emotive imagery in the treatment of darkness phobia in children. *Behaviour Change, 13,* 223–229.

Costello, E., Angold, A., Burns, B. J., Stangl, D. K., Tweed, D. L., Erkanli, A., & Worthman, C. M. (1996). The Great Smoky Mountains Study of youth: Goals, design, methods, and the prevalence of DSM-III-R disorders. *Archives of General Psychiatry, 53,* 1129–1136.

Costello, E. J., Costello, A. J., Edelbrock, C., Burns, B. J., Dulcan, M. K., Brent, D., & Janiszewski, S. (1988). Psychiatric disorders in pediatric primary care: Prevalence and risk factors. *Archives of General Psychiatry, 45,* 1107–1116.

Costello, E., Egger, H. L., & Angold, A. (2004). Developmental epidemiology of anxiety disorders. In T. H. Ollendick & J. S. March (Eds.), *Phobic and anxiety disorders in children and adolescents: A clinician's guide to effective psychosocial and pharmacological interventions* (pp. 61–91). New York: Oxford University Press.

Costello, E., Egger, H. L., & Angold, A. (2005). The developmental epidemiology of anxiety disorders: Phenomenology, prevalence, and comorbidity. *Child and Adolescent Psychiatric Clinics of North America, 14*, 631–648.

Costello, E., Farmer, E. M., Angold, A., Burns, B. J., & Erkanli, E. (1997). Psychiatric Disorders among American Indian and White Youth in Appalachia: The Great Smoky Mountains Study. *American Journal of Public Health, 87*, 827–832.

Costello, E., Mustillo, S., Erkanli, A., Keeler, G., & Angold, A. (2003). Prevalence and development of psychiatric disorders in childhood and adolescence. *Archives of General Psychiatry, 60*, 837–844.

Cowart, M. W., & Ollendick, T. H. (2010). Attentional biases in children: Implications for treatment. In J. A. Hadwin & A. P. Field (Eds.), *Information processing biases and anxiety: A developmental perspective* (pp. 297–319). Oxford, UK: Wiley-Blackwell.

Creswell, C., & O'Connor, T. G. (2011). Interpretation bias and anxiety in childhood: Stability, specificity and longitudinal associations. *Behavioural and Cognitive Psychotherapy, 39*, 191–204.

Creswell, C., Schniering, C. A., & Rapee, R. M. (2005). Threat interpretation in anxious children and their mothers: Comparison with nonclinical children and the effects of treatment. *Behaviour Research and Therapy, 43*, 1375–1381.

Crick, N. R., & Ladd, G. (1993). Children's perceptions of their peer experiences: Attributions, loneliness, social anxiety, and social avoidance. *Developmental Psychology, 29*, 244–254.

Cunningham, M. J., Wuthrich, V. M., Rapee, R. M., Lyneham, H. J., Schniering, C. A., & Hudson, J. L. (2009). The Cool Teens CD-ROM for anxiety disorders in adolescents: A pilot case series. *European Child and Adolescent Psychiatry, 18*, 125–129.

Curry, J. F., March, J. S., & Hervey, A. S. (2004). Comorbidity of childhood and adolescent anxiety disorders: Prevalence and implications. In T. H. Ollendick, & J. S. March (Eds.), *Phobic and anxiety disorders in children and adolescents: A clinician's guide to effective psychosocial and pharmacological interventions* (pp. 116–140). New York: Oxford University Press.

Dadds, M. R., Barrett, P. M., Rapee, R. M., & Ryan, S. (1996). Family processes and child anxiety and aggression: An observational analysis. *Journal of Abnormal Child Psychology, 24,* 715–734.

Dadds, M. R., Spence, S. H., Holland, D. E., Barrett, P. M., & Laurens, K. R. (1997). Prevention and early intervention for anxiety disorders: A controlled trial. *Journal of Consulting and Clinical Psychology, 65*, 627–635.

Danielson, C., McCart, M. R., de Arellano, M. A., Macdonald, A., Doherty, L. S., & Resnick, H. S. (2010). Risk reduction for substance use and trauma-related psychopathology in adolescent sexual assault victims: Findings from an open trial. *Child Maltreatment, 15*, 261–268.

Davis, T., May, A., & Whiting, S. E. (2011). Evidence-based treatment of anxiety and phobia in children and adolescents: Current status and effects on the emotional response. *Clinical Psychology Review, 31*, 592–602.

Davis, T., Ollendick, T. H., & Öst, L. (2009). Intensive treatment of specific phobias in children and adolescents. *Cognitive and Behavioral Practice, 16*, 294–303.

Daviss, W., Racusin, R., Fleischer, A., Mooney, D., Ford, J. D., & McHugo, G. J. (2000). Acute stress disorder symptomatology during hospitalization for pediatric injury. *Journal of the American Academy of Child and Adolescent Psychiatry, 39*, 569–575.

Deacon, B., & Olatunji, B. O. (2007). Specificity of disgust sensitivity in the prediction of behavioral avoidance in contamination fear. *Behaviour Research and Therapy, 45*, 2110–2120.

De Bellis, M. D., Casey, B. J., Dahl, R. E., Birmaher, B., Williamson, D. E., Thomas, K. M., ... Ryan, N. D. (2000). A pilot study of amygdala volumes in pediatric generalized anxiety disorder. *Biological Psychiatry, 48,* 51–57.

Deblinger, E., Steer, R. A., & Lippmann, J. (1999). Two-year follow-up study of cognitive behavioral therapy for sexually abused children suffering post-traumatic stress symptoms. *Child Abuse and Neglect, 23*, 1371–1378.

Degnan, K. A., Almas, A. N., & Fox, N. A. (2010). Temperament and the environment in the etiology of childhood anxiety. *Journal of Child Psychology and Psychiatry, 51*, 497–517.

de Haan, E., Hoogduin, K., Buitelaar, J., & Keijsers, G. (1998). Behavior therapy versus clomipramine for the treatment of obsessive-compulsive disorder in children and adolescents. *Journal of the American Academy of Child and Adolescent Psychiatry, 37*, 1022–1029.

de Jong, P. J., Andrea, H., & Muris, P. (1997). Spider phobia in children: Disgust and fear before and after treatment. *Behaviour Research and Therapy, 35*, 559–562.

de Jong, P. J., & Muris, P. (2002). Spider phobia: Interaction of disgust and perceived likelihood of involuntary physical contact. *Journal of Anxiety Disorders, 16*, 51–65.

De Los Reyes, A., & Kazdin, A. E. (2005). Informant discrepancies in the assessment of childhood psychopathology: A critical review, theoretical framework, and recommendations for further study. *Psychological Bulletin, 131*, 483–509.

de Rosnay, M., Cooper, P. J., Tsigaras, N., & Murray, L. (2006). Transmission of social anxiety from mother to infant: An experimental study using a social referencing paradigm. *Behaviour Research and Therapy, 44*, 1165–1175.

de Wilde, A., & Rapee, R. M. (2008). Do controlling maternal behaviours increase state anxiety in children's responses to a social threat? A pilot study. *Journal of Behavior Therapy and Experimental Psychiatry, 39*, 526–537.

Dewis, L. M., Kirkby, K. C., Martin, F., Daniels, B. A., Gilroy, L. J., & Menzies, R. G. (2001). Computer-aided vicarious exposure versus live graded exposure for spider phobia in children. *Journal of Behavior Therapy and Experimental Psychiatry, 32*, 17–27.

DiBartolo, P. M., & Grills, A. E. (2006). Multiple informant reliability and the prediction of socially anxious behavior in children. *Journal of Anxiety Disorders, 20*, 630–645.

DiBartolo, P., & Helt, M. (2007). Theoretical models of affectionate versus affectionless control in anxious families: A critical examination based on observations of parent–child interactions. *Clinical Child and Family Psychology Review, 10*, 253–274.

Doerfler, L. A., Connor, D. F., Volungis, A. M., & Toscano, P. (2007). Panic disorder in clinically referred children and adolescents. *Child Psychiatry and Human Development, 38*, 57–71.

Douglass, H. M., Moffitt, T. E., Dar, R., & McGee, R. (1995). Obsessive-compulsive disorder in a birth cohort of 18-year-olds: Prevalence and predictors. *Journal of the American Academy of Child and Adolescent Psychiatry, 34*, 1424–1431.

Dufton, L. M., Dunn, M. J., & Compas, B. E. (2009). Anxiety and somatic complaints in children with recurrent abdominal pain and anxiety disorders. *Journal of Pediatric Psychology, 34*, 176–186.

Dufton, L. M., Dunn, M. J., Slosky, L. S., & Compas, B. E. (2011). Self-reported and laboratory-based responses to stress in children with recurrent pain and anxiety. *Journal of Pediatric Psychology, 36*, 95–105.

Eaves, L., Silberg, J., Meyer, J., Maes, H., Simonoff, E., Pickles, A., ... Hewitt, J. (1997). Genetics and developmental psychopathology: Part 2: The main effects of genes and environment on behavioral problems in the Virginia Twin Study of Adolescent Behavioral Development. *Journal of Child Psychology and Psychiatry, and Allied Disciplines, 38*, 965–980.

Edwards, S. L., Rapee, R. M., Kennedy, S. J., & Spence, S. H. (2010). The assessment of anxiety symptoms in preschool-aged children: the Revised Preschool Anxiety Scale. *Journal of Clinical Child and Adolescent Psychology, 39*, 400–409.

Egger, H., & Angold, A. (2006). Common emotional and behavioral disorders in preschool children: Presentation, nosology, and epidemiology. *Journal of Child Psychology and Psychiatry, 47*(3-4), 313–337.

Egger, H. L., Costello, E. J., & Angold, A. (2003). School refusal and psychiatric disorders: A community study. *Journal of the American Academy of Child and Adolescent Psychiatry, 42*, 797–807.

Egger, H. L., Erkanli, A., Keeler, G., Potts, E., Walter, B., & Angold, A. (2006). Test-retest reliability of the preschool age psychiatric assessment (PAPA). *Journal of the American Academy of Child and Adolescent Psychiatry, 45*, 538–549.

Ehlers, A. (1993). Somatic symptoms and panic attacks: A retrospective study of learning experiences. *Behaviour Research and Therapy, 31*, 269–278.

Eisen, A. R., Brien, L. K., Bowers, J., & Strudler, A. (2001). Separation anxiety disorder. In C. A. Essau & F. Petermann (Eds.), *Anxiety disorders in children and adolescents: Epidemiology, risk factors, and treatment.* London, UK: Harwood Academic.

Eisenberg, N., & Spinrad, T. L. (2004). Emotion-related regulation: Sharpening the definition. *Child Development, 75*, 334–339.

Eley, T. C., Gregory, A. M., Clark, D. M., & Ehlers, A. (2007). Feeling anxious: A twin study of panic/somatic ratings, anxiety sensitivity and heartbeat perception in children. *Journal of Child Psychology and Psychiatry, 48*, 1184–1191.

Ellis, C. R., & Singh, N. N. (1999). Psychopharmacological approaches. In S. Russ & T. H. Ollendick (Eds.), *Handbook of psychotherapies with children and families* (pp. 199–216). Dordrecht, Netherlands: Kluwer Academic.

Erath, S. A., Flanagan, K. S., & Bierman, K. L. (2007). Social anxiety and peer relations in early adolescence: Behavioral and cognitive factors. *Journal of Abnormal Child Psychology, 35*, 405–416.

Esbjørn, B., Hoeyer, M., Dyrborg, J., Leth, I., & Kendall, P. C. (2010). Prevalence and co-morbidity among anxiety disorders in a national cohort of psychiatrically referred children and adolescents. *Journal of Anxiety Disorders, 24*, 866–872.

Essau, C. A. (2005). Frequency and patterns of mental health services utilization among adolescents with anxiety and depressive disorders. *Depression and Anxiety, 22*, 130–137.

Essau, C. A., Conradt, J., & Petermann, F. (2000). Frequency, comorbidity, and psychosocial impairment of anxiety disorders in German adolescents. *Journal of Anxiety Disorders, 14*, 263–279.

Essex, M. J., Klein, M. H., Slattery, M. J., Goldsmith, H. H., Kalin, N. H. (2010). Early risk factors and developmental pathways to chronic high inhibition and social anxiety disorder in adolescence. *American Journal of Psychiatry, 167*, 40–46.

Feng, X., Shaw, D., & Silk, J. (2008). Developmental trajectories of anxiety symptoms among boys across early and middle childhood. *Journal of Abnormal Psychology, 117*, 32–47.

Ferrell, C. B., Beidel, D. C., & Turner, S. M. (2004). Assessment and treatment of socially phobic children: A cross cultural comparison. *Journal of Clinical Child and Adolescent Psychology, 33*, 260–268.

Field, A. (2006). Watch out for the beast: fear information and attentional bias in children. *Journal of Clinical Child and Adolescent Psychology, 35*, 431–439.

Field, A. P., Argyris, N. G., & Knowles, K. A. (2001). Who's afraid of the big bad wolf: A prospective paradigm to test Rachman's indirect pathways in children. *Behaviour Research and Therapy, 39*, 1259–1276.

Field, A. P., & Lawson, J. J. (2003). Fear information and the development of fears during childhood: Effects on implicit fear responses and behavioural avoidance. *Behaviour Research and Therapy, 41*, 1277–1293.

Field, A. P., Lawson, J., & Banerjee, R. (2008). The verbal threat information pathway to fear in children: The longitudinal effects on fear cognitions and the immediate effects on avoidance behavior. *Journal of Abnormal Psychology, 117*, 214–224.

Field, A. P., & Lester, K. J. (2010). Is there room for 'development' in developmental models of information processing biases to threat in children and adolescents? *Clinical Child and Family Psychology Review, 13*, 315–332.

Fisak, B. R., & Grills-Taquechel, A. E. (2007). Parental modeling, reinforcement, and information transfer: Risk factors in the development of child anxiety? *Clinical Child and Family Psychology Review, 10*, 213–231.

Fjermestad, K. W., Haugland, B., Heiervang, E., & Öst, L. (2009). Relationship factors and outcome in child anxiety treatment studies. *Clinical Child Psychology and Psychiatry, 14*, 195–214.

Foa, E. H., Johnson, K., Feeny N. C., & Treadwell, K. R. H. (2001). The Child PTSD Symptom Scale: A preliminary examination of its psychometric properties. *Journal of Clinical Child Psychology*, *30*, 376–384.

Forbes, E. E., Shaw, D. S., Fox, N. A., Cohn, J. F., Silk, J. S., & Kovacs, M. (2006). Maternal depression, child frontal asymmetry, and child affective behavior as factors in child behavior problems. *Journal of Child Psychology and Psychiatry*, *47*, 79–87.

Fox, N., Henderson, H., Marshall, P., Nichols, K., & Ghera, M. (2005). Behavioral inhibition: Linking biology and behavior within a developmental framework. *Annual Review of Psychology, 56*, 235–262.

Francis, S. E., & Chorpita, B. F. (2011). Parental beliefs about child anxiety as a mediator of parent and child anxiety. *Cognitive Therapy and Research*, *35*, 21–29.

Freeman, J. B., Garcia, A. M., Coyne, L., Ale, C., Przeworski, A., Himle, M., ... Leonard, H. L. (2008). Early childhood OCD: Preliminary findings from a family-based cognitive-behavioral approach. *Journal of the American Academy of Child and Adolescent Psychiatry*, *47*, 593–602.

Gar, N. S., & Hudson, J. L. (2009). The association between maternal anxiety and treatment outcome for childhood anxiety disorders. *Behaviour Change*, *26*, 1–15.

Gar, N. S., Hudson, J. L., & Rapee, R. M. (2005). Family factors and the development of anxiety disorders. In J. L. Hudson & R. M. Rapee (Eds.), *Psychopathology and the family* (pp. 125–145). New York: Elsevier Science.

Gau, S., Chong, M., Chen, T., & Cheng, A. (2005). A 3-year panel study of mental disorders among adolescents in Taiwan. *American Journal of Psychiatry, 162*, 1344–1350.

Geller, D., Biederman, J., Stewart, S., Mullin, B., Martin, A., Spencer, T., & Faraone, S. (2003). Which SSRI? A meta-analysis of pharmacotherapy trials in pediatric obsessive-compulsive disorder. *American Journal of Psychiatry*, *160*, 1919–1928.

Geller, D. A., Hoog, S. L., Heiligenstein, J. H., Ricardi, R. K., Tamura, R., Kluszynski, S., & Jacobson, J. G. (2001). Fluoxetine treatment for obsessive-compulsive disorder in children and adolescents: A placebo-controlled clinical trial. *Journal of the American Academy of Child and Adolescent Psychiatry*, *40*, 773–779.

Geller, D. A., Wagner, K., Emslie, G., Murphy, T., Carpenter, D. J., Wetherhold, E., & ... Gardiner, C. (2004). Paroxetine treatment in children and adolescents with obsessive-compulsive disorder: A randomized, multicenter, double-blind, placebo-controlled trial. *Journal of the American Academy of Child and Adolescent Psychiatry*, *43*, 1387–1396.

Gerull, F., & Rapee, R. (2002). Mother knows best: effects of maternal modeling on the acquisition of fear and avoidance behaviour in toddlers. *Behaviour Research and Therapy*, *40*, 279–287.

Ginsburg, G. (2009). The child anxiety prevention study: Intervention model and primary outcomes. *Journal of Consulting and Clinical Psychology*, *77*, 580–587.

Ginsburg, G. S., Burstein, M., Becker, K. D., & Drake, K. L. (2011). Treatment of obsessive compulsive disorder in young children: An intervention model and case series. *Child and Family Behavior Therapy*, *33*, 97–122.

Ginsburg, G. S., Kingery, J., Drake, K. L., & Grados, M. A. (2008). Predictors of treatment response in pediatric obsessive-compulsive disorder. *Journal of the American Academy of Child and Adolescent Psychiatry*, *47*, 868–878.

Graae, F., Milner, J., Rizzotto, L., & Klein, R. G. (1994). Clonazepam in childhood anxiety disorders. *Journal of the American Academy of Child and Adolescent Psychiatry*, *33*, 372–376.

Greco, L. A., & Morris, T. L. (2002). Paternal child-rearing style and child social anxiety: Investigation of child perceptions and actual father behavior. *Journal of Psychopathology and Behavioral Assessment*, *24*, 259–267.

Gregory, A. C., & Eley, T. C. (2007). Genetic influences on anxiety in children: What we've learned and where we're heading. *Clinical Child and Family Psychology Review*, *10*, 199–212.

Gregory, A. M., Caspi, A., Moffitt, T. E., Koenen, K., Eley, T. C., & Poulton, R. (2007). Juvenile mental health histories of adults with anxiety disorders. *American Journal of Psychiatry*, *164*, 301–308.

Gresham, F. M. (2002). Teaching social skills to high-risk children and youth: Preventive and remedial strategies. In M. R. Shinn, H. M. Walker, & G. Stoner (Eds.), *Interventions for academic and behavior problems Part II: Preventive and remedial approaches* (pp. 403–432). Bethesda, MD: National Association of School Psychologists.

Grills, A. E. (2003). *Long-term relations among peer victimization and internalizing symptoms in children* (Unpublished doctoral dissertation). Virginia Tech, Blacksburg, VA.

Grills, A. E., & Ollendick, T. H. (2002a). Peer victimization, global self-worth, and anxiety in middle school children. *Journal of Clinical Child and Adolescent Psychology, 31,* 59–68.

Grills, A. E., & Ollendick, T. H. (2002b). Issues in parent-child agreement: The case of structured diagnostic interviews. *Clinical Child and Family Psychology Review, 5,* 57–83.

Grills-Taquechel, A. E., Fletcher, J. M., Vaughn, S. R., & Stuebing, K. K. (2011). Anxiety and reading problems in early elementary school: Evidence for unidirectional or bidirectional relations? *Child Psychiatry and Human Development.*

Grills-Taquechel, A. E., & Ollendick, T. H. (2008). Diagnostic interviewing. In M. Hersen & A. M. Gross (Eds.), *Handbook of clinical psychology* (Vol. 2. Children). New York: John Wiley.

Grills-Taquechel, A. E. & Ollendick, T. H. (2012). *A review of randomized clinical trials research on child anxiety disorders.* Unpublished manuscript.

Grover, R. L., Ginsburg, G. S., & Ialongo, N. (2005). Childhood predictors of anxiety symptoms: A longitudinal study. *Child Psychiatry and Human Development, 36,* 133–153.

Grüner, K., Muris, P., & Merckelbach, H. (1999). The relationship between anxious rearing behaviours and anxiety disorders symptomatology in normal children. *Journal of Behavior Therapy and Experimental Psychiatry, 30,* 27–35.

Hadwin, J., & Field, A. (2010). *Information processing biases and anxiety: A developmental perspective.* Oxford, UK: Wiley-Blackwell.

Hagopian, L. P., & Ollendick, T. H. (1993). Simple phobia in children. In R. T. Ammerman & M. Hersen (Eds.), *Handbook of behavior therapy with children and adults: A developmental and longitudinal perspective* (Vol. 171). Boston, MA: Allyn & Bacon.

Hannesdottir, D., & Ollendick, T. H. (2007). The role of emotion regulation in the treatment of child anxiety disorders. *Clinical Child and Family Psychology Review, 10,* 275–293.

Hettema, J. M., Prescott, C. A., Myers, J. M., Neale, M. C., & Kendler, K. S. (2005). The structure of genetic and environmental risk factors for anxiety disorders in men and women. *Archives of General Psychiatry, 62,* 182–189.

Heyman, I. I., Fombonne, E. E., Simmons, H. H., Ford, T. T., Meltzer, H. H., & Goodman, R. R. (2003). Prevalence of obsessive-compulsive disorder in the British nationwide survey of child mental health. *International Review of Psychiatry, 15,* 178–184.

Hirshfeld-Becker, D. R., Masek, B., Henin, A., Blakely, L., Pollock-Wurman, R. A., McQuade, J., ... Biederman, J. (2010). Cognitive behavioral therapy for 4- to 7-year-old children with anxiety disorders: A randomized clinical trial. *Journal of Consulting and Clinical Psychology, 78,* 498–510.

Hirshfeld-Becker, D., Micco, J., Simoes, N., & Henin, A. (2008). High risk studies and developmental antecedents of anxiety disorders. *American Journal of Medical Genetics, 148C,* 99–117.

Hoffman, E. C., & Mattis, S. G. (2000). A developmental adaptation of panic control treatment for panic disorder in adolescence. *Cognitive and Behavioral Practice, 7,* 253–261.

Howard, B., Chu, B. C., Krain, A. L., Marrs-Garcia, A. L., & Kendall, P. C. (2000). *Cognitive-Behavioral Family Therapy for Anxious Children: Therapist manual* (2nd ed.). Ardmore, PA: Workbook Publishing.

Hudson, J. L., & Rapee, R. M. (2000). The origins of social phobia. *Behavior Modification, 24,* 102–129.

Hudson, J. L., & Rapee, R. M. (2001). Parent-child interactions and anxiety disorders: An observational study. *Behaviour Research and Therapy, 39,* 1411–1427.

Hudson, J. L., Rapee, R. M., Deveney, C., Schniering, C. A., Lyneham, H. J., & Bovopoulos, N. (2009). Cognitive-behavioral treatment versus an active control for children and adolescents with anxiety disorders: A randomized trial. *Journal of the American Academy of Child and Adolescent Psychiatry, 48,* 533–544.

Hughes, A. A., & Kendall, P. C. (2007). Prediction of cognitive behavior treatment outcome for children with anxiety disorders: Therapeutic relationship and homework compliance. *Behavioural and Cognitive Psychotherapy*, *35*, 487–494.

Hummel, R. M., & Gross, A. M. (2001). Socially anxious children: An observational study of parent-child interaction. *Child and Family Behavior Therapy*, *23*, 19–41.

Ialongo, N., Edelsohn, G., Werthamer-Larsson, L., & Crockett, L. (1994). The significance of self-reported anxious symptoms in first-grade children. *Journal of Abnormal Child Psychology*, *22*, 441–455.

Ishikawa, S., Okajima, I., Matsuoka, H., & Sakano, Y. (2007). Cognitive behavioural therapy for anxiety disorders in children and adolescents: A meta-analysis. *Child and Adolescent Mental Health*, *12*, 164–172.

James, A., Soler, A., & Weatherall, R. (2005). Cognitive behavioural therapy for anxiety disorders in children and adolescents. *Cochrane Database of Systematic Reviews (Online)*, *4*, CD004690.

Kaplow, J. B., Curran, P. J., Angold, A., & Costello, E. (2001). The prospective relation between dimensions of anxiety and the initiation of adolescent alcohol use. *Journal of Clinical Child Psychology*, *30*, 316–326.

Karevold, E., Røysamb, E., Ystrom, E., & Mathiesen, K. S. (2009). Predictors and pathways from infancy to symptoms of anxiety and depression in early adolescence. *Developmental Psychology*, *45*, 1051–1060.

Karver, M. S. (2006). Determinants of multiple informant agreement on child and adolescent behavior. *Journal of Abnormal Child Psychology, 34,* 251–262.

Karver, M. S., Handelsman, J. B., Fields, S., & Bickman, L. (2006). Meta-analysis of therapeutic relationship variables in youth and family therapy: The evidence for different relationship variables in the child and adolescent treatment outcome literature. *Clinical Psychology Review*, *26*, 50–65.

Kashani, J. H., Beck, N. C., Hoeper, E. W., Fallahi, C., Corcoran, C. M., McAllister, J. A., Rosenberg, T. K., & Reid, J. C. (1987). Psychiatric disorders in a community sample of adolescents. *American Journal of Psychiatry, 144,* 584–589.

Kashani, J. H., & Orvaschel, H. (1988). Anxiety disorders in mid-adolescence: A community sample. *American Journal of Psychiatry*, *145*, 960–964.

Kashani, J. H., & Orvaschel, H. (1990). A community study of anxiety in children and adolescents. *American Journal of Psychiatry*, *147*, 313–318.

Kassam-Adams, N., & Winston, F. (2004). Predicting child PTSD: The relationship between acute stress disorder and PTSD in injured children. *Journal of the American Academy of Child and Adolescent Psychiatry*, *43*, 403–411.

Katon, W., Lozano, P., Russo, J., McCauley, E., Richardson, L., & Bush, T. (2007). The prevalence of DSM-IV anxiety and depressive disorders in youth with asthma compared with controls. *Journal of Adolescent Health*, *41*, 455–463.

Katon, W., Richardson, L., Lozano, P., & McCauley, E. (2004). The relationship of asthma and anxiety disorders. *Psychosomatic Medicine*, *66*, 349–355.

Kaufman, J., Birmaher, B., Brent, D., Rao, U., Flynn, C., Moreci, P., Williamson, D., & Ryan, N. (1997). Schedule for Affective Disorders and Schizophrenia for School-Age Children-Present and Lifetime version (K-SADS-PL): Initial reliability and validity data. *Journal of the American Academy of Child and Adolescent Psychiatry, 36,* 980–988.

Kazdin, A. E., & Bass, D. (1989). Power to detect differences between alternative treatments in comparative psychotherapy outcome research. *Journal of Consulting and Clinical Psychology, 57,* 138–147.

Kendall, P. C. (1990). *Coping Cat workbook*. Ardmore, PA: Workbook.

Kendall, P.C. (1994). Treating anxiety disorders in children: Results of a randomized clinical trial. *Journal of Consulting and Clinical Psychology, 62,* 100–110.

Kendall, P. C., Choudhury, M., Hudson, J., & Webb, A. (2002). *The C. A. T. Project manual for the cognitive behavioral treatment of anxious adolescents*. Ardmore, PA: Workbook Publishing.

Kendall, P. C., Comer, J. S., Marker, C. D., Creed, T. A., Puliafico, A. C., Hughes, A. A., ... Hudson, J. (2009). In-session exposure tasks and therapeutic alliance across the treatment of childhood anxiety disorders. *Journal of Consulting and Clinical Psychology*, *77*, 517–525.

Kendall, P. C., Compton, S. N., Walkup, J. T., Birmaher, B., Albano, A. M., & Sherril J. (2010). Clinical characteristics of anxiety disordered youth. *Journal of Anxiety Disorders, 24,* 360–365.

Kendall, P. C., Flannery-Schroeder, E., Panichelli-Mindel, S. M., Southam-Gerow, M., Henin, A., & Warman, M. (1997). Therapy for youths with anxiety disorders: A second randomized clinical trial. *Journal of Consulting and Clinical Psychology, 65,* 366–380.

Kendall, P. C., & Hedtke, K. (2006). Coping Cat workbook (2nd ed.). Ardmore, PA: Workbook.

Kendall, P. C., Hudson, J., Gosch, E., Flannery-Schroeder, E., & Suveg, C. (2008). Child and family therapy for anxiety-disordered youth: Results of a randomized clinical trial. *Journal of Consulting and Clinical Psychology, 76,* 282–297.

Kendall, P. C., & Southam-Gerow, M. A. (1996). Long-term follow-up of a cognitive-behavioral therapy for anxiety disordered youth. *Journal of Consulting and Clinical Psychology, 64,* 724–730.

Kendall, P. C., & Treadwell, K. H (2007). The role of self-statements as a mediator in treatment for youth with anxiety disorders. *Journal of Consulting and Clinical Psychology*, *75*, 380–389.

Kessler, R. C., Berglund, P., Demler, O., Jin, R., Merikangas, K. R., & Walters, E. E. (2005). Lifetime prevalence and age-of-onset distributions of DSM-IV disorders in the national comorbidity Survey Replication. *Archives of General Psychiatry*, *62*, 593–602.

Khanna, M. S., & Kendall, P. C. (2009). Exploring the role of parent training in the treatment of childhood anxiety. *Journal of Consulting and Clinical Psychology*, *77*, 981–986.

King, N. J., Heyne, D., & Ollendick, T. H. (2005). Cognitive-behavioral treatments for anxiety and phobic disorders in children and adolescents: A review. *Behavioral Disorders*, *30*, 241–257.

Kingery, J., Erdley, C., Marshall, K., Whitaker, K., & Reuter, T. (2010). Peer experiences of anxious and socially withdrawn youth: An integrative review of the developmental and clinical literature. *Clinical Child and Family Psychology Review*, *13*, 91–128.

Klein, R. G., Koplewicz, H. S., & Kanner, A. (1992). Imipramine treatment of children with separation anxiety disorder. *Journal of the American Academy of Child and Adolescent Psychiatry*, *31*, 21–28.

Kovacs, M., Gatsonis, C., Paulauskas, S., & Richards, C. (1989). Depressive disorders in childhood: Part IV: A longitudinal study of comorbidity with and risk for anxiety disorders. *Archives of General Psychiatry*, *46*, 776–782.

Kowalik, J., Weller, J., Venter, J., & Drachman, D. (2011). Cognitive behavioral therapy for the treatment of pediatric posttraumatic stress disorder: A review and meta-analysis. *Journal of Behavior Therapy and Experimental Psychiatry*, *42*, 405–413.

Kratochvil, C., Kutcher, S., Reiter, S., & March, J. S. (1999). Pharmacotherapy of pediatric anxiety disorders. In S. Russ & T. H. Ollendick (Eds.), *Handbook of psychotherapies with children and families* (pp. 345–366). Dordrecht, Netherlands: Kluwer Academic.

Kroes, M., Kalff, A. C., Steyaert, J., Kessels, A. H., Feron, F. M., Hendriksen, J. M., ... Vles, J. H. (2002). A longitudinal community study: Do psychosocial risk factors and Child Behavior Checklist scores at 5 years of age predict psychiatric diagnoses at a later age? *Journal of the American Academy of Child and Adolescent Psychiatry*, *41*, 955–963.

Kupersmidt, J. B., Coie, J. D., & Dodge, K. A. (1990). The role of poor peer relationships in the development of disorder. In S. R. Asher & J. D. Coie (Eds.), *Peer rejection in childhood* (pp. 274–305). New York: Cambridge University Press.

Ladd, G. (2006). Peer rejection, aggressive or withdrawn behavior, and psychological maladjustment from ages 5 to 12: An examination of four predictive models. *Child Development*, *77*, 822–846.

La Greca, A. L., & Stone, W. L. (1993). Social Anxiety Scale for Children-Revised: Factor Structure and Concurrent Validity. *Journal of Clinical Child Psychology*, *22*, 17–28.

La Greca, A. M. (2001). Friends or foes? Peer influences on anxiety among children and adolescents. In W. K. Silverman & P. A. Treffers (Eds.), *Anxiety disorders in children and adolescents: Research, assessment and intervention* (pp. 159–186). New York: Cambridge University Press.

La Greca, A. M., & Fetter, M. D. (1995). Peer relations. In A. R. Eisen, C. A. Kearney, & C. E. Schaefer (Eds.), *Clinical handbook of anxiety disorders in children and adolescents* (pp. 82–130). Lanham, MD: Jason Aronson.

La Greca, A. M., & Harrison, H. (2005). Adolescent peer relations, friendships, and romantic relationships: Do they predict social anxiety and depression? *Journal of Clinical Child and Adolescent Psychology, 34*, 49–61.

La Greca, A. M., & Lopez, N. (1998). Social anxiety among adolescents: Linkages with peer relations and friendships. *Journal of Abnormal Child Psychology, 26*, 83–94.

La Greca, A. M., & Prinstein, M. J. (1999). Peer group. In W. K. Silverman & T. H. Ollendick (Eds.), *Developmental issues in the clinical treatment of children* (pp. 171–198). Needham Heights, MA: Allyn & Bacon.

Last, C. G., Hansen, C., & Francis, N. (1997). Anxious children in adulthood: A prospective study of adjustment. *Journal of the American Academy of Child and Adolescent Psychiatry, 36*, 645–652.

Last, C. G., Perrin, S., Hersen, M., & Kazdin, A. E. (1992). DSM-IIIR anxiety disorders in children: Sociodemographic and clinical characteristics. *Journal of the American Academy of Child and Adolescent Psychiatry, 31*, 1070–1076.

Last, C. G., Perrin, S., Hersen, M., & Kazdin, A. E. (1996). A prospective study of childhood anxiety disorders. *Journal of the American Academy of Child and Adolescent Psychiatry, 35*, 1502–1510.

Last, C. G., & Strauss, C. C. (1989). Obsessive-compulsive disorder in childhood. *Journal of Anxiety Disorders, 3*, 295–302.

Lau, W., Chan, C., Li, J., & Au, T. (2010). Effectiveness of group cognitive-behavioral treatment for childhood anxiety in community clinics. *Behaviour Research and Therapy, 48,* 1067–1077.

Lavigne, J. J., LeBailly, S.A., Hopkins, J., Gouze, K. R., & Binns, H. J. (2009). The prevalence of ADHD, ODD, depression, and anxiety in a community sample of 4-year-olds. *Journal of Clinical Child and Adolescent Psychology, 38*, 315–328.

Leitenberg, H., Yost, L. W., & Carroll-Wilson, M. (1986). Negative cognitive errors in children: Questionnaire development, normative data, and comparisons between children with and without self-reported symptoms of depression, low self-esteem, and evaluation anxiety. *Journal of Consulting and Clinical Psychology, 54*, 528–536.

Lewin, A. B., Storch, E. A., Merlo, L. J., Adkins, J. W., Murphy, T., & Geffken, G. A. (2005). Intensive cognitive behavioral therapy for pediatric obsessive compulsive disorder: A treatment protocol for mental health providers. *Psychological Services, 2*, 91–104.

Lewinsohn, P., Gotlib, I., Lewinsohn, M., Seeley, J., & Allen, N. (1998). Gender differences in anxiety disorders and anxiety symptoms in adolescents. *Journal of Abnormal Psychology, 107*, 109–117.

Lewinsohn, P. M., Zinbarg, R., Seeley, J. R., Lewinsohn, M., & Sack, W. H. (1997). Lifetime comorbidity among anxiety disorders and between anxiety disorders and other mental disorders in adolescents. *Journal of Anxiety Disorders, 11*, 377–394.

Liber, J. M., McLeod, B. D., Van Widenfelt, B. M., Goedhart, A. W., van der Leeden, A. M., Utens, E. J., & Treffers, P. A. (2010). Examining the relation between the therapeutic alliance, treatment adherence, and outcome of cognitive behavioral therapy for children with anxiety disorders. *Behavior Therapy, 41*, 172–186.

Liebowitz, M. R., Turner, S. M., Piacentini, J., Beidel, D. C., Clarvit, S. R., Davies, S. O., ... Simpson, H. (2002). Fluoxetine in children and adolescents with OCD: A placebo-controlled trial. *Journal of the American Academy of Child and Adolescent Psychiatry, 41*, 1431–1438.

Løhre, A., Lydersen, S., & Vatten, L. J. (2010). Factors associated with internalizing or somatic symptoms in a cross-sectional study of school children in grades 1–10. *Child and Adolescent Psychiatry and Mental Health, 4.*

Lonigan, C. J., Vasey, M. W., Phillips, B. M., & Hazen, R. A. (2004). Temperament, anxiety, and the processing of threat-relevant stimuli. *Journal of Clinical Child and Adolescent Psychology, 33,* 8–20.

Manassis, K. (2001). Child–parent relations: Attachment and anxiety disorders. In W. K. Silverman & P. A. Treffers (Eds.), *Anxiety disorders in children and adolescents: Research, assessment and intervention* (pp. 255–272). New York: Cambridge University Press.

Mancuso, E., Faro, A., Joshi, G., & Geller, D. A. (2010). Treatment of pediatric obsessive-compulsive disorder: A review. *Journal of Child and Adolescent Psychopharmacology, 20,* 299–308.

March, J. S., Biederman, J., Wolkow, R., Safferman, A., Mardekian, J., Cook, E. H., … Wagner, K. D. (1998). Sertraline in children and adolescents with obsessive–compulsive disorder: A multicenter randomized controlled trial. *Journal of the American Medical Association, 280,* 1752–1756.

March, J. S., Entusah, A., Rynn, M., Albano, A., & Tourian, K. A. (2007). A randomized controlled trial of venlafaxine ER versus placebo in pediatric social anxiety disorder. *Biological Psychiatry, 62,* 1149–1154.

March, J. S., & Mulle, K. (1998). *OCD in children and adolescents: A cognitive-behavioral treatment manual.* New York: Guilford Press.

March, J. S., Parker, J. D. A., Sullivan, K., Stallings, P., & Conners, C. K. (1997). The Multidimensional Anxiety Scale for Children (MASC): Factor structure, reliability, and validity. *Journal of the American Academy of Child and Adolescent Psychiatry, 36,* 554–565.

Marmorstein, N. R. (2006). Generalized versus performance-focused social phobia: Patterns of comorbidity among youth. *Journal of Anxiety Disorders, 20,* 778–793.

Masi, G., Favilla, L., Mucci, M., & Millepiedi, S. (2000a). Panic disorder in clinically referred children and adolescents. *Child Psychiatry and Human Development, 31,* 139–151.

Masi, G., Favilla, L., Mucci, M., & Millepiedi, S. (2000b). Depressive comorbidity in children and adolescents with Generalized Anxiety Disorder. *Child Psychiatry and Human Development, 30,* 205–215

Masi, G., Mucci, M., Favilla, L., Romano, R., & Poli, P. (1999). Symptomatology and comorbidity of generalized anxiety disorder in children and adolescents. *Comprehensive Psychiatry, 40,* 210–215.

Masia-Warner, C., Storch, E. A., Pincus, D. B., Klein, R. G., Heimberg, R. G., & Liebowitz, M. R. (2003). The Liebowitz Social Anxiety Scale for Children and Adolescents: An initial psychometric investigation. *Journal of the American Academy of Child and Adolescent Psychiatry, 42,* 1076–1084.

Matchett, G., & Davey, G. C. (1991). A test of a disease-avoidance model of animal phobias. *Behaviour Research and Therapy, 29,* 91–94.

Mathews, A., Mogg, K., Kentish, J., & Eysenck, M. (1995). Effect of psychological treatment on cognitive bias in generalized anxiety disorder. *Behaviour Research and Therapy, 33,* 293–303.

Matson, J. L., Bamburg, J. W., Cherry, K. E., & Paclawskyj, T. R. (1999). A validity study on the Questions About Behavioral Function (QABF) scale: Predicting treatment success for self-injury, aggression, and stereotypies. *Research in Developmental Disabilities, 20,* 163–175.

Mattis, S. G., & Ollendick, T. H. (2002). School refusal and separation anxiety. In M. Hersen (Ed.), *Clinical behavior therapy: Adults and children* (pp. 304–325). Hoboken, NJ: John Wiley.

McConaughy, S. H., & Achenbach, T. M. (2004). *Manual for the Test Observation Form for Ages 2–18.* Burlington, VT: UVM, Center for Children, Youth, & Families.

McGee, R., Feehan, M., Williams, S., & Anderson, J. (1992). DSM-III disorders from age 11–15 years. *Journal of the American Academy of Child and Adolescent Psychiatry, 31,* 50–59.

McGee, R., Feehan, M., Williams, S., & Partridge, F. (1990). DSM-III disorders in a large sample of adolescents. *Journal of the American Academy of Child and Adolescent Psychiatry*, *29*, 611–619.

McLeod, B. D., & Weisz, J. R. (2005). The Therapy Process Observational Coding System-Alliance Scale: Measure characteristics and prediction of outcome in usual clinical practice. *Journal of Consulting and Clinical Psychology*, *73*, 323–333.

McLeod, B. D., Wood, J. J., & Weisz, J. R. (2007). Examining the association between parenting and childhood anxiety: A meta-analysis. *Clinical Psychology Review*, *27*, 155–172.

McNally, R. J. (2002). Disgust has arrived. *Journal of Anxiety Disorders*, *16*, 561–566.

McNeil, C. B., & Ware, L. M. (2003). Parent training. In T. H. Ollendick & C. S. Schroeder (Eds.), *Encyclopedia of pediatric and clinical child psychology* (pp. 443–445). New York: Kluwer.

McQuaid, E. L., Kopel, S. J., & Nassau, J. H. (2001). Behavioral adjustment in children with asthma: A meta-analysis. *Journal of Developmental and Behavioral Pediatrics*, *22*, 430–439.

Meiser-Stedman, R., Smith, P., Glucksman, E., Yule, W., & Dalgleish, T. (2007). Parent and child agreement for acute stress disorder, post-traumatic stress disorder and other psychopathology in a prospective study of children and adolescents exposed to single-event trauma. *Journal of Abnormal Child Psychology*, *35*, 191–201.

Melfsen, S., Kühnemund, M., Schwieger, J., Warnke, A., Stadler, C., Poustka, F., & Stangier, U. (2011). Cognitive behavioral therapy of socially phobic children focusing on cognition: A randomised wait-list control study. *Child and Adolescent Psychiatry and Mental Health, 5,* 5.

Merikangas, K., He, J., Brody, D., Fisher, P. W., Bourdon, K., & Koretz, D. S. (2010). Prevalence and treatment of mental disorders among US children in the 2001–2004 NHANES. *Pediatrics*, *125*, 75–81.

Merikangas, K., He, J., Burstein, M., Swanson, S. A., Avenevoli, S., Cui, L., ... Swendsen, J. (2010). Lifetime prevalence of mental disorders in U.S. adolescents: Results from the National Comorbidity Survey Replication-Adolescent Supplement (NCS-A). *Journal of the American Academy of Child and Adolescent Psychiatry*, *49*, 980–989.

Merikangas, K. R., Mehta, R. L., Molnar, B. E., Walters, E. E., Swendsen, J. D., Auilar-Gaziola, S., ... Kessler, R. C. (1998). Comorbidity of substance use disorders with mood and anxiety disorders: Results of the international consortium in psychiatric epidemiology. *Addictive Behaviors*, *23*, 893–908.

Mian, N. D., Wainwright, L., Briggs-Gowan, M. J., & Carter, A. S. (2011). An ecological risk model for early childhood anxiety: The importance of early child symptoms and temperament. *Journal of Abnormal Child Psychology, 39,* 501–512.

Micco, J. A., Choate-Summers, M. L., Ehrenreich, J. T., Pincus, D. B., & Mattis, S. G. (2007). Efficacious treatment components of panic control treatment for adolescents: A preliminary examination. *Child and Family Behavior Therapy, 29,* 1–23.

Mifsud, C., & Rapee, R. M. (2005). Early intervention for childhood anxiety in a school setting: Outcomes for an economically disadvantaged population. *Journal of the American Academy of Child and Adolescent Psychiatry*, *44*, 996–1004.

Miles, H., MacLeod, A. K., & Pote, H. (2004). Retrospective and prospective cognitions in adolescents: Anxiety, depression, and positive and negative affect. *Journal of Adolescence*, *27*, 691–701.

Miller, A., Enlow, M., Reich, W., & Saxe, G. (2009). A diagnostic interview for acute stress disorder for children and adolescents. *Journal of Traumatic Stress*, *22*, 549–556.

Mills, R. L., & Rubin, K. H. (1993). Socialization factors in the development of social withdrawal. In K. H. Rubin & J. B. Asendorpf (Eds.), *Social withdrawal, inhibition, and shyness in childhood* (pp. 117–148). Hillsdale, NJ: Lawrence Erlbaum.

Moehler, E., Kagan, J., Oelkers-Ax, R., Brunner, R., Poustka, L., Haffner, J., & Resch, F. (2008). Infant predictors of behavioural inhibition. *British Journal of Developmental Psychology*, *26*, 145–150.

Mogg, K., Bradley, B. P., Millar, N., & White, J. (1995). A follow-up study of cognitive bias in generalized anxiety disorder. *Behaviour Research and Therapy, 33*, 927–935.

Monga, S., Young, A., & Owens, M. (2009). Evaluating a cognitive behavioral therapy group program for anxious five to seven year old children: A pilot study. *Depression and Anxiety, 26*, 243–250.

Moore, P. S., Whaley, S. E., & Sigman, M. (2004). Interactions between mothers and children: Impacts of maternal and child anxiety. *Journal of Abnormal Psychology, 113*, 471–476.

Moradi, A. R., Taghavi, R., Neshat-Doost, H. T., Yule, W., & Dalgleish, T. (2000). Memory bias for emotional information in children and adolescents with posttraumatic stress disorder: A preliminary study. *Journal of Anxiety Disorders, 14*, 521–534.

Morgan, J., & Banerjee, R. (2006). Social anxiety and self-evaluation of social performance in a nonclinical sample of children. *Journal of Clinical Child and Adolescent Psychology, 35*, 292–301.

Morren, M., Kindt, M., van den Hout, M., & van Kasteren, H. (2003). Anxiety and the processing of threat in children: Further examination of the cognitive inhibition hypothesis. *Behaviour Change, 20*, 131–142.

Muris, P. (2002). An expanded Childhood Anxiety Sensitivity Index: Its factor structure, reliability, and validity in a non-clinical adolescent sample. *Behaviour Research and Therapy, 40*, 299–311.

Muris, P., Huijding, J., Mayer, B., Leemreis, W., Passchier, S., & Bouwmeester, S. (2009). The effects of verbal disgust- and threat-related information about novel animals on disgust and fear beliefs and avoidance in children. *Journal of Clinical Child and Adolescent Psychology, 38*, 551–563.

Muris, P., Mayer, B., den Adel, M., Roos, T., & van Wamelen, J. (2009). Predictors of change following cognitive-behavioral treatment of children with anxiety problems: A preliminary investigation on negative automatic thoughts and anxiety control. *Child Psychiatry and Human Development, 40*, 139–151.

Muris, P., Mayer, B., Huijding, J., & Konings, T. (2008). A dirty animal is a scary animal! Effects of disgust-related information on fear beliefs in children. *Behaviour Research and Therapy, 46*, 137–144.

Muris, P., Meesters, C., Mayer, B., Bogie, N., Luijten, M., Geebelen, E., ... Smit, C. (2003). The Koala Fear Questionnaire: A standardized self-report scale for assessing fears and fearfulness in pre-school and primary school children. *Behaviour Research and Therapy, 41*, 597–617.

Muris, P., Meesters, C., Merckelbach, H., & Hülsenbeck, P. (2000). Worry in children is related to perceived parental rearing and attachment. *Behaviour Research and Therapy, 38*, 487–497

Muris, P., & Merckelbach, H. (2001). The etiology of childhood specific phobia: A multifactorial model. In M. W. Vasey & M. R. Dadds (Eds.), *The developmental psychopathology of anxiety* (pp. 355–385). New York: Oxford University Press.

Muris, P., Merckelbach, H., Gadet, B., & Moulaert, V. (2000). Fears, worries, and scary dreams in 4- to 12-year-old children: Their content, developmental pattern, and origins. *Journal of Clinical Child Psychology, 29*, 43–52

Muris, P., Merckelbach, H., Holdrinet, I., & Sijsenaar, M. (1998). Treating phobic children: Effects of EMDR versus exposure. *Journal of Consulting and Clinical Psychology, 66*, 193–198.

Muris, P., Merckelbach, H., & Meesters, C. (2001). Learning experiences and anxiety sensitivity in normal adolescents. *Journal of Psychopathology and Behavioral Assessment, 23*, 279–283.

Muris, P., Merckelbach, H., Schmidt, H., & Tierney, S. (1999). Disgust sensitivity, trait anxiety and anxiety disorders symptoms in normal children. *Behaviour Research and Therapy, 37*, 953–961.

Muris, P., & Ollendick, T. H. (2005). The role of temperament in the etiology of child psychopathology. *Clinical Child and Family Psychology Review, 8*, 271–289.

Muris, P., van Brakel, A. L., Arntz, A., & Schouten, E. (2011). Behavioral inhibition as a risk factor for the development of childhood anxiety disorders: A longitudinal study. *Journal of Child and Family Studies, 20,* 157–170.

Muris, P., van der Heiden, S., & Rassin, E. (2008). Disgust sensitivity and psychopathological symptoms in non-clinical children. *Journal of Behavior Therapy and Experimental Psychiatry, 39,* 133–146.

Muris, P., van Zwol, L., Huijding, J., & Mayer, B. (2010). Mom told me scary things about this animal: Parents installing fear beliefs in their children via the verbal information pathway. *Behaviour Research and Therapy, 48,* 341–346.

Murray, L., de Rosnay, M., Pearson, J., Bergeron, C., Schofield, E., Royal-Lawson, M., & Cooper, P. J. (2008). Intergenerational transmission of social anxiety: The role of social referencing processes in infancy. *Child Development, 79,* 1049–1064.

Nakamura, B. J., Pestle, S. L., & Chorpita, B. F. (2009). Differential sequencing of cognitive-behavioral techniques for reducing child and adolescent anxiety. *Journal of Cognitive Psychotherapy, 23,* 114–135.

Noël, V. A., & Francis, S. E. (2011). A meta-analytic review of the role of child anxiety sensitivity in child anxiety. *Journal of Abnormal Child Psychology, 39,* 721–733.

Norberg, M., Krystal, J., & Tolin, D. (2008). A meta-analysis of D-cycloserine and the facilitation of fear extinction and exposure therapy. *Biological Psychiatry, 63,* 1118–1126.

Oh, W., Rubin, K. H., Bowker, J. C., Booth-LaForce, C., Rose-Krasno, L., & Laursen, B. (2008). Trajectories of social withdrawal from middle childhood to early adolescence. *Journal of Abnormal Child Psychology, 36,* 553–566.

Olatunji, B., Cisler, J., McKay, D., & Phillips, M. L. (2010). Is disgust associated with psychopathology? Emerging research in the anxiety disorders. *Psychiatry Research, 175,* 1–10.

Olatunji, B., & Deacon, B. (2008). Specificity of disgust sensitivity in the prediction of fear and disgust responding to a brief spider exposure. *Journal of Anxiety Disorders, 22,* 328–336.

Ollendick, T. H. (1983). Reliability and validity of the Revised Fear Survey Schedule for Children (FSSC-R). *Behaviour Research and Therapy, 21,* 685–692.

Ollendick, T. H. (1995). Cognitive behavioral treatment of panic disorder with agoraphobia in adolescents: A multiple baseline design analysis. *Behavior Therapy, 26,* 517–531.

Ollendick, T., Allen, B., Benoit, K., & Cowart, M. (2011). The tripartite model of fear in children with specific phobias: Assessing concordance and discordance using the behavioral approach test. *Behaviour Research and Therapy, 49,* 459–465.

Ollendick, T. H., Birmaher, B., & Mattis, S. G. (2004). Panic Disorder. In T. L. Morris & J. S. March (Eds.), *Anxiety disorders in children and adolescents* (2nd ed., pp. 189–211). New York: Guilford Press.

Ollendick, T. H., & Cerny, J. A. (1981). *Clinical behavior therapy with children.* New York: Plenum Press.

Ollendick, T. H., Grills, A. E., & Alexander, K. (2001). Fear and anxiety in children and adolescents. In C. A. Essau and F. Petermann (Eds.), *Anxiety in children and adolescents: Epidemiology, risk factors, and treatment.* London, UK: Harwood Academic.

Ollendick, T. H., Grills, A. E., & King, N. (2001). Applying developmental theory to the assessment and treatment of childhood disorders: Does it make a difference? *Clinical Psychology and Psychotherapy, 8,* 304–314.

Ollendick, T. H., Hagopian, L. P., & King, N. J. (1997). Specific phobias in children. In G. C. L. Davey (Ed.), *Phobias: A handbook of theory, research, and treatment.* Chichester, UK: Wiley.

Ollendick, T. H., Jarrett, M. A., Grills-Taquechel, A. E., Hovey, L. D., & Wolff, J. C. (2008). Comorbidity as a predictor and moderator of treatment outcome in youth with anxiety, affective, attention deficit/hyperactivity disorder, and oppositional/conduct disorders. *Clinical Psychology Review, 28,* 1447–1471.

Ollendick, T. H., & King, N. J. (1991). Origins of childhood fears: An evaluation of Rachman's theory of fear acquisition. *Behaviour Research and Therapy, 29,* 117–123.

Ollendick, T. H., King, N. J., & Muris, P. (2002). Fears and phobias in children: Phenomenology, epidemiology, and aetiology. *Child and Adolescent Mental Health*, *7*, 98–106.

Ollendick, T. H., & Yule, W. (1990). Depression in British and American children and its relation to anxiety and fear. *Journal of Consulting and Clinical Psychology*, *58*, 126–129.

Ollendick, T. H., Öst, L., Reuterskiöld, L., Costa, N., Cederlund, R., Sirbu, C., ... Jarrett, M. A. (2009). One-session treatment of specific phobias in youth: A randomized clinical trial in the United States and Sweden. *Journal of Consulting and Clinical Psychology*, *77*, 504–516.

Orvaschel, H. (1995). *Schedule for Affective Disorders and Schizophrenia for School-Age Children Epidemiologic Version-5*. Ft. Lauderdale, FL: Center for Psychological Studies, Nova Southeastern University.

Öst, L.-G. (1989). One-session treatment for specific phobias. *Behaviour Research and Therapy*, *27*, 1–7.

Öst, L.-G. (1997). Rapid treatment of specific phobias. In G. C. L. Davey (Ed.), *Phobias: A handbook of theory, research and treatment* (pp.227–247). Oxford, England: Wiley.

Öst, L. G., Svensson, L., Hellstrom, K., & Lindwall, R. (2001). One-session treatment of specific phobias in youths: A randomized clinical trial. *Journal of Consulting and Clinical Psychology, 69,* 814–824.

Pagani, L. S., Japel, C., Vaillancourt, T., Côté, S., & Tremblay, R. E. (2008). Links between life course trajectories of family dysfunction and anxiety during middle childhood. *Journal of Abnormal Child Psychology, 36,* 41–53.

Pahl, K. M., & Barrett, P. M. (2010). Preventing anxiety and promoting social and emotional strength in preschool children: A universal evaluation of the Fun FRIENDS program. *Advances in School Mental Health Promotion*, *3*, 14–25.

Pawlak, C. C., Pascual-Sanchez, T. T., Raë, P. P., Fischer, W. W., & Ladame, F. F. (1999). Anxiety disorders, comorbidity, and suicide attempts in adolescence: A preliminary investigation. *European Psychiatry*, *14*, 132–136.

Payne, S., Bolton, D., & Perrin, S. (2011). A pilot investigation of cognitive therapy for generalized anxiety disorder in children aged 7–17 years. *Cognitive Therapy and Research*, *35*, 171–178.

Pediatric OCD Treatment Study Team (POTS). (2004). Cognitive-behavior therapy, Sertraline, and their combination for children and adolescents with Obsessive-Compulsive Disorder: The pediatric OCD treatment study (POTS) randomized controlled trial. *Journal of the American Medical Association*, *292*, 1969–1976.

Piacentini, J., & Langley, A. K. (2004). Cognitive-behavioral therapy for children who have obsessive-compulsive disorder. *Journal of Clinical Psychology*, *60*, 1181–1194.

Pina, A. A., Silverman, W. K., Fuentes, R. M., Kurtines, W. M., & Weems, C. F. (2003). Exposure-based cognitive-behavioral treatment for phobic and anxiety disorders: Treatment effects and maintenance for Hispanic/Latino relative to European-American youths. *Journal of the American Academy of Child and Adolescent Psychiatry*, *42*, 1179–1187.

Pina, A. A., Villalta, I. K., & Zerr, A. A. (2009). Exposure-based cognitive behavioral treatment of anxiety in youth: An emerging culturally-prescriptive framework. *Behavioral Psychology/Psicología Conductual*, *17*, 111–135.

Pincus, D. B., Santucci, L. C., Ehrenreich, J. T., & Eyberg, S. M. (2008). The implementation of modified parent-child interaction therapy for youth with separation anxiety disorder. *Cognitive and Behavioral Practice*, *15*, 118–125.

Pine, D. (2009). Integrating research on development and fear learning: A vision for clinical neuroscience? *Depression and Anxiety*, *26*, 775–779.

Pine, D. S., Cohen, P., Gurley, D., Brook, J., & Ma, Y. (1998). The risk for early-adulthood anxiety and depressive disorders in adolescents with anxiety and depressive disorders. *Archives of General Psychiatry*, *55*, 56–64.

Pine, D., Helfinstein, S., Bar-Haim, Y., Nelson, E., & Fox, N. (2009). Challenges in developing novel treatments for childhood disorders: Lessons from research on anxiety. *Neuropsychopharmacology*, *34*, 213–228.

Pliszka, S. R. (2011). Anxiety disorders. In S. Goldstein & C. R. Reynolds (Eds.), *Handbook of neurodevelopmental and genetic disorders in children* (2nd ed., pp. 188–208). New York: Guilford Press.

Puliafico, A. C., & Kendall, P. C. (2006). Threat-related attentional bias in anxious youth: A review. *Clinical Child and Family Psychology Review, 9*, 162–180.

Rao, P. A., Beidel, D. C., Turner, S. M., Ammerman, R. T., Crosby, L. E., & Sallee, F. R. (2007). Social anxiety disorder in childhood and adolescence: Descriptive psychopathology. *Behaviour Research and Therapy, 45*, 1181–1191.

Rapee, R. M. (1997). Potential role of childrearing practices in the development of anxiety and depression. *Clinical Psychology Review, 17*, 47–67.

Rapee, R. M. (2001). The development of generalized anxiety. In M. W. Vasey & M. R. Dadds (Eds.), *The developmental psychopathology of anxiety* (pp. 481–503). New York: Oxford University Press.

Rapee, R. M., Abbott, M. J., & Lyneham, H. J. (2006). Bibliotherapy for children with anxiety disorders using written materials for parents: A randomized controlled trial. *Journal of Consulting and Clinical Psychology, 74*, 436–444.

Rapee, R. M., Schniering, C. A., & Hudson, J. L. (2009). Anxiety disorders during childhood and adolescence: Origins and treatment. *Annual Review of Clinical Psychology, 5*, 311–341.

Reed, L. J., Carter, B. D., & Miller, L. C. (1995). Fear and anxiety in children. In C. E. Walker & M. C. Roberts (Eds.), *Handbook of clinical child psychology*. New York: Wiley.

Reich, W. (2000). Diagnostic Interview for Children and Adolescents (DICA). *Journal of the American Academy of Child and Adolescent Psychiatry, 39*, 59–66.

Reijntjes, A., Thomaes, S., Boelen, P., van der Schoot, M., de Castro, B. O., & Telch, M. J. (2011). Delighted when approved by others, to pieces when rejected: Children's social anxiety magnifies the linkage between self- and other evaluations. *Journal of Child Psychology and Psychiatry, 52*, 774–781.

Reiss, S. (1991). Expectancy model of fear, anxiety, and panic. *Clinical Psychology Review, 11*, 141–153.

Reynolds, C. R., & Kamphaus, R. W. (2004). *BASC-2: Behavior Assessment System for Children, Second Edition Manual*. Circle Pines, MN: American Guidance Service.

Reynolds, C. R., & Richmond, B. O. (2008). *Revised Children's Manifest Anxiety Scale* (2nd ed.). Torrance, CA: Western Psychological Services.

Riddle, M. A., Reeve, E. A., Yaryura-Tobias, J. A., Yang, H., Claghorn, J. L., Gaffney, G., ... Walkup, J. T. (2001). Fluvoxamine for children and adolescents with obsessive-compulsive disorder: A randomized, controlled, multicenter trial. *Journal of the American Academy of Child and Adolescent Psychiatry, 40*, 222–229.

Roberts, R. E., & Roberts, C. (2007). Ethnicity and risk of psychiatric disorder among adolescents. *Research in Human Development, 4*, 89–117.

Roberts, R. E., Roberts, C., & Xing, Y. (2007). Rates of DSM-IV psychiatric disorders among adolescents in a large metropolitan area. *Journal of Psychiatric Research, 41*, 959–967.

Roelofs, J., Meesters, C., Ter Huurne, M., Bamelis, L., & Muris, P. (2006). On the links between attachment style, parental rearing behaviors, and internalizing and externalizing problems in non-clinical children. *Journal of Child and Family Studies, 15*, 331–344.

Rolfsnes, E. S., & Idsoe, T. (2011). School-based intervention programs for PTSD symptoms: A review and meta-analysis. *Journal of Traumatic Stress, 24*, 155–165.

Ronan, K. R., Finnis, K., & Johnston, D. M. (2006). Interventions with youth and families: A prevention and stepped care model. In G. Reyes & G. A. Jacobs (Eds.), *Handbook of international disaster psychology: Practices and programs* (Vol. 2, pp. 13–35). Westport, CT: Praeger / Greenwood.

Rork, K. E., & Morris, T. L. (2009). Influence of parenting factors on childhood social anxiety: Direct observation of parental warmth and control. *Child and Family Behavior Therapy, 31*, 220–235.

Ross, C. M., Davis, T. A., & Hogg, D. Y. (2007). Screening and assessing adolescent asthmatics for anxiety disorders. *Clinical Nursing Research*, *16*, 5–24.

Rozenman, M., Weersing, V., & Amir, N. (2011). A case series of attention modification in clinically anxious youths. *Behaviour Research and Therapy*, *49*, 324–330.

Rynn, M., Puliafico, A., Heleniak, C., Rikhi, P., Ghalib, K., & Vidair, H. (2011). Advances in pharmacotherapy for pediatric anxiety disorders. *Depression and Anxiety*, *28*, 76–87.

Rynn, M. A., Riddle, M. A., Yeung, P. P., & Kunz, N. R. (2007). Efficacy and safety of extended-release venlafaxine in the treatment of generalized anxiety disorder in children and adolescents: Two placebo-controlled trials. *American Journal of Psychiatry*, *164*, 290–300.

Rynn, M. A., Siqueland, L., & Rickels, K. (2001). Placebo-controlled trial of sertraline in the treatment of children with generalized anxiety disorder. *American Journal of Psychiatry*, *158*, 2008–2014.

Salloum, A. (2010). Minimal therapist-assisted cognitive-behavioral therapy interventions in stepped care for childhood anxiety. *Professional Psychology: Research and Practice*, *41*, 41–47.

Sattler, J. M., & Hoge, R. (2006). *Assessment of children: Behavioral and clinical applications* (5th ed.). San Diego, CA: Author.

Saxe, G., Stoddard, F., Hall, E., Chawla, N., Lopez, C., Sheridan, R., ... Yehuda, R. (2005). Pathways to PTSD: Part I: Children with burns. *American Journal of Psychiatry*, *162*, 1299–1304.

Sburlati, E. S., Schniering, C. A., Lyneham, H. J., & Rapee, R. M. (2011). A model of therapist competencies for the empirically supported cognitive behavioral treatment of child and adolescent anxiety and depressive disorders. *Clinical Child and Family Psychology Review*, *14*, 89–109.

Scahill, L., Riddle, M., McSwiggin-Hardin, M., Ort, S., King, R., Goodman, W., ... Leckman, J. (1997). Children's Yale-Brown Obsessive Compulsive Scale: Reliability and validity. *Journal of the American Academy of Child and Adolescent Psychiatry*, *36*, 844–852.

Schneider, B. H., & Tessier, N. G. (2007). Close friendship as understood by socially withdrawn, anxious early adolescents. *Child Psychiatry and Human Development*, *38*, 339–351.

Scott, T., Short, E., Singer, L., Russ, S., & Minnes, S. (2006). Psychometric properties of the Dominic Interactive Assessment: A computerized self-report for children. *Assessment*, *13*, 16–26.

Seligman, L. D., & Ollendick, T. H. (2011). Cognitive-behavioral therapy for anxiety disorders in youth. *Child and Adolescent Psychiatric Clinics of North America*, *20*, 217–238.

Shaffer, D., Fisher, P., Lucas, C. P., Dulcan, M. K., & Schwab-Stone, M. E. (2000). NIMH Diagnostic Interview Schedule for Children Version IV (NIMH DISC-IV): Description, differences from previous versions, and reliability of some common diagnoses. *Journal of the American Academy of Child and Adolescent Psychiatry, 39*, 28–38.

Shamir-Essakow, G., Ungerer, J. A., & Rapee, R. M. (2005). Attachment, behavioral inhibition, and anxiety in preschool children. *Journal of Abnormal Child Psychology, 33*, 131–143.

Shanahan, L., Copeland, W., Costello, E., & Angold, A. (2008). Specificity of putative psychosocial risk factors for psychiatric disorders in children and adolescents. *Journal of Child Psychology and Psychiatry*, *49*, 34–42.

Sherrill, J., & Kovacs, M. (2000). Interview Schedule for Children and Adolescents (ISCA). *Journal of the American Academy of Child and Adolescent Psychiatry*, *39*, 67–75.

Shortt, A. L., Barrett, P. M., & Fox, T. L. (2001). Evaluating the FRIENDS program: A cognitive-behavioral group treatment for anxious children and their parents. *Journal of Clinical Child Psychology, 30*, 525–535.

Silverman, W. K., & Albano, A. M. (1996). *Anxiety Disorders Interview Schedule, Parent/Child version*. New York: Oxford University Press.

Silverman, W. K., Fleisig, W., Rabian, B., & Peterson, R. A. (1991). Child Anxiety Sensitivity Index. *Journal of Clinical Child Psychology*, *20*, 162–168.

Silverman, W. K., Kurtines, W. M., Ginsburg, G. S., Weems, C. F., Rabian, B., & Serafini, L. T. (1999). Contingency management, self-control, and education support in the treatment of childhood phobic disorders: A randomized clinical trial. *Journal of Consulting and Clinical Psychology, 67,* 675–687.

Silverman, W. K., & Ollendick, T.H. (2008). Assessment of child and adolescent anxiety disorders. In J. Hunsley & E. Mash (Eds.), *A Guide to assessments that work.* New York: Oxford University Press.

Silverman, W., Pina, A. A., & Viswesvaran, C. (2008). Evidence-based psychosocial treatments for phobic and anxiety disorders in children and adolescents. *Journal of Clinical Child and Adolescent Psychology, 37,* 105–130.

Simeon, J. G., Ferguson, H., Knott, V., & Roberts, N. (1992). Clinical, cognitive, and neurophysiological effects of alprazolam in children and adolescents with overanxious and avoidant disorders. *Journal of the American Academy of Child and Adolescent Psychiatry, 31,* 29–33.

Southam-Gerow, M. A., & Kendall, P. C. (2000). A preliminary study of the emotion understanding of youths referred for treatment of anxiety disorders. *Journal of Clinical Child Psychology, 29,* 319–327.

Southam-Gerow, M. A., Kendall, P. C., & Weesing, V. R. (2001). Examining outcome variability: Correlates of treatment response in a child and adolescent anxiety clinic. *Journal of Clinical Child Psychology, 30,* 422–436.

Spence, S. H. (1995). *Social skills training: Enhancing social competence with children and adolescents.* London, UK: NFER Nelson.

Spence, S. H. (1998). A measure of anxiety symptoms among children. *Behaviour Research and Therapy, 36,* 545–566.

Spence, S. H. (2003). Social skills training with children and young people: Theory, evidence and practice. *Child and Adolescent Mental Health, 8,* 84–96.

Spence, S.H., Donovan, C., & Brechman-Toussaint, M. (2000). The treatment of childhood social phobia: The effectiveness of a social skills training-based, cognitive-behavioral intervention, with and without parental involvement. *Journal of Child Psychology and Psychiatry and Allied Disciplines, 41,* 713–726.

Spence, S. H., Donovan, C. L., March, S., Gamble, A., Anderson, R. E., Prosser, S., & Kenardy, J. (2011). A randomized controlled trial of online versus clinic-based CBT for adolescent anxiety. *Journal of Consulting and Clinical Psychology, 79,* 629–642.

Spence, S. H., Najman, J. M., Bor, W., O'Callaghan, M., & Williams, G. M. (2002). Maternal anxiety and depression, poverty and marital relationship factors during early childhood as predictors of anxiety and depressive symptoms in adolescence. *Journal of Child Psychology and Psychiatry, 43,* 457–470.

Spielberger, C. D. (1973). *Manual for the State-Trait Anxiety Inventory for Children.* Palo Alto, CA: Consulting Psychologists Press.

Spielmans, G. I., Pasek, L. F., & Mcfall, J. P. (2007). What are the active ingredients in cognitive and behavioral psychotherapy for anxious and depressed children? A meta-analytic review. *Clinical Psychology Review, 27,* 642–654.

Spokas, M., & Heimberg, R. G. (2009). Overprotective parenting, social anxiety, and external locus of control: Cross-sectional and longitudinal relationships. *Cognitive Therapy and Research, 33,* 543–551.

Stallard, P., Simpson, N., Anderson, S., Carter, T., Osborn, C., & Bush, S. (2005). An evaluation of the FRIENDS programme: A cognitive behaviour therapy intervention to promote emotional resilience. *Archives of Disease in Childhood, 90,* 1016–1019.

Stallard, P., Simpson, N., Anderson, S., Hibbert, S., & Osborn, C. (2007). The FRIENDS Emotional Health Programme: Initial findings from a school-based project. *Child and Adolescent Mental Health, 12,* 32–37.

Stopa, J. E., Barrett, P. M., & Golingi, F. (2010). The prevention of childhood anxiety in socioeconomically disadvantaged communities: A universal school-based trial. *Advances in School Mental Health Promotion, 3,* 5–24.

Storch, E. L., Brassard, M. R., & Masia-Warner, C. L. (2003). The relationship of peer victimization to social anxiety and loneliness in adolescence. *Child Study Journal, 33,* 1–18.

Storch, E. A., Masia-Warner, C., Heidgerken, A. D., Fisher, P. H., Pincus, D. B., & Liebowitz, M. R. (2006). Factor structure of the Liebowitz Social Anxiety Scale for Children and Adolescents. *Child Psychiatry and Human Development*, *37*, 25–37.

Storch, E. A., Murphy, T. K., Adkins, J. W., Lewin, A. B., Geffken, G. R., Johns, N. B., ... Goodman, W. K. (2006). The Children's Yale-Brown Obsessive-Compulsive Scale: Psychometric properties of child- and parent-report formats. *Journal of Anxiety Disorders*, *20*, 1055–1070.

Storch, E., Murphy, T., Goodman, W., Geffken, G., Lewin, A., Henin, A., ... Geller, D. (2010). A preliminary study of D-cycloserine augmentation of cognitive-behavioral therapy in pediatric obsessive-compulsive disorder. *Biological Psychiatry*, *68*, 1073–1076.

Strauss, C. C., & Last, C. G. (1993). Social and simple phobias in children. *Journal of Anxiety Disorders*, *7*, 141–152.

Strauss, C. C., Last, C. G., Hersen, M., & Kazdin, A. E. (1988). Association between anxiety and depression in children and adolescents with anxiety disorders. *Journal of Abnormal Child Psychology*, *16*, 57–68.

Suárez, L. M., Bennett, S. M., Goldstein, C. R., & Barlow, D. H. (2009). Understanding anxiety disorders from a 'triple vulnerability' framework. In M. M. Antony & M. B. Stein (Eds.), *Oxford handbook of anxiety and related disorders* (pp. 153–172). New York: Oxford University Press.

Suveg, C., Hudson, J. L., Brewer, G., Flannery-Schroeder, E., Gosch, E., & Kendall, P. C. (2009). Cognitive-behavioral therapy for anxiety-disordered youth: Secondary outcomes from a randomized clinical trial evaluating child and family modalities. *Journal of Anxiety Disorders*, *23*, 341–349.

Suveg, C., & Zeman, J. (2004). Emotion regulation in children with anxiety disorders. *Journal of Clinical Child and Adolescent Psychology*, 33, 750–759.

Swedo, S. E., Leonard, H. L., Garvey, M., Mittleman, B., Allen, A. J., Perlmutter, S., ... Lougee, L. (1998). Pediatric autoimmune neuropsychiatric disorders associated with streptococcal infections: Clinical description of the first 50 cases. *American Journal of Psychiatry*, *155*, 264–271.

Thapar, A., & McGuffin, P. (1995). Are anxiety symptoms in childhood heritable? *Journal of Child Psychology and Psychiatry*, *36*, 439–447.

Thibodeau, R., Jorgensen, R. S., & Kim, S. (2006). Depression, anxiety, and resting frontal EEG asymmetry: A meta-analytic review. *Journal of Abnormal Psychology*, *115*, 715–729.

Tiwari, S., Podell, J. C., Martin, E. D., Mychailyszyn, M. P., Furr, J. M., & Kendall, P. C. (2008). Experiential avoidance in the parenting of anxious youth: Theory, research, and future directions. *Cognition and Emotion*, *22*, 480–496.

Turner, S. M., Beidel, D. C., & Costello, A. (1987). Psychopathology in the offspring of anxiety disorders patients. *Journal of Consulting and Clinical Psychology*, *55*, 229–235.

Valla, J., Bergeron, L., & Smolla, N. (2000). The Dominic-R: A pictorial interview for 6- to 11-year-old children. *Journal of the American Academy of Child and Adolescent Psychiatry*, *39*, 85–93.

Valla, J., Kovess, V., Chan Chee, C., Berthiaume, C., Vantalon, V., Piquet, C., ...Alles-Jardel, M. (2002). A French study of the Dominic Interactive. *Social Psychiatry and Psychiatric Epidemiology*, *37*, 441.

Van Ameringen, M., Mancini, C., & Farvolden, P. (2003). The impact of anxiety disorders on educational achievement. *Journal of Anxiety Disorders, 17,* 561–571.

van der Bruggen, C. O., Stams, G. M., & Bögels, S. M. (2008). Research review: The relation between child and parent anxiety and parental control: A meta-analytic review. *Journal of Child Psychology and Psychiatry*, *49*, 1257–1269

van der Leeden, A. M., van Widenfelt, B. M., van der Leeden, R., Liber, J. M., Utens, E. J., & Treffers, P. A. (2011). Stepped care cognitive behavioural therapy for children with anxiety disorders: A new treatment approach. *Behavioural and Cognitive Psychotherapy*, *39*, 55–75.

Van Oort, F. V. A., Greaves-Lord, K., Verhulst, F. C., Ormel, J., & Huizink, A. C. (2009) The developmental course of anxiety symptoms during adolescence: The TRIALS study. *Journal of Child Psychology and Psychiatry*, *50*, 1209–1217.

Vasey, M., & Dadds, M. (2001). *The developmental psychopathology of anxiety*. New York: Oxford University Press.

Vasey, M. W., & MacLeod, C. (2001). Information-processing factors in childhood anxiety: A review and developmental perspective. In M. W. Vasey & M. R. Dadds (Eds.), *The developmental psychopathology of anxiety* (pp. 253–277). New York, NY: Oxford University Press.

Vasey, M. W., & Ollendick, T. H. (2000). Anxiety. In A. J. Sameroff, M. Lewis, & S. M. Miller (Eds.), *Handbook of developmental psychopathology (2nd ed.)* (pp. 511–529). Dordrecht, Netherlands: Kluwer Academic.

Verduin, T. L., & Kendall, P. C. (2003). Differential occurrence of comorbidity within childhood anxiety disorders. *Journal of Clinical Child and Adolescent Psychology*, *32*, 290–295.

Verduin, T. L., & Kendall, P. C. (2008). Peer perceptions and liking of children with anxiety disorders. *Journal of Abnormal Child Psychology, 36,* 459–469.

Verhulst, F., van der Ende, J., Ferdinand, R., & Kasius, M. (1997). The prevalence of DSM-III-R diagnoses in a national sample of Dutch adolescents. *Archives of General Psychiatry*, *54*, 329–336.

Viana, A. G., Rabian, B., & Beidel, D. C. (2008). Self-report measures in the study of comorbidity in children and adolescents with social phobia: Research and clinical utility. *Journal of Anxiety Disorders*, *22*, 781–792.

Vitiello, B., & Waslick, B. (2010). Pharmacotherapy for children and adolescents with anxiety disorders. *Psychiatric Annals*, *40*, 185–191.

Wagner, K., Berard, R., Stein, M. B., Wetherhold, E., Carpenter, D. J., Perera, P., ... Machin, A. (2004). A multicenter, randomized, double-blind, placebo-controlled trial of paroxetine in children and adolescents with social anxiety disorder. *Archives of General Psychiatry*, *61*, 1153–1162.

Walker, J. L., Lahey, B. B., Russo, M. F., & Frick, P. J. (1991). Anxiety, inhibition, and conduct disorder in children: Part I: Relations to social impairment. *Journal of the American Academy of Child and Adolescent Psychiatry*, *30*, 187–191.

Walkup, J. T., Albano, A., Piacentini, J., Birmaher, B., Compton, S. N., Sherrill, J. T., ... Kendall, P. C. (2008). Cognitive behavioral therapy, sertraline, or a combination in childhood anxiety. *New England Journal of Medicine*, *359*, 2753–2766.

Walkup, J. T., Labellarte, M. J., Riddle, M. A., Pine, D. S., Greenhill, L., Klein, R., & ... Roper, M. (2001). Fluvoxamine for the treatment of anxiety disorders in children and adolescents. *New England Journal of Medicine*, *344,* 1279–1285.

Warren, S. L., & Sroufe, L. (2004). Developmental issues. In T. H. Ollendick & J. S. March (Eds.), *Phobic and anxiety disorders in children and adolescents: A clinician's guide to effective psychosocial and pharmacological interventions* (pp. 92–115). New York: Oxford University Press.

Waters, A. M., Lipp, O. V., & Spence, S. H. (2004). Attentional bias toward fear-related stimuli: An investigation with nonselected children and adults and children with anxiety disorders. *Journal of Experimental Child Psychology*, *89*, 320–337.

Waters, A., Wharton, T., Zimmer-Gembeck, M., & Craske, M. (2008). Threat-based cognitive biases in anxious children: comparison with non-anxious children before and after cognitive behavioural treatment. *Behaviour Research and Therapy*, *46*, 358–374.

Watson, H. S., & Rees, C. S. (2008). Meta-analysis of randomized, controlled treatment trials for pediatric obsessive-compulsive disorder. *Journal of Child Psychology and Psychiatry*, *49*, 489–498.

Watt, M. C., & Stewart, S. H. (2000). Anxiety sensitivity mediates the relationships between childhood learning experiences and elevated hypochondriacal concerns in young adulthood. *Journal of Psychosomatic Research, 49,* 107–118.

Watts, S. E., & Weems, C. F. (2006). Associations among selective attention, memory bias, cognitive errors and symptoms of anxiety in youth. *Journal of Abnormal Child Psychology, 34,* 841–852.

Weeks, M., Coplan, R. J., & Kingsbury, A. (2009). The correlates and consequences of early appearing social anxiety in young children. *Journal of Anxiety Disorders, 23*, 965–972.

Weems, C. F., Costa, N. M., Watts, S. E., Taylor, L. K., & Cannon, M. F. (2007). Cognitive errors, anxiety sensitivity, and anxiety control beliefs: Their unique and specific associations with childhood anxiety symptoms. *Behavior Modification, 31*, 174–201.

Weich, S., Patterson, J., Shaw, R., & Stewart-Brown, S. (2009). Family relationships in childhood and common psychiatric disorders in later life: Systematic review of prospective studies. *The British Journal of Psychiatry, 194*, 392–398.

Weller, E. B., Weller, R. A., Fristad, M. A., Rooney, M. T., & Schecter, J. (2000). Children's Interview for Psychiatric Syndromes (ChIPS). *Journal of the American Academy of Child and Adolescent Psychiatry, 39*, 76–84.

Wells, J., Browne, M., Scott, K. M., McGee, M. A., Baxter, J., & Kokaua, J. (2006). Prevalence, interference with life and severity of 12 month DSM-IV disorders in Te Rau Hinengaro: The New Zealand Mental Health Survey. *Australian and New Zealand Journal of Psychiatry, 40*, 845–854.

Wever, C., & Rey, J. M. (1997). Juvenile obsessive-compulsive disorder. *Australian and New Zealand Journal of Psychiatry, 31*, 105–113.

Wheatcroft, R., & Creswell, C. (2007). Parents' cognitions and expectations about their preschool children: The contribution of parental anxiety and child anxiety. *British Journal of Developmental Psychology, 25*, 435–441.

Williams, T. I., Salkovskis, P. M., Forrester, L., Turner, S., White, H., & Allsopp, M. A. (2010). A randomised controlled trial of cognitive behavioural treatment for obsessive compulsive disorder in children and adolescents. *European Child and Adolescent Psychiatry, 19*, 449–456.

Wittchen, H., Nelson, C. B., & Lachner, G. G. (1998). Prevalence of mental disorders and psychosocial impairments in adolescents and young adults. *Psychological Medicine: A Journal of Research in Psychiatry and the Allied Sciences, 28*, 109–126.

Wittchen, H., Reed, V., & Kessler, R. C. (1998). The relationship of agoraphobia and panic in a community sample of adolescents and young adults. *Archives of General Psychiatry, 55*, 1017–1024.

Wolfe, V. V. (2002). *The Children's Impact of Traumatic Events Scale (CITES-R).* Available from Vicky V. Wolfe, PhD, Department of Psychology, London Health Sciences Center, London, Ontario, Canada N6A 4G5 (Vicky.Wolfe@LHSC.ON.CA)

Wolpe, J. (1958). *Psychotherapy by reciprocal inhibition.* Stanford, CA: Stanford University Press.

Wood, J. J. (2006). Parental intrusiveness and children's Separation Anxiety in a clinical sample. *Child Psychiatry and Human Development, 37*, 73–87.

Wood, J. J., McLeod, B. D., Piacentini, J. C., & Sigman, M. (2009). One-year follow-up of family versus child CBT for anxiety disorders: Exploring the roles of child age and parental intrusiveness. *Child Psychiatry and Human Development, 40*, 301–316.

Wood, J. J., McLeod, B. D., Sigman, M., Hwang, W., & Chu, B. C. (2003). Parenting and childhood anxiety: Theory, empirical findings, and future directions. *Journal of Child Psychology and Psychiatry, 44*, 134–151.

Wood, J. J., Piacentini, J. C., Southam-Gerow, M., Chu, B. C., & Sigman, M. (2006). Family cognitive behavioral therapy for child anxiety disorders. *Journal of the American Academy of Child and Adolescent Psychiatry, 45*, 314–321.

Woodward, L. J., & Fergusson, D. M. (2001). Life course outcomes of young people with anxiety disorders in adolescence. *Journal of the American Academy of Child and Adolescent Psychiatry, 40*, 1086–1093.

World Health Organization. (2007). ICD-10 (version 2007). Retrieved from: http://apps.who.int/classifications/apps/icd/icd10online/

Zimmermann, P. P., Wittchen, H. U., Höfler, M. M., Pfister, H. H., Kessler, R. C., & Lieb, R. (2003). Primary anxiety disorders and the development of subsequent alcohol use disorders: A 4-year community study of adolescents and young adults. *Psychological Medicine: A Journal of Research in Psychiatry and the Allied Sciences, 33*, 1211–1222.

8

Appendix: Tools and Resources

Appendix 1

Information About Child Anxiety Disorders

Specific Phobia

The main feature of specific phobia is a persistent and excessive fear that is cued to, or triggered by, the presence or anticipation of a specific object or situation. Exposure to a phobic object immediately and always results in an anxiety response that may be characterized by panic. Many children and adolescents do not realize that their anxiety is excessive or unreasonable and may believe that their fearful responses are justified. In other words, young people may fully believe that the threatening object or event will really harm them if they do not avoid it. The anxiety response causes considerable distress for the child or adolescent and/or interferes with normal everyday functioning at home, at school, or with friends.

Social Phobia

The main feature of social phobia is a significant and persistent fear of social or performance situations. The child or adolescent fears that he/she will act in a way that would be humiliating or embarrassing, and being exposed to feared social situations almost always causes anxiety. These situations are either avoided or endured with distress (e.g., crying, freezing). Further, the avoidance, anxious anticipation, or distress related to the feared situation significantly interferes with the child or youth's life functioning and is not due to the direct effects of substances (e.g., medication) or general medical conditions.

Separation Anxiety Disorder

Separation anxiety, which can be defined as the experience of distress upon being separated from one's parent or caregiver, is a temporary and age-appropriate phenomenon observed in infants and toddlers between 6 and 18 months of age. Separation anxiety disorder (SAD), on the other hand, is characterized by significant and recurrent amounts of worry upon (or in anticipation of) separation from a child or adolescent's home or from those to whom the child or adolescent is attached. Those suffering from SAD may worry about losing their parents and/or getting lost or kidnapped. They often refuse to go to certain places (e.g., school) because of fears of separation, or become extremely fearful when they are left alone without their parents. These children and adolescents may also refuse to sleep alone, may experience nightmares about separation, or experience various physical complaints (e.g., body aches, nausea) when separated from their parents. Separation anxiety may cause significant impairment in important areas of functioning, (e.g., academic and social). The duration of this problem must last for at least 4 weeks and must present itself before the child or youth is 18 years of age.

Generalized Anxiety Disorder

Generalized anxiety disorder (GAD) is characterized by large amounts of uncontrollable worry. The anxiety experienced here extends to a number of events or activities and is not associated with any one object or situation. The child or adolescent with generalized anxiety disorder is frequently described as a "worrier" or "worrywart." This anxiety and worry is associated with restlessness, fatigue, difficulty concentrating, irritability, muscle tension, and/or sleep disturbances.

Obsessive-Compulsive Disorder

Obsessions are recurrent and persistent thoughts, impulses, or images that are intrusive, inappropriate, and cause significant amounts of anxiety or distress. These obsessions are not excessive worries about real-life problems, and the person suffering from them realizes that they are irrational and products of his/her own mind. Persons suffering from obsessions try their best to ignore them or to neutralize them with some other thought or action. Common obsessions include thoughts about contamination, repeated doubts, a need to have things in a particular order, aggressive or scary impulses, and sexual imagery. Compulsions are defined by rigidly applied repetitive behaviors or mental acts that a person feels a need to perform in response to an obsession. The purpose of compulsions is to prevent or reduce distress or prevent some feared event or situation. Further, these behaviors or mental acts are excessive and not realistically connected to what they are supposed to neutralize or prevent. Common compulsions include hand washing, ordering, checking, praying, counting, and repeating words silently. Obsessive-compulsive disorder is characterized by recurrent and severe obsessions and/or compulsions that are time consuming (i.e., more than 1 hour per day) or cause large amounts of distress or impairment.

Panic Disorder

A panic attack is a discrete period of intense fear that occurs in the absence of real danger with four or more of the following symptoms: an increased heart rate, sweating, trembling or shaking, shortness of breath, feeling like you are choking, chest pain, nausea, feeling dizzy, feelings of unreality or being detached from oneself, fear of going crazy, fear of dying, numbness, and/or chills or hot flashes.

There are three types of panic attacks:
1. Unexpected (uncued) panic attacks (i.e., those that occur "out of the blue");
2. Situationally bound (cued) panic attacks (i.e., these almost always occur immediately in anticipation of, in response to, or during an exposure to certain situations);
3. Situationally predisposed panic attacks (i.e., these tend to, but do not always, occur in conjunction with certain situations).

Those suffering from panic disorder experience recurrent, unexpected panic attacks followed by at least 1 month of persistent concern about having another attack, worrying about the meanings or consequences of the attacks (e.g., "I'm going crazy"), and/or with significant changes in behavior related to the attacks. These panic attacks are not due to the direct effects of a substance (e.g., caffeine) or a general medical condition (e.g., hyperthyroidism). In terms of variable diagnoses, panic disorder either occurs as panic disorder without agoraphobia or panic disorder with agoraphobia.

Agoraphobia

The main feature of agoraphobia is worry about being in situations in which escape might be difficult or embarrassing in the event of an unexpected or situationally predisposed panic attack or panic-like symptoms. This worry may also come from anxiety about not having help available in the event of a panic attack. Those suffering from agoraphobia are typically fearful of the types of public situations that may include being outside of the home, being in a crowded place, or traveling. These situations are often avoided or endured with extreme anxiety about having a panic attack or panic-like symptoms. Those suffering from agoraphobia often times ask friends to keep them company in situations in which escape may be difficult or embarrassing. In terms of variable diagnoses, agoraphobia either occurs as panic disorder with agoraphobia or agoraphobia without history of panic disorder.

Posttraumatic Stress Disorder

Those suffering from posttraumatic stress disorder (PTSD) develop symptoms following exposure to a traumatic event involving actual or threatened death or serious injury or harmful threats to oneself or others. The child or adolescent's response to the traumatic event involves intense fear, helplessness, horror, and/or disorganized or agitated behavior. A primary feature of posttraumatic stress is that the traumatic event is persistently re-experienced by the victim in the form of recurrent, intrusive, and frightening recollections or dreams. The child or adolescent often acts as if the event were about to reoccur through feelings of intense distress or arousal in response to symbolic cues that resemble some aspect of the event. In addition, affected children or youths generally avoid objects, people, or places associated with the trauma, fail to remember important details about the event, as well as tend to experience a severe loss of interest in activities, feelings of detachment, restriction of feelings, and/or a sense of shortened future. Further, the child or adolescent will often experience associated symptoms such as difficulty sleeping, irritability or angry outbursts, difficulty concentrating, being overly vigilant, and/or exaggerated startle responses. The disturbance occurs for more than 1 month and causes marked distress for the child.

Appendix 2

Sample Anxiety Measures

Revised Fear Survey Schedule for Children

SELF-RATING QUESTIONAIRE (FSSC-R)

Name:_____ Age:_____ Date:_____

DIRECTIONS: A number of statements which boys and girls use to describe the fears they have are given below. Read each carefully and put an **X** in the box in front of the words that best describe your fear. There are no right or wrong answers. Remember, find the words which best describe how much fear you have.

1. Giving an oral report .... ❑ None   ❑ Some   ❑ A lot
2. Riding in the car or bus .... ❑ None   ❑ Some   ❑ A lot
3. Getting punished by mother .... ❑ None   ❑ Some   ❑ A lot
4. Lizards .... ❑ None   ❑ Some   ❑ A lot
5. Looking foolish .... ❑ None   ❑ Some   ❑ A lot
6. Ghosts or spooky things .... ❑ None   ❑ Some   ❑ A lot
7. Sharp objects... ❑ None   ❑ Some   ❑ A lot
8. Having to go to the hospital .... ❑ None   ❑ Some   ❑ A lot
9. Death or dead people .... ❑ None   ❑ Some   ❑ A lot
10. Getting lost in a strange place .... ❑ None   ❑ Some   ❑ A lot
11. Snakes .... ❑ None   ❑ Some   ❑ A lot
12. Talking on the telephone .... ❑ None   ❑ Some   ❑ A lot
13. Roller coaster or carnival rides .... ❑ None   ❑ Some   ❑ A lot
14. Getting sick at school .... ❑ None   ❑ Some   ❑ A lot
15. Being sent to the principal .... ❑ None   ❑ Some   ❑ A lot
16. Riding on the train .... ❑ None   ❑ Some   ❑ A lot
17. Being left at home with a sitter .... ❑ None   ❑ Some   ❑ A lot
18. Bears or wolves .... ❑ None   ❑ Some   ❑ A lot
19. Meeting someone for the first time .... ❑ None   ❑ Some   ❑ A lot
20. Bombing attacks – being invaded .... ❑ None   ❑ Some   ❑ A lot
21. Getting a shot from the nurse or doctor .... ❑ None   ❑ Some   ❑ A lot
22. Going to the dentist .... ❑ None   ❑ Some   ❑ A lot
23. High places like mountains .... ❑ None   ❑ Some   ❑ A lot
24. Being teased .... ❑ None   ❑ Some   ❑ A lot
25. Spiders .... ❑ None   ❑ Some   ❑ A lot
26. A burglar breaking into our house .... ❑ None   ❑ Some   ❑ A lot

27. Flying in an airplane.. ❑ None   ❑ Some   ❑ A lot

28. Being called on by the teacher .... ❑ None   ❑ Some   ❑ A lot

29. Getting poor grades .... ❑ None   ❑ Some   ❑ A lot

30. Bats or birds .... ❑ None   ❑ Some   ❑ A lot

31. My parents criticizing me .... ❑ None   ❑ Some   ❑ A lot

32. Guns .... ❑ None   ❑ Some   ❑ A lot

33. Being in a fight .... ❑ None   ❑ Some   ❑ A lot

34. Fire – getting burned .... ❑ None   ❑ Some   ❑ A lot

35. Getting a cut or injury .... ❑ None   ❑ Some   ❑ A lot

36. Being in a big crowd... ❑ None   ❑ Some   ❑ A lot

37. Thunderstorms... ❑ None   ❑ Some   ❑ A lot

38. Having to eat some food I don't like .... ❑ None   ❑ Some   ❑ A lot

39. Cats .... ❑ None   ❑ Some   ❑ A lot

40. Failing a test .... ❑ None   ❑ Some   ❑ A lot

41. Being hit by a car or truck .... ❑ None   ❑ Some   ❑ A lot

42. Having to go to school .... ❑ None   ❑ Some   ❑ A lot

43. Playing rough games during recess .... ❑ None   ❑ Some   ❑ A lot

44. Having my parents argue .... ❑ None   ❑ Some   ❑ A lot

45. Dark rooms or closets .... ❑ None   ❑ Some   ❑ A lot

46. Having to put on a recital .... ❑ None   ❑ Some   ❑ A lot

47. Ants or beetles .... ❑ None   ❑ Some   ❑ A lot

48. Being criticized by others .... ❑ None   ❑ Some   ❑ A lot

49. Strange looking people .... ❑ None   ❑ Some   ❑ A lot

50. The sight of blood... ❑ None   ❑ Some   ❑ A lot

51. Going to the doctor .... ❑ None   ❑ Some   ❑ A lot

52. Strange or mean looking dogs .... ❑ None   ❑ Some   ❑ A lot

53. Cemeteries.. ❑ None   ❑ Some   ❑ A lot

54. Getting a report card .... ❑ None   ❑ Some   ❑ A lot

55. Getting a haircut .... ❑ None   ❑ Some   ❑ A lot

56. Deep water or the ocean .... ❑ None   ❑ Some   ❑ A lot

57. Nightmares .... ❑ None   ❑ Some   ❑ A lot

58. Falling from high places .... ❑ None   ❑ Some   ❑ A lot

59. Getting a shock from electricity .... ❑ None   ❑ Some   ❑ A lot

60. Going to bed in the dark .... ❑ None   ❑ Some   ❑ A lot

61. Getting car sick .... ❑ None   ❑ Some   ❑ A lot

62. Being alone .... ❑ None   ❑ Some   ❑ A lot

63. Having to wear clothes different from others .... ❑ None   ❑ Some   ❑ A lot

64. Getting punished by my father .... ❏ None ❏ Some ❏ A lot

65. Having to stay after school .... ❏ None ❏ Some ❏ A lot

66. Making mistakes .... ❏ None ❏ Some ❏ A lot

67. Mystery movies .... ❏ None ❏ Some ❏ A lot

68. Loud sirens .... ❏ None ❏ Some ❏ A lot

69. Doing something new .... ❏ None ❏ Some ❏ A lot

70. Germs or getting a serious illness .... ❏ None ❏ Some ❏ A lot

71. Closed spaces .... ❏ None ❏ Some ❏ A lot

72. Earthquakes .... ❏ None ❏ Some ❏ A lot

73. Terrorists.. ❏ None ❏ Some ❏ A lot

74. Elevators .... ❏ None ❏ Some ❏ A lot

75. Dark places .... ❏ None ❏ Some ❏ A lot

76. Not being able to breathe .... ❏ None ❏ Some ❏ A lot

77. Getting a bee sting .... ❏ None ❏ Some ❏ A lot

78. Worms or snails .... ❏ None ❏ Some ❏ A lot

79. Rats or mice .... ❏ None ❏ Some ❏ A lot

80. Taking a test .... ❏ None ❏ Some ❏ A lot

Spence Children's Anxiety Scale

SPENCE CHILDREN'S ANXIETY SCALE (Parent Report)

Your Name: _____   Date: _____

Your Child's Name: _____

Below is a list of items that describe children. For each item please circle the response that best describes your child. Please answer all the items

1.	My child worries about things	Never	Sometimes	Often	Always
2.	My child is scared of the dark	Never	Sometimes	Often	Always
3.	When my child has a problem, s(he) complains of having a funny feeling in his / her stomach	Never	Sometimes	Often	Always
4.	My child complains of feeling afraid.	Never	Sometimes	Often	Always
5.	My child would feel afraid of being on his/her own at home	Never	Sometimes	Often	Always
6.	My child is scared when s(he) has to take a test	Never	Sometimes	Often	Always
7.	My child is afraid when (s)he has to use public toilets or bathrooms	Never	Sometimes	Often	Always
8.	My child worries about being away from us / me	Never	Sometimes	Often	Always
9.	My child feels afraid that (s)he will make a fool of him/herself in front of people	Never	Sometimes	Often	Always
10.	My child worries that (s)he will do badly at school	Never	Sometimes	Often	Always
11.	My child worries that something awful will happen to someone in our family	Never	Sometimes	Often	Always
12.	My child complains of suddenly feeling as if (s)he can't breathe when there is no reason for this	Never	Sometimes	Often	Always
13.	My child has to keep checking that (s)he has done things right (like the switch is off, or the door is locked)	Never	Sometimes	Often	Always
14.	My child is scared if (s)he has to sleep on his/her own	Never	Sometimes	Often	Always
15.	My child has trouble going to school in the mornings because (s)he feels nervous or afraid	Never	Sometimes	Often	Always
16.	My child is scared of dogs	Never	Sometimes	Often	Always
17.	My child can't seem to get bad or silly thoughts out of his / her head	Never	Sometimes	Often	Always
18.	When my child has a problem, s(he) complains of his/her heart beating really fast	Never	Sometimes	Often	Always
19.	My child suddenly starts to tremble or shake when there is no reason for this	Never	Sometimes	Often	Always
20.	My child worries that something bad will happen to him/her	Never	Sometimes	Often	Always
21.	My child is scared of going to the doctor or dentist	Never	Sometimes	Often	Always
22.	When my child has a problem, (s)he feels shaky	Never	Sometimes	Often	Always
23.	My child is scared of heights (eg., being at the top of a cliff)	Never	Sometimes	Often	Always

24. My child has to think special thoughts (like numbers or words) to stop bad things from happening	Never	Sometimes	Often	Always
25. My child feels scared if (s)he has to travel in the car, or on a bus or train	Never	Sometimes	Often	Always
26. My child worries what other people think of him/her	Never	Sometimes	Often	Always
27. My child is afraid of being in crowded places (like shopping centres, the movies, buses, busy playgrounds)	Never	Sometimes	Often	Always
28. All of a sudden my child feels really scared for no reason at all	Never	Sometimes	Often	Always
29. My child is scared of insects or spiders	Never	Sometimes	Often	Always
30. My child complains of suddenly becoming dizzy or faint when there is no reason for this	Never	Sometimes	Often	Always
31. My child feels afraid when (s)he has to talk in front of the class	Never	Sometimes	Often	Always
32. My child's complains of his / her heart suddenly starting to beat too quickly for no reason	Never	Sometimes	Often	Always
33. My child worries that (s)he will suddenly get a scared feeling when there is nothing to be afraid of	Never	Sometimes	Often	Always
34. My child is afraid of being in small closed places, like tunnels or small rooms	Never	Sometimes	Often	Always
35. My child has to do some things over and over again (like washing his / her hands, cleaning or putting things in a certain order)	Never	Sometimes	Often	Always
36. My child gets bothered by bad or silly thoughts or pictures in his/her head	Never	Sometimes	Often	Always
37. My child has to do certain things in just the right way to stop bad things from happening	Never	Sometimes	Often	Always
38. My child would feel scared if (s)he had to stay away from home overnight	Never	Sometimes	Often	Always
39. Is there anything else that your child is really afraid of?	Never	Sometimes	Often	Always
Please write down what it is, and fill out how often (s)he is afraid of this thing:				

Appendix 3

Sample Scripts and Recording Sheets

Muscle Relaxation Training Scripts

Hands and Arms
Make a fist with your left hand. Squeeze it hard. Feel the tightness in your hand and arm as you squeeze. Now let your hand go and relax. See how much better your hand and arm feel when they are relaxed. Once again, make a fist with your left hand and squeeze hard. Good. Now relax and let your hand go. (Repeat the process for the right hand and arm.)

Arms and Shoulders
Stretch your arms out in front of you. Raise them high up over your head. Way back. Feel the pull in your shoulders. Stretch higher. Now just let your arms drop back to your side. Okay, let's stretch again. Stretch your arms out in front of you. Raise them over your head. Pull them back, way back. Pull hard. Now let them drop quickly. Good. Notice how your shoulders feel more relaxed. This time let's have a great big stretch. Try to touch the ceiling. Stretch your arms way out in front of you. Raise them way up high over your head.Push them way, way back. Notice the tension and pull in your arms and shoulders. Hold tight now. Great. Let them drop very quickly and feel how good it is to be relaxed. It feels good and warm and lazy.

Shoulders and Neck
Try to pull your shoulders up to your ears and push your head down into your shoulders. Hold in tight. Okay, now relax and feel the warmth. Again, pull your shoulders up to your ears and push your head down into your shoulders. Do it tightly. Okay, you can relax now. Bring your head out and let your shoulders relax. Notice how much better it feels to be relaxed than to be all tight. One more time now. Push your head down and your shoulders way up to your ears. Hold it. Feel the tenseness in your neck and shoulders. Okay. You can relax now and feel comfortable. You feel good.

Jaw
Put your teeth together real hard. Let your neck muscles help you. Now relax. Just let your jaw hang loose. Notice how good it feels just to let your jaw drop. Okay, bite down again hard. That's good. Now relax again. Just let your jaw drop. It feels so good just to let go. Okay, one more time. Bite down. Hard as you can. Harder. Oh, you're really working hard. Good. Now relax. Try to relax your whole body. Let yourself go as loose as you can.

Face and Nose
Wrinkle up your nose. Make as many wrinkles in your nose as you can. Scrunch your nose up real hard. Good. Now you can relax your nose. Now wrinkle up your nose again. Wrinkle it up hard. Hold it just as tight as you can. Okay. You can relax your face. Notice that when you scrunch up your nose that your cheeks and your mouth and your forehead all help you and they get tight, too. So when you relax your nose, your whole face relaxes too, and that feels good. Now make lots of wrinkles on your forehead. Hold it tight now. Okay, you can let go. Now you can just relax. Let your face go smooth. No wrinkles anywhere. Your face feels nice and smooth and relaxed.

Stomach
Now tighten up your stomach muscles real tight. Make your stomach real hard. Don't move. Hold it. You can relax now. Let your stomach go soft. Let it be as relaxed as you can. That feels so much bet-

ter. Okay, again. Tighten your stomach real hard. Good. You can relax now. Kind of settle down, get comfortable, and relax. Notice the difference between a tight stomach and a relaxed one. That's how we want it to feel. Nice and loose and relaxed. Okay. Once more. Tighten up. Tighten hard. Good. Now you can relax completely. You can feel nice and relaxed.

This time, try to pull your stomach in. Try to squeeze it against your backbone. Try to be as skinny as you can. Now relax. You don't have to be skinny now. Just relax and feel your stomach being warm and loose. Okay, squeeze in your stomach again. Make it touch your backbone. Get it real small and tight. Get as skinny as you can. Hold tight now. You can relax now. Settle back and let your stomach come back out where it belongs. You can really feel good now. You've done fine.

Legs and Feet

Push your toes down on the floor real hard. You'll probably need your legs to help you push. Push down, spread your toes apart. Now relax your feet. Let your toes go loose and feel how nice that is. It feels good to be relaxed. Okay. Now push your toes down. Let your leg muscles help you push your feet down. Push your feet. Hard. Okay. Relax your feet, relax your legs, relax your toes. It feels so good to be relaxed. No tenseness anywhere. You feel kind of warm and tingly.

Adapted from *Clinical Behavior Therapy With Children*, by T. H. Ollendick & J. A. Cerny, 1981, New York: Plenum Press, pp.70–72. © 1981 by Plenum Press. Reproduced with permission.

Appendix 4

Sample Scripts and Recording Sheets

Imaginal Relaxation Training Script

Hands and Arms

Pretend you have a whole lemon in your left hand. Now squeeze it hard. Try to squeeze all the juice out. Feel the tightness in your hand and arm as you squeeze. Now drop the lemon. Notice how your muscles feel when they are relaxed. Take another lemon and squeeze it. Try to squeeze this one harder than you did the first one. That's right. Real hard. Now drop your lemon and relax. See how much better your hand and arm feel when they are relaxed. Once again, take a lemon in your left hand and squeeze all the juice out. Don't leave a single drop. Squeeze hard. Good. Now relax and let the lemon fall from your hand. (Repeat the process for the right hand and arm.)

Arms and Shoulders

Pretend you are a furry, lazy cat. You want to stretch. Stretch your arms out in front of you. Raise them up high over your head. Way back. Feel the pull in your shoulders. Stretch higher. Now just let your arms drop back to your side. Okay, kitten, stretch again. Stretch your arms out in front of you. Raise them over your head. Pull them back, way back. Pull hard. Now let them drop quickly. Good. Notice how your shoulders feel more relaxed. This time let's have a great big stretch. Try to touch the ceiling. Stretch your arms way out in front of you. Raise them way up high over your head. Push them way, way back. Notice the tension and pull in your arms and shoulders. Hold tight now. Great. Let them drop very quickly and feel how good it is to be relaxed. It feels good and warm and lazy.

Shoulders and Neck

Now pretend you are a turtle. You're sitting out on a rock by a nice, peaceful pond, just relaxing in the warm sun. It feels nice and warm and safe here. Oh-oh! You sense danger. Pull your head into your house. Try to pull your shoulders up to your ears and push your head down into your shoulders. Hold in tight. It isn't easy to be a turtle in a shell. The danger is past now. You can come out into the warm sunshine and, once again, you can relax and feel the warm sunshine. Watch out now! More danger. Hurry, pull your head back into your house and hold it tight. You have to be closed in tight to protect yourself. Okay, you can relax now. Bring your head out and let your shoulders relax. Notice how much better it feels to be relaxed than to be all tight. Once more time, now. Danger! Pull your head in. Push your shoulders way up to your ears and hold tight. Don't let even a tiny piece of your head show outside your shell. Hold it. Feel the tenseness in your neck and shoulders. Okay. You can come out now. It's safe again. Relax and feel comfortable in your safety. There's no more danger. Nothing to worry about. Nothing to be afraid of. You feel good.

Jaw

You have a giant jawbreaker bubble gum in your mouth. It's very hard to chew. Bite down on it. Hard! Let your neck muscles help you. Now relax. Just let your jaw hang loose. Notice how good it feels just to let your jaw drop. Okay, let's tackle that jawbreaker again now. Bite down. Hard! Try to squeeze it out between your teeth. That's good. You're really tearing that gum up. Now relax again. Just let your jaw drop off your face. It feels so good just to let go and not have to fight that bubble gum. Okay, one more time. We're really going to tear it up this time. Bite down. Hard as you can. Harder. Oh, you're really working hard. Good. Now relax. Try to relax your whole body. You've beaten the bubble gum. Let yourself go as loose as you can.

Face and Nose

Here comes a pesky old fly. He has landed on your nose. Try to get him off without using your hands. That's right, wrinkle up your nose. Make as many wrinkles in your nose as you can. Scrunch your nose up real hard. Good. You've chased him away. Now you can relax your nose. Oops, here he comes back again. Shoo him off. Wrinkle it up hard. Hold it just as tight as you can. Okay, he flew away. You can relax your face. Notice that when you scrunch up your nose that your cheeks and your mouth and your forehead and your eyes all help you, and they get tight too. So when you relax your nose, your whole face relaxes too, and that feels good. Oh-oh! This time that old fly has come back, but this time he's on your forehead. Make lots of wrinkles. Try to catch him between all those wrinkles. Hold it tight now. Okay, you can let go. He's gone for good. Now you can just relax. Let your face go smooth, no wrinkles anywhere. Your face feels nice and smooth and relaxed.

Stomach

Hey! Here comes a cute baby elephant. But he's not watching where he's going. He doesn't see you lying there in the grass, and he's about to step on your stomach. Don't move. You don't have time to get out of the way. Just get ready for him. Make your stomach very hard. Tighten up your stomach muscles real tight. Hold it. It looks like he is going the other way. You can relax now. Let your stomach go soft. Let it be as relaxed as you can. That feels so much better. Oops, he's coming this way again. Get ready. Tighten up your stomach. Real hard. If he steps on you when your stomach is hard, it won't hurt. Make your stomach into a rock. Okay, he's moving away again. You can relax now. Kind of settle down, get comfortable, and relax. Notice the difference between a tight stomach and a relaxed one. That's how we want it to feel: nice and loose and relaxed. You won't believe this, but this time he's really coming your way and no turning around. He's headed straight for you. Tighten up. Tighten hard. Here he comes. This is really it. You've got to hold on tight. He's stepping on you. He's stepped over you. Now he's gone for good. You can relax completely. You're safe. Everything is okay, and you can feel nice and relaxed.

This time imagine that you want to squeeze through a narrow fence and the boards have splinters on them. You'll have to make yourself very skinny if you're going to make it through. Suck your stomach in. Try to squeeze it up against your backbone. Try to be as skinny as you can. You've got to get through. Now relax. You don't have to be skinny now. Just relax and feel your stomach being warm and loose. Okay, let's try to get through that fence now. Squeeze up your stomach. Make it touch your backbone. Get it real small and tight. Get as skinny as you can. Hold tight now. You've got to squeeze through. You got through that skinny little fence and no splinters. You can relax now. Settle back and let your stomach come back out where it belongs. You can feel really good now. You've done fine.

Legs and Feet

Now pretend you are standing barefoot in a big, fat mud puddle. Squish your toes down deep into the mud. Try to get your feet down to the bottom of the mud puddle. You'll probably need your legs to help you push. Push down, spread your toes apart, and feel the mud squish up between your toes. Now step out of the mud puddle. Relax your feet. Let your toes go loose and feel how nice that is. It feels good to be relaxed. Back into the mud puddle. Squish your toes down. Let your leg muscles help you push your feet down. Push your feet. Hard. Try to squeeze that mud puddle dry. Okay. Come back out now. Relax your feet, relax your legs, relax your toes. It feels so good to be relaxed. No tenseness anywhere. You feel kind of warm and tingly.

Adapted from *Clinical Behavior Therapy With Children*, by T. H. Ollendick & J. A. Cerny, 1981, New York: Plenum Press, pp. 68–70. © 1981 by Plenum Press. Reproduced with permission.

Peter Jaffe, David A. Wolfe, Marcie Campbell

Growing Up with Domestic Violence

Advances in Psychotherapy – Evidence-Based Practice, Vol. 23

2012, x + 78 pages, ISBN 978-0-88937-336-5
US $29.80 / £ 19.90 / € 24.95, (Series Standing Order: US $24.80 / £ 15.90 / € 19.95)

Intimate partner violence (IPV) can have a profound impact on the children - this book shows to recognize these effects and provide effective clinical interventions and preventive measures

This compact and easy-to-read text by leading experts shows practitioners and students how to recognize the impact of intimate partner violence (IPV) on children and youth and to provide effective clinical interventions and school-based prevention programs.

Exposure to IPV is defined using examples from different ages and developmental stages. The book describes the effects of exposure to IPV and reviews epidemiology and etiology. Its main focus is on proven assessment, intervention, and prevention strategies. Relevant and current theories regarding the impact of exposure on children and youth are reviewed, and illustrative real-life case studies from the clinical experiences of the authors are described.

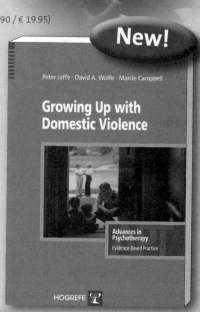

New!

Peter Jaffe · David A. Wolfe · Marcie Campbell

Growing Up with Domestic Violence

Advances in Psychotherapy
Evidence-Based Practice

HOGREFE

Table of Contents:

Hogrefe Publishing
30 Amberwood Parkway · Ashland, OH 44805 · USA
Tel: (800) 228-3749 · Fax: (419) 281-6883
E-Mail: customerservice@hogrefe.com

Hogrefe Publishing
Merkelstr. 3 · 37085 Göttingen · Germany
Tel: +49 551 999 500 · Fax: +49 551 999 50 111
E-Mail: customerservice@hogrefe.de

Hogrefe Publishing c/o Marston Book Services Ltd
PO Box 269 · Abingdon, OX14 4YN · UK
Tel: +44 1235 465577 · Fax +44 1235 465556
E-mail: direct.orders@marston.co.uk

HOGREFE

Order online at **www.hogrefe.com**
or call toll-free **(800) 228-3749** (US only)

Craig Marker & Alyson Aylward

Generalized Anxiety Disorder

Advances in Psychotherapy — Evidence-Based Practice, Vol. 24

2012, viii + 84 pages, ISBN 978-0-88937-335-8
US $29.80 / £ 19.90 / € 24.95, (Series Standing Order: US $24.80 / £ 15.90 / € 19.95)

A practical book outlining a new, evidence-based treatment protocol for this debilitating and difficult-to-treat disorder

Generalized anxiety disorder (GAD) is a debilitating disorder that has often proved difficult to treat. Advances in conceptualization, diagnosis, and treatment now allow an empirically supported approach to its diagnosis and treatment. After briefly outlining theoretical models, this clear and concise book presents an integrative, up-to-date treatment protocol for GAD. Suitable both for practitioners and for students, it guides readers through assessment and differential diagnosis, etiological models such as cognitive avoidance, positive beliefs about worry, and intolerance of uncertainty, and treatment techniques. The therapeutic approach described here integrates techniques from CBT, mindfulness- and acceptance-based therapy, as well as motivational interviewing. This practical volume is rounded off by case vignettes, handouts, questionnaires, and other useful tools.

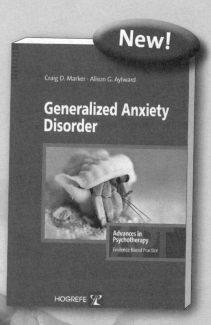

Table of Contents:

Preface, Acknowledgments
1 Description
1.1 Terminology
1.2 Definition
1.3 Epidemiology
1.4 Course and Prognosis
1.5 Differential Diagnosis
1.6 Comorbidities
1.7 Diagnostic Procedures
2 Theories and Models of Generalized Anxiety Disorder
2.1 Worry as Cognitive Avoidance
2.2 Positive Beliefs About Worry
2.3 Uncertainty and Worry
2.4 Information-Processing Biases Associated with GAD
2.5 Metaworry

2.6 Implications for Treatment
3 Diagnosis and Treatment Indications
3.1 Key Features to be Assessed
3.2 Overview of Effective Treatment Strategies
3.3 Factors that Influence Treatment Decisions
4 Treatment
4.1 Methods of CBT
4.2 Mechanisms of Action
4.3 Efficacy and Prognosis
4.4 Combination Treatments
4.5 Overcoming Barriers to Treatment
4.6 Adapting Treatment for Different Age Groups
4.7 Adapting Treatment for Different Cultures
Case Vignettes, Further Reading, References, Appendices: Tools and Resources

Hogrefe Publishing
30 Amberwood Parkway · Ashland, OH 44805 · USA
Tel: (800) 228-3749 · Fax: (419) 281-6883
E-Mail: customerservice@hogrefe.com

Hogrefe Publishing
Merkelstr. 3 · 37085 Göttingen · Germany
Tel: +49 551 999 500 · Fax: +49 551 999 50 111
E-Mail: customerservice@hogrefe.de

Hogrefe Publishing c/o Marston Book Services Ltd
PO Box 269 · Abingdon, OX14 4YN · UK
Tel: +44 1235 465577 · Fax +44 1235 465556
E-mail: direct.orders@marston.co.uk

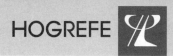

Order online at **www.hogrefe.com**
or call toll-free **(800) 228-3749** (US only)

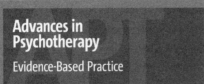

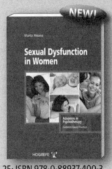
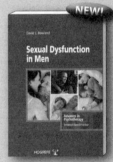